D1268092

BRAZIL

THE INFINITE COUNTRY

BY WILLIAM LYTLE SCHURZ

The Manila Galleon

Latin America: A Descriptive Survey

This New World: The Civilization of Latin America

American Foreign Affairs

Brazil, The Infinite Country

BRAZIL

THE INFINITE COUNTRY

BY WILLIAM LYTLE SCHURZ

E. P. DUTTON & CO., INC., NEW YORK

FIRST EDITION

Published simultaneously in Canada by Clarke, Irwin & Co., Ltd., of Toronto

Library of Congress Catalog Card Number: 61-5038

"I have had long time dwelling with me a man, who for the space of ten or twelve years had dwelt in that other world, which in our age was lately discovered in those parts where *Villegaignon* first landed, and surnamed *Antartike France.* This discoverie of so infinit and vast a countrie, seemeth worthy great consideration."

———From the John Florio translation of the essay entitled "Of the Canibals," by Michel de Montaigne, 1580.

Contents

BRAZIL

THE INFINITE COUNTRY

PART I
THE SCENE

CHAPTER 1

The Immensity

BRAZIL RANKS FIFTH IN SIZE AMONG THE NATIONS OF THE world. Only the Soviet Union, Canada, China, and the United States have a larger area. But of these, Brazil is bigger than continental United States or China proper. It is larger than Australia, and, with one-sixth the population, has 2,000,000 more square miles than India. It occupies nearly half the surface of South America, and its 14,000-odd miles of land frontier adjoin every nation of the continent except Chile and Ecuador. Its single coast is nearly 4,600 miles long. It is, indeed, a spacious land.

Like the two other "United States" of the Western Hemisphere, Brazil is a federal republic. It is composed of 21 states, four territories, and a federal district, in which the new capital, Brasilia, is situated. The former federal district is now the state of Guanabara. One of the 21 states, Amazonas, is bigger than Alaska. Three are larger than Texas and six are larger than California. Bahia, sixth in size, is almost as big as France. The adjoining country of Bolivia would fit into the state of Mato Grosso, with room enough left over for Uruguay.

At the other extreme, Sergipe, the smallest state, is almost the size of Massachusetts. Alagoas, its neighbor across the river, is equal in area to Maryland. Portugal, the mother country, is only a little larger than Paraiba, one of the minor states of the Northeast.

The main feature of the lay of the land is its roughness. There are no wide plains like the Argentine pampa, the Ukraine or much of our own Middle West. Most of Brazil is up-and-downhill. South of Salvador the country is walled off from the sea by the rugged escarpment of the Serra da Mar which so daunted the early Portuguese settlers. Beyond the mountain wall the great Brazilian plateau stretches westward to the trough of the Paraná and beyond to the Paraguay and the marshy flood-plain of the Pantanães. Everywhere in between are rolling hills and mountain ranges that follow no regular pattern of direction or distance. In this vast helter-skelter landscape the sprawling ranges bear Portuguese or Tupí names like Mantiqueira and Apucarana and Taguatinga. Far to the northwest, across the *despovoado* or "unpeopled" wilderness that borders the ultimate confines of Bolivia, the lonely Serra dos Parecís reaches almost to the Madeira, to form the divide between the Amazonian and Platine river systems.

These are not high mountains in the lofty sense of the Andes or the Himalayas, or even of our Rockies, but are more like the Appalachians. The highest peaks in Brazil, Itatiaia in the state of São Paulo, and the Bandeira, on the border between Minas Gerais and Espirito Santo, are under 10,000 feet in elevation. They are old mountains, long settled in their final resting place in a geologically ancient land, so that earthquakes are not among the hazards of human existence. The important fact is that hills or mountains are ubiquitous, and the majority of the Brazilian people dwell among them. Wherever one goes, he is never far from them. Sailing up the jungle-fringed Amazon from Belém, the hills are evident along the irregular skyline back of Monte Alegre. And I remember once climbing a hill on the banks of the lower Tapajóz from whose top the long vista to the east was reminiscent of the Adirondacks. One may see them to advantage in many places. Typical are the everlasting hills, set in iron, that surround the city of Belo Horizonte and spread far out over the historic heart of Minas Gerais. An alternative spectacle is the gently rolling ridges of the Borborema, inland from Recife on the north coast, across which the highway climbs to the pleasant city of Garanhúns at over 4,000 feet above sea level. Or the traveler may view the rugged face of the Brazilian earth in its most dramatic guises from any open spot in Rio. A short drive up over the new road by the rock-bound hill city of Petropolis leads among the basaltic pinnacles and crags of the Organ Mountains, over which planes from the north fly low into the airports on Guanabara Bay. A longer ride takes one up the winding trunk highway out of Rio into the valley of the Paraiba and on within sight of the Itatiaia into São Paulo. Where the ground levels off in the semblance of a plain, as in Rio Grande do Sul or southern Mato Grosso, or where some river from out the uplands slows down its course and curves lazily across the narrow shelf by the sea, the land is almost never flat for long.

Aside from any esthetic considerations of natural beauty or variety of prospect, to which the Brazilian, like the Portuguese, is singularly indifferent anyway, the uneven terrain has left its marks on the national life, as in its physiognomy. It has been a barrier to the attainment of a surface transportation system needed to pull together the parts of so gigantic a nation, to facilitate its fuller occupation and development, and to assure the very preservation of its unity. While an obstacle to continuous navigation of its rivers, the rough terrain is responsible for the large hydroelectric potential of sites like the Paulo Affonso falls on the São Francisco or the rapids of the Paraná. Also, as a result of the erosion of a land that nearly always leans at an angle from the horizontal, much of what was once Brazil—and its most fruitful layers—now lies at the bottom of the Atlantic Ocean.

Of the major river systems of Brazil, only one, that of the São Francisco, seems to fit properly into the natural scheme of things.

In spite of certain limitations, it has been a traditional link between the north and south of the country, and is still so used by those who are not in a hurry. No other river serves as a "course of empire," and on none of them south of the Amazon is there a city of 50,000 people. The Amazon, with its network of giant tributaries, is virtually detached from the realities of Brazilian life. The Paraguay and Paraná, of the Platine fluvial system, flow southward out of the back of Brazil into other countries. Smaller rivers like the Doce and the Paraiba tumble down out of the highlands into the Atlantic. The streams which originate in the Serra da Mar follow the tilt of the land west into the Paraná. Thus the Brazilian rivers either flow in the wrong place or in the wrong direction, or their course is too broken, except for short stretches, where local navigation is possible. The country is practically lakeless. But as for its rivers, Brazil is, in the words of Roy Nash, who knew them well, "the best watered of all the great land masses."

Nor, in spite of the reckless devastation of its forests as the principal source of thermal energy and artificial heat, or for no purpose whatever other than to see them burn, is any other land of its proportions probably so well wooded. The forests differ greatly in general appearance, density, and dominant species, depending on climate, soil, topography, and propinquity of other areas with special characteristics. Thus in southwestern Mato Grosso the hard *quebracho* tree and other examples of Chaco vegetation occur, as the ilex Paraguayensis or *Yerba Mate* tree grows wild in Paraná. The largest single expanse of forest reaches from the northern border and the coast of Pará and Maranhão deep into the western side of Mato Grosso. As the Amazonian Hyleia, this is the true equatorial jungle, yet it is not uniform in character, and varies from the open forest of the *terra firme* or high ground to the tangled maze of the *varzea* in the flood-plain of the great rivers. Occasionally its continuity is broken by large islands of open grasslands, as in the remote Territory of Rio Branco and the upper basin of the Tapajóz. Beginning in a relatively narrow strip along the northeast coast and extending down into the northern part of Rio Grande do Sul is another area of Brazil's forest primeval. Below the latitude of Salvador it widened out deeper and deeper into the hinterland, until it originally covered the states of São Paulo and most of Paraná and Santa Catarina. Much of this forested area has been cleared for farming or to utilize its trees for firewood, and efforts at reforestation with eucalyptus and other species have done little to restore the original forest cover. In Paraná the nature of the forest changes with the appearance of the araucaria or Paraná pine with its familiar telltale branches. In southern Bahia, Espirito Santo, and on down the waterlogged ridges of the Serra da Mar there remains a true rain forest that evokes the image of the Amazonia. It forms a barrier to movement between the Bahia country and the populous south, so that such through land-transport lines as exist detour behind the forest curtain. On the 40-mile drive between São Paulo and Santos, or lower down the coast on the railroad between Curitiba and Paranaguá, one passes through this dense zone of dripping jungle.

Inside this belt of true forest there begins the vast domain of the *caatinga* that is largely coterminous with the drought region of the Northeast. This, the "white"—or gray—forest of the Tupí aborigines, is similar to the scrub mesquite lands of our southwest. In an area of low and uncertain rainfall, the dry atmosphere has set the dull tones of nature. Here in the *sertão* the sparse ground cover is composed of low gnarled trees, with a scant and brownish foliage, and a variety of xerophytic plants and thorn-covered bushes where the horsemen who penetrate these inhospitable lands dress in leather for protection. Since the *caatinga* extends into Goiás, the traveler may observe a good demonstration of its features on his way from the airport of the new city of Brasilia. Out beyond the wide zone of the *caatinga,* though sometimes interspersed with it, are the open grasslands of the *campo cerrado* or "closed country." Its openness is often qualified by the presence of *buritý* or clusters of palms. And though its grass may appear deceptively high, it provides little nourishment for livestock, since the "hard-pan" soil which underlies the surface of the ground lacks the basic elements of fertility. Similar conditions exist in the Campos Gerais, the large break in the Amazonian forest which appears in the upper basin of the distant Rio Branco, and wherever open *campos* lands occur in the green solidarity of the jungle.

In pleasing contrast to the *cerrado* are the *Campos Limpos,* or "clean lands," which cover much of Rio Grande do Sul and the so-called *Campos de Vaccaría,* or "cow-country" in southern Mato Grosso. These farmed lands have a good natural growth of grasses that are suitable for pasturage.

A Brazilian poet, then residing in Portugal, wrote a nostalgic poem that begins with the words "My land has palm trees" (*Minha terra tem palmeiras*). Of all the rich flora of Brazil, the palm is its most distinctive feature. Probably nowhere on earth is there a greater profusion of palm trees than along the Madeira-Mamoré Railroad, in the remote corner of Amazonia that is now known as the Territory of Rondonia. *Cocoteiros* line long stretches of the coast. Royal palms border the avenues of Rio and many other cities, and in the center of São Paulo they seem to challenge the tall skyscrapers that wall them in. On Marajó and the tidal flats of the lower Amazon the *murumurú* form a curtain at the edge of the chaotic plant life of the flooded lands. Through the interior of Maranhão and Piauí the *babassú* palm is the characteristic mark of the landscape, and farther to the south the carnauba takes its place in the depressions closer to the coast. About the headwaters of streams in the north country one may find clusters of the tall *buritý* palm. For Brazil, its billions of palm trees serve a multiplicity of purposes, some of which are beyond the realm of statistics to measure. They provide food and drink, fuel and fiber, and building materials. The *babassú* is not only a major source of vegetable oil, but in default of coal, thousands of tons of the tough-shelled nuts are annually shoveled into the grates of antiquated locomotives on the railroads of the north. The *caboclo* may split the hard outer layer of the *paxiuba* palm's trunk for the walls of his hut, and he thatches its roof with palm fronds. Caught in the jungle at nightfall, he improvises in a matter of minutes a lean-to of poles and fronds that will shield him from a tropical downpour. From the fronds of the carnauba palm, a waxy secretion is derived that has many uses in industry. And palm trees add grace to many a Brazilian landscape and break the monotony of the wide spaces.

Much of the story of Brazil is told in its place names. It was originally christened as the Island of Santa Cruz by its nonchalant Portuguese discoverers, for no other reason than that they had just erected a wooden cross as a sign of possession. After a period of neglect by the government at Lisbon, roving sailors found in the forests along its coast a tree which yielded a brick-red dye known to the textile industry of the time as brazilwood, from the word *brasa* or glowing coal. So the lonely land, no longer an island, gained an economic basis of sorts, to supplement the parrots and monkeys in the cargoes of trading ships, and became known henceforth in popular parlance as Brazil.

Few place names were transplanted from the mother country. While there are eight Lisbons in the United States, there are none in Brazil. The largest single concentration of Lusitanian place names is on the lower Amazon, where they include the towns of Alemquer, Almeirím, Bragança, Obidos, and Santarém.

As was customary in the Hispanic colonies in the New World, the Church contributed many names to the geography of Brazil. Three of the 21 states, Espirito Santo, São Paulo, and Santa Catarina, bear religious names. The calendar of saints was liberally drawn on in the designating of towns and cities, like São Vicente, São Miguel Arcanjo, and São José dos Campos. In the same category, the early settlement of Todos os Santos and the important port of Santos were all-inclusive. The so-called three A-B-C suburbs of São Paulo are Santo Amaro, São Braz, and São Caetano. There are also the Portuguese equivalents of Bethlehem and Nazareth, of the Good Jesus and the "Cross of Souls."

Most typical of place names in Brazil are those borrowed from the rich and expressive *lingua geral* of the Tupí race. Some are words compounded of *assú* (big) and *mirím* (little), like Iguassú and Mogi-mirím, or combinations of terms from the nature lore of the aborigines, like Itabira and Paranaguá. They are words with strong final accents, like Caxambú and Cuiabá and Corumbá, Botucatú and Caruarú, and melodious names like Araraquara and Inhanguera and Ipiranga, Guanabara and Pirapora and Piratininga.

Many place names are evocative of natural features of the land or of some dominant form of vegetation of the locality. Among the former are Bahia and Belo Horizonte and Recife, which was named for a reef that lies off its shore. Rio de Janeiro received its name from the error of its discoverer who mistook its dead-end harbor for the estuary of a river. Places associated with the plant life of the area are Palmares and Bananeiras, Bacabal and Xique Xique, Campos and Campinas, and Campo Grande and Campo Formoso, or "beautiful field."

Sometimes places are named for famous individuals. For example, there are towns that commemorate the fathers of the republic, like Ruy Barbosa and Benjamin Constant or dignitaries of the Empire, like Joaquim Nabuco. In the western part of the state of São Paulo there are five towns which bear the names of former presidents. Many towns are monuments to local dignitaries, like Miguel Calmón and João Pessoa, and to Padre Cicero, the priest of the *sertão*. A river in the basin of the Madeira is named for Theodore Roosevelt, and the Territory through which it flows is a perpetual memorial to his companion, the great explorer and friend of the Indians, Marshall Rondón.

Few place names in Brazil are reminiscent of foreign lands. Most of them are the sites of German colonies, like Blumenau and Novo Friburgo, São Leopoldo and Frederico Westphalen. Above Campinas, on the railroad between São Paulo and Ribeirão Preto, is Americana, which marks the post-Civil War settlement of southerners in that locality. There are two Clevelands in Brazil and in Goiás there is a Filadelfia. In the back of Maranhão a village is dubbed Nova Iorque, which is Brazilian for New York, as *uisque* is whiskey and *airixtú* is Irish stew. In Rio Bay, reminiscent of the short-lived French occupation in the 1500's, is the isle of Villegagnon. And the name of Copacabana, the city's famous oceanshore area, is not Brazilian at all, but was imported from the Andes, like the woolen fabrics which Otavalo Indians from Ecuador now peddle along its avenues.

Brazilians are in the habit of naming their towns with combinations like Fordlandia and Petrolandia, and with compounds of the Greek root *polis*. Among these are Indianapolis and Florianopolis, or Floriano's City, the capital of Santa Catarina, and Petropolis and Theresopolis, in the hills near Rio. On the north coast there is a Salinopolis that no longer produces salt, and in the hinterland some devotee of universal language evidently named the town of Esperantinopolis, or perhaps it was meant to be the City of Hope.

Some of the most picturesque place names in Brazil are of subjective origin. They preserve the mood or memory of some individual who once passed that way. The Abrolhos, the shoals off Caravellas, on which many ships have gone down, means "Open your eyes!" In Rio Grande do Sul, a town is named Não-me-Toque or "Don't touch me!" In the Acre, a place is named Deixa-falar, or "Let him talk," and another in the same region is Livre-nos Deus, which means "Free us, God!" In Maranhão there is a Vamos Ver, or "Let's see." In the mouth of the Juruá, there is an island called Conciencia because men bound for the rubber forests were supposed to leave their consciences in its keeping. There are places suggestive of unpleasant forms of animal life, like Cascabel (rattlesnake), Jacaré (alligator), Carrapateiras (ticks), and Carapanatuba (mosquitoes). There must have once been drownings at Afogados da Ingazeira and dead women by the Rio das Mortas. The Paraisos on the map seem to tell a tale of men who had found what they were seeking. But in the loneliness of the back country there are more "Solitudes" than "Paradises." Spix, the German naturalist, who visited Brazil in 1817, comments on the place names with which "the settlers eternalized their mood at the moment of their arrival, such as Bomfím, Bemposto, Boa-Morte, Sossego, Sem-Dentes, Foge Homem, and Arrependido."

It is one of the miracles of history that Brazil is still of one piece. In view of the predatory habits of seafaring nations in the sixteenth century, its fragmentation would have seemed inevitable from the beginning. However, a variety of circumstances have combined to preserve its territorial integrity both against breakup from within and conquest from without.

For a long time Portugal could devote only a small residue of her scanty store of resources and energies to her giant colony. Her limited manpower was already spread too thin over the East and the African coasts, and there was little to spare for Brazil. Portugal may have hoped, by a policy of silence, to avoid calling the attention of other nations to her overseas enterprises. Perhaps the silence may have been due to the fact that the Portuguese were not a writing folk. When Brazil became an independent empire in 1822 and a republic in 1889, she was still intact. The skill of her great diplomat, the Baron of Rio Branco, finally cemented her long frontiers in their present form by a series of negotiated agreements with her neighbors.

The claims implied in the papal Line of Demarcation of 1493 and their westward extension under the terms of the Treaty of Tordesillas could only have affected Portugal's relations with Spain. They were hardly a deterrent against the covetousness of the French, the Dutch, and the English in an age when even "The Most Christian King" of France mocked the validity of the Borgian title to Brazil.

After all, the Spaniards were preoccupied with the exploration of their mineralized colonies on the west coast of South America and in Mexico, and they had little interest in the forbidding world which lay to the east of Potosí. But even so the Portuguese were apprehensive of danger from that quarter, as was demonstrated by the stone forts which they built in the jungle of the Guaporé and at Tabatinga, where the Amazon enters Brazil from Peru. Meanwhile, the long line of Jesuit missions that reached from Argentina and Paraguay across eastern Bolivia into the upper Amazon basin created an international barrier between the colonies of the two Hispanic peoples. Even during the 60 years of "captivity" between 1580 and 1640, when Portugal was a dependency of Spain, the Spaniards made no move to dismember Brazil; their overlordship of Portugal did have the effect of opening Brazil to aggression from the enemies of Spain. The only area where Portuguese and Spaniards were in contact during the colonial period was in the open lands in the far south between the coast and the Rio Uruguay, but the potential seeds of conflict in that region did not bear their full fruit until the time of the imperial regime in Brazil. Among other European powers, armed aggressions against the Portuguese in Brazil were made by the Dutch, which resulted in the occupation of a large part of northern Brazil in the latter 1600's, but none was of long duration or seriously threatened the hegemony of Portugal.

After all, as the world was constituted in the sixteenth century, there was too little in Brazil to attract the long-term cupidity of rival colonial powers. If gold had been discovered in Minas during that period instead of in the late 1600's, there might well have been a different story to tell. As things were, almost all that Brazil then offered at first glance was space, and there was room aplenty lying about unoccupied in other more accessible quarters of the globe. The wooded zone that bordered the coast was hard going for the European, who was a creature of the open country, and his still medieval imagination peopled its recesses with formidable terrors. The primitive aborigines, who were liable to be as waspish as they were curious about the newcomers, added another element of uneasiness and apprehension to those who dared penetrate beyond the security of the landing beaches. Moreover, the well-established reputation of the natives for anthropophagy further discouraged Frenchmen and others of more conventional gastronomic habits from imposing on the hospitality of their hosts. In this connection, it is significant that Montaigne, who received firsthand reports on the subject from a repatriated and intact fellow countryman, entitled his famous essay "Of the Cannibals." Aside from brazilwood and a few natural oddities like birds and animals and exotic fruits which the Indians brought down to the shore to barter for the baubles and trinkets of Europe, the new land offered little that might be taken away for profit and that would repay the long and trying voyage from the ports of Brittany and the Low Countries.

So much for the external threats to Brazilian unity. By its very size, if for no other reason, the territorial solidarity of this sprawling world was exposed to dangers from within. There was lacking some natural feature such as the Nile River, the pampa in Argentina, the insular character of Britain, or the bordering ocean in narrow Chile to help bind the land together. Nor is there yet an artificial substitute in the form of a truly natural transportation system, no Union Pacific Railroad or Inca Highway, to mitigate the disunion of nature.

It appeared likely that, with growing inequalities of regional development, the clash of antagonistic or incompatible local interests might break up the country into several independent nations, as occurred with the original Central American Union. This came near happening in the United States and presumably it was possible in Brazil. That it did not was the result of a combination of favorable circumstances. As it was, Brazil survived a number of major crises, which included the abolition of slavery, a radical shift in political forms from empire to republic, and, except for the revolt of the state of São Paulo against the Union in 1923, the increasing unbalance of regional growth, without serious menace to the basic oneness of the nation.

In this problem of the attainment and maintenance of a true national unity against the potential forces of separatism and disintegration, the Indian played an important, if silent, role. The very presence of the widespread Tupí race served the purposes of Portuguese policy. It did not constitute a powerful organized Indian state with a strong national consciousness of its own, comparable to the Inca Empire or the warrior federation of the Araucanians in Chile. There was no central authority around whose strength or prestige—or memories of former greatness—the Indian population of Brazil might rally to create a racial dualism in the country. If the native peoples refused to co-operate in the Portuguese efforts to take over their home preserves, they at least did not offer a mass resistance to the white intruders; they only withdrew farther into the wilderness as the Tupí-nambás did by their epic migration from the south to their ultimate island refuge between the Madeira and the Solimões.

In the contacts between Portuguese and Indians, miscegenation early became a more important factor than hostility, which tended to be only temporary and piecemeal anyway. The same pattern of racial *rapprochement* had prevailed in Paraguay between the Spaniards and the Guaranís, who were cousins of the Brazilian Tupís, and with the same results in the creation of a mestizo race. In both cases, those of mixed breed became active partners of their European progenitors and indispensable aides in the process of occupation. More adapted than the Portuguese to survival under the conditions which prevailed in the back country, the mestizos became, like the French-Canadian *habitants,* the accepted instrument of penetration into the interior. Typical of them were the hardy Mamelucos of São Paulo, who as *bandeirantes* or frontiersmen conducted the *entradas* deep into the hinterland of Brazil that gave some substance of reality to the claims of Portugal to the area of the papal donation. A similar service was performed by the *caboclo* cattlemen in the zone behind the coastal settlements of the Northeast.

During the early period of the colony the *lingua geral* served a useful purpose as a medium of communication, as a sort of "pidgin English." However, its use was gradually supplanted by the Portuguese language, which became for all practical purposes the universal tongue of Brazil, as it has remained to this day.

Whatever its drawbacks in opening up the interior, the pattern of dispersion of the small Portuguese population around a few cities along the seaboard had its advantages. At least it enabled the colonists to keep open their lines of communication with the mother country. It also enabled these isolated centers of settlement to succor one another by sea in the event of threats from the outside.

There was more good hard sense in the colonial policies of Portugal than has generally been credited. There were few illusions of glory or glamor in those who were responsible for the governance of the Lusitanian *Ultramar*. But there was much that was down-to-earth, shrewd, and sound. The important thing was to hold what they had, to make the most of what it offered them at the particular time, and to wait for the ultimate rewards of their patience and foresight, as the potential wealth of the country might be revealed and developed. They had too little to work with and too much on their minds to hurry what could come by its own momentum as the population grew and the vast land was gradually occupied and put to use. They created no ponderous mechanism of government, as the Spaniards did in their great viceroyalties, but entrusted much of the actual responsibility for administration to those who were already on the ground and who had a personal stake in the future of the land. So they left much of the initiative for dealing with local problems to the big landowners and other leaders with roots in Brazil, men who were more familiar with local conditions than officialdom in Lisbon could ever be. When there was a crisis in the affairs of the colony, they generally rose to the occasion. For example, they were aware of the advantages of guerrilla warfare as a strategy adapted to the peculiarities of the local terrain, and on occasion resorted to such informal methods as a technique of military defense.

After a system of rule that often seemed little better than improvised and lightly imposed had been tightened and formalized by the reforms of Pombal, the chief minister, the changes had too little time to mature before the country became independent from Portugal in 1822. The Empire which followed the breaking of colonial ties proved to be a strong force for unity during the period when Brazil was taking shape as a sovereign nation in its own right. The process was immensely aided by the public devotion to the person of the second emperor, Dom Pedro II.

Among other influences which contributed to the final consolidation of Brazilian unity was the interest of the United States and England in preserving the integrity of Brazil against any dangers which might have menaced it from the designs of colonial-minded powers of the time. Though American and British motivation may have been different, even if equally selfish, the results for Brazil were similar.

The federal system which was adopted as the form of government for the republic from its inception in 1889 proved to be a valuable device for reconciling regional differences of opinion and interest and for absorbing the shocks of potential conflict between the various parts of the country.

Finally, the predominance of a rural civilization, whose members lacked overpowering local attachments that might qualify the potency of national feelings, was an asset for the survival of the republic as a single country. The Brazilians were a people on the move and were long accustomed to wandering freely over the length and breadth of the open land without local barriers to their nomadism.

Since, in most respects, Brazil is too large to be treated as a whole, it is customary to consider the facts of Brazilian life on a regional basis. The identity of the various regions is dictated by a number of factors—geographical, historic, economic, racial, or sentimental. Some of the generally accepted regions are grounded in old tradition and their distinguishing peculiarities have become part of the folklore of Brazil. The conventional divisions of the country may sometimes be ill-defined, like such amorphous areas as the Middle East or our own Middle West. However, in spite of the lack of precision in fixing their limits, the traditional regions serve a practical purpose of convenience in the story of Brazilian problems. They also reflect differences of culture and customs which add an appeal of interest to a national panorama that might otherwise seem monotonous.

A region whose separate identity is incontestable is the Amazonia. It not only has special distinguishing characteristics, but its geographic locale is clearly determined by the watershed of the Amazon and its far-flung fluvial system, or at least by those areas which find their principal outlet through the main river itself. It is really international in its scope and includes parts of several neighboring countries.

The regional character of the Northeast is rather historic than geographic. It has a sort of classic status like New England, the German Rhineland, or the French Midi. It was the original seat of Portuguese colonization and rule, and it early became the setting of a multi-racial society which marked it off from the rest of Brazil and which it has preserved in large part to the present. Yet there is much cultural variety within the region, particularly as between the coast and the *sertão* or backlands. It also lacks both climatic and economic unity. It includes the layer of maritime states of the so-called "bulge" and extends north into Maranhão, where it merges into the physical world of Amazonia, and south into Bahia and the margins of another area of tropical rain forest.

Some regions are little more than prolongations or enlargements of dominant states like São Paulo and Minas. These states possess definite personalities of their own and their rights to a regional position in the Brazilian Union are supported by large populations and a certain dynamic sense of destiny, particularly in the case of São Paulo. Beyond their borders they have recognized spheres of influence in other states, established by propinquity and confirmed by lines of communication. Control of some of these dependent areas is competitive, as in the "triangle" of Minas or in the Platine basin of Mato Grosso, a large state which still lacks economic and political cohesion and a consciousness of separate individuality. As Goiás develops around the new federal capital and lines of communication by way of Belo Horizonte are improved, the influence of Minas within its borders may increase. Though the state of Paraná is still within the zone of attraction of São Paulo, it possesses a certain potential for independence, including its own outlet to the sea, direct lines of communication with the republic of Paraguay, a flourishing coffee industry, and a growing and enterprising capital city. Similarly, the city of Rio de Janeiro is the center of a dependent area which embraces the somewhat amorphous state of the same name. It also has a certain limited influence beyond the line of the Rio Doce and the port city of Vitoria in the nondescript state of Espirito Santo. However, its over-all attraction is still national rather than local, and the great city itself has a certain personality of its own that sets it off from other cities and regions of Brazil. To the far south the state of Rio Grande do Sul has earned a unique and separate place among the components of Brazil. This special status is due not only to its location, relatively isolated from the body of the federation, but to certain circumstances of history and race. Its people are an assertive and vigorous folk, with an economy and way of life more like that of their Spanish-speaking neighbors than of the majority of their fellow-Brazilians. There is also a considerable admixture of German and Italian blood in the population, whose sentimental ties with Brazil are still more local than national in their reach. The smaller state of Santa Catarina, which borders Rio Grande do Sul to the north, lies more properly within its effective zone of attraction than within the sphere of influence of São Paulo.

The central governments of nations in the process of violent change or forced development tend to be impatient with any survivals of deep-seated regional loyalties or mentality that might make agreement on national policy or action more difficult. This situation occurred in France in the 1790's, when local

BOA VISTA
RIO BRANCO
AMAPA
MACAPÁ
EQUATOR
MANAUS
BELÉM
SÃO LUIZ
FORTALEZA
AMAZONAS
PARÁ
MARANHÃO
CEARÁ
TERESINA
NATAL
PARAIBA
PÔRTO VELHO
PIAUÍ
PERNAMBUCO
RECIFE
ACRE
RONDÔNIA
(GUAPORÉ)
RIO BRANCO
BRAZIL
ALAGOAS
MACEIÓ
SERGIPE
ARACADU
BAHIA
GOIÁS
MATO GROSSO
CUIABÁ
SALVADOR
BRASILIA
GOIÂNIA
MINAS GERAIS
BELO HORIZONTE
ESPÍRITO SANTO
VITÓRIA
SÃO PAULO
RIO DE JANEIRO
NITERÓI
SÃO PAULO
RIO DE JANEIRO
PARANÁ
QUANABARA
CURITIBA
SANTA CATARINA
ATLANTIC OCEAN
FLORIANÓPOLIS
RIO GRANDE DO SUL
PÔRTO ALEGRE
BRAZIL

attachments and memories proved to be an obstacle to a nation-wide acceptance of the principles of the French Revolution. Spain, always a prey to the disruptive force of regionalism at home, faced a similar problem in her overseas empires as political habits and thinking became crystallized around a particular locality after three centuries of rule. The alternative would have been the frank adoption of a policy of "divide-and-rule," which was a hidden feature of Spanish colonialism anyway. Instead, the strengthening of the Spanish monarchy under Charles III led to administrative reforms in the colonies which were calculated to shift the affiliation of the creoles to new units of government, as the French provincials were to become citizens of new departments that lacked a subjective base.

While the Brazilian government has a natural concern for unity of outlook on issues which it considers vital to the welfare of the state as a whole, it has avoided provoking a serious display of regional sentiment. It seems to have resigned itself to living as harmoniously as possible with a certain heritage of regionalism and all that that implies. However, the government's deeper sentiments may be reflected in the apparently arbitrary divisions of the country which appear in the official *Atlas do Brasil* produced by the National Council of Geography. This regional breakdown has been determined by purely physical considerations and thus ignores old ties of tradition and sentiment. The six regions, which frequently cut across accepted or established boundaries, are identified in purely directional terms, like North, East, South, and West-Central.

Since most of Brazil lies within the so-called Torrid Zone, the presumption is of unmitigated heat, a sort of year-round season of dog-days. But when Gilberto Freyre uses the term "world in the tropics," he evidently means it in the sense of a land bounded by Cancer and Capricorn, the latter of which crosses Brazil between Rio and São Paulo. The Equator very appropriately enters Brazil by the mouth of the Amazon. It later passes unnoticed through the village of São Joaquim at the junction of the Negro and the Uaupés before disappearing to the west into Colombia and its namesake, Ecuador.

Though latitude does have much to do with the climate of Brazil, its force is tempered by a number of other elements. Most important of these is altitude, the wide spread of the brown areas that dominate the green of the relief maps over most of the country south of the Amazon. While there are no elevations comparable to the Andes, prevailing levels of between 2,000 and 4,000 feet above sea level for much of Brazil account for a climate that is at least subtropical and often temperate. Extremes of temperature have a narrower range than in most of the United States, and it can be as uncomfortably hot in Washington, D.C., Kansas City, or Houston as anywhere in Brazil. And thermometer readings do not reach the heights of Phoenix or El Paso in midsummer. The principal difference is in the monotony and duration of the heat. At Manaus, in the middle of the Amazon Valley, the mean temperature in February, the coolest month, is 78 degrees, and in the warmest month, October, it is only three degrees higher. The over-all range for the year is between 67 and 99 degrees. But the average humidity at Manaus is 87 per cent, a little lower than in steamy Belém. At Porto Alegre, at the opposite extremity of the country, the weather can be as hot in January as in Manaus in October, but in the southern July there may be chilly mornings with the temperature hovering a little above freezing. The average humidity in Porto Alegre is only about 10 per cent below that of Manaus and almost as high as that of Rio. The normal yearly spread of temperatures at Rio is between 55 and 102 degrees, but the mean ranges only from 69 degrees for July to 78 degrees for December. Except for Manaus, which though almost 1,000 miles from the mouth of the Amazon lies only a few feet above sea level, these are coastal cities and therefore subject to the climatic influence of the sea.

For among the other factors which make climate and weather in Brazil are the trade winds that blow in from the northeast across the coastal zone and into the interior, the movement of continental air masses over the hinterland, and the influence of the ocean current from the South Atlantic whose cooling touch the traveler feels as his ship passes Cape Frio above Rio. There are other local phenomena, like refreshing breezes that blow off the wide rivers onto the land and the rapid lifting after nightfall of the heavy curtain of heat which envelops the jungle by day. I have slept during many months in a hammock hung between trees and always under a blanket, and I have lain shivering on the bottom of a dugout canoe only a few degrees below the Equator. Anyone who has lived through a sweltering afternoon in Belém is familiar with the welcome wave of coolness which settles over the city after the downpour of rain that regularly relieves the charged atmosphere in late afternoon.

While heavy thunderstorms are a normal accompaniment of life in Brazil, the country is free from the plague of tornadoes and hurricanes. However, there are infrequent land gales like the one that blew up out of Paraná in July, 1959, and did considerable damage to towns in its path. A freakish feature of nature at Rio is the occasional *resaca* or strong ground swell in the ocean which originates in storm areas beyond the horizon and pounds the shore at Copacabana in quiet weather, sometimes undermining the Avenida Atlántica and buildings on the ocean front.

Of cities in the interior, Belo Horizonte, situated at about 3,000 feet above sea level, has some of the marks of a typical continental climate. The temperature may fall into the 40's in the southern winter and rise into the high 90's in the summer. But the humidity is noticeably lower than along the coast, so that the climate is generally pleasant and healthful.

In São Paulo, the thermometer has fallen to 34 degrees, though frost is rare. In summer the humidity may make the weather uncomfortable at times, but never to the same point as in sweltering Rio. In winter the weather can be very chilly and damp, and dense morning fogs sometimes close in its busy airport. Like that of San Francisco, its climate is somewhat unpredictable and temperamental, if invigorating and bracing. In the summer months torrential rains may suddenly descend on the city and continue for hours. In the interior of the state of São Paulo winter temperatures tend to be progressively lower until one reaches the valley of the Paraná. Eventually the roads cross the frost frontier, beyond which the cultivation of coffee becomes a highly speculative venture.

The range of rainfall in Brazil is much wider than that of temperature. Over most of the country there are definite wet and dry seasons, though their duration and intensity vary considerably from one area to another. Even in the Amazon Valley it rains much more at one season of the year than at another. This marked seasonality may create serious problems for agriculture, for highway transportation and river navigation, for domestic and municipal water supply, for hydroelectric installations and the construction industry, and for the health and comfort of the individual.

The rates for some Brazilian cities, as averaged over a period of years, and American cities of comparable rainfall, are as follows: Natal, 41 inches (Boston), Recife, 70 inches (Mobile), Rio de Janeiro, 46 inches (Washington, D.C.), Curitiba, 54 inches (Jacksonville), and Porto Alegre, 63 inches (New Orleans). Of interior cities, Belo Horizonte has an average rate of 38 inches, or about that of Cincinnati.

The heaviest rainfall recorded in Brazil is not, as might be expected, in the Amazon Valley but far to the south in the Serra da Mar at the edge of the Temperate Zone. Against 107 inches for Manaus, in the heart of the world's largest rain forest, a fall of 178 inches has been registered in the locality of Itapanhau near Mogi das Cruzes. In this water-logged belt of high jungle which borders the coast in the states of Rio de Janeiro and São Paulo, the prevailing precipitation for the year is above 130 inches. Farther south in the coastal zone of Paraná the level is generally around 100 inches.

The most extraordinary climatic feature of Brazil is the existence of the vast semi-arid area in the Northeast known to geographers as the *Polígono das Seccas* or "polygon of drought." The region includes parts of nine states and extends from within the borders of Piauí in a southwesterly direction across the *sertão* into northern Minas. Though its uneven-sided bulk lies behind the coastal belt of adequate rainfall, it touches the sea in Rio Grande do Norte. It embraces roughly 365,000 square miles of land, or about the combined size of Texas and Colorado. It has over three-fourths of the total area of the Northeast and about two-thirds of its people. In 1950 it had a population of about 10,500,000. It contains only one city of over 100,000, Campina Grande in Paraiba, and about 23 towns of more than 10,000 inhabitants.

The region is cursed by recurrent droughts that are almost periodic in their regularity. Though the rainless cycle is scarcely mathematical in its operation, the natives anticipate a *secca* of serious intensity in every decade. In "normal" years there is generally sufficient rainfall for the limited needs of its ascetic and fatalistic population. The sparse xerophytic vegetation of the Caatinga is green and the large ponds or puddles that pass for storage reservoirs contain enough water for people and livestock. There is even enough moisture in the ground for cultivation of the subsistence crops on which the population depends for its food supply. Probably typical of the localities in the area is Queixeramobím in Ceará, whose rainfall in "good years" averages around 25 inches.

But when the rains fail to appear at the end of the long dry season, the land and its occupants face a time of tragedy that may be prolonged for a year or more. The story is told in the long chronicle of the great droughts that has been kept since the early centuries of the colony. It includes the five-year period from 1723 to 1727, the devastating *secca grande* of 1790–93, about a dozen more droughts of from two to three years' duration, and at least 16 other rainless years. In the period 1915–19 the rainfall over most of the area was less than 40 per cent of normal. In the three-year drought of 1877–79 over 60,000 people died and twice as many more immigrated to other parts of Brazil. The backlands of Ceará lost over half their population. In the four years that began in 1915, 30,000 died and many more made the long trek into the Amazon Valley. The plight of the survivors was greatly aggravated by the virtual extinction of the herds and flocks in the stricken areas.

The latest drought occurred in 1958, and affected chiefly the states of Ceará, Paraiba, and Rio Grande do Norte, with an estimated population of 6,300,000. Due to better-organized relief measures, the toll in human lives was kept to a minimum, but the economic losses were very heavy. It has been calculated that the beef supply available to the population declined by 300,000 tons and the stock of basic foodstuff by a total of 700,000 tons. The yield of corn and beans fell to 15 per cent of normal, and the yield of manioc and bananas, the other staples in the subsistence diet of the *sertão,* was cut by half. Over 45,000 tons of cotton, the "cash crop" of the region, were lost to the drought.

A special government organization, known as the Inspectoría Federal de Obras Contra as Seccas, is primarily responsible for relief measures in the drought area of the Northeast. In the early 1920's an ambitious program of irrigation works was initiated by the federal government, but the system of dams and canals was never completed. Only about 15,000 acres are actually under irrigation and an additional 45,000 are planted to crops in lands adjacent to the local streams or in semi-dry strips of ground. The ultimate possibilities of irrigation are limited by circumstances of topography and rainfall to a maximum of about 2,000,000 acres, or approximately sufficient land for about 400,000 persons. However, the population of the drought regions is increasing at the rate of about 500,000 a year, and the current of migration to other parts of Brazil drains off only a minority of this human increment. In the drought of 1958 some 200,000, who represented less than half the normal growth of population, left the area for the south and the Goiás country beyond the São Francisco where Brasilia is situated. Two years later much damage was done in the same region of the Northeast by heavy floods!

A comprehensive program of the federal government looks to revolutionary reforms in the economic structure of the *sertão* that would alleviate the permanent menace of drought. However, the potentiality of the *sertão* is necessarily restricted by the dearth of basic natural resources within the stricken region. Beyond the production of the traditional subsistence food crops, the bases of the area's precarious economy largely consist of an old and "extensive" livestock industry, the cultivation of cotton in the Seridó region of Rio Grande de Norte and other localities, and a few small centers of vegetable and tobacco farming that are dependent on a regular supply of ground water. Pending the realization of official projects for the amelioration of present conditions, the efforts of government are restricted to emergency measures in periods of crisis. For example, during the latest drought employment on public works was provided for over 400,000 persons at a minimum wage of 40 cruzeiros, about 25 cents, a day. Those who managed to make their way into Fortaleza and other cities along the coast were cared for by relief stations until the situation in the interior improved with the final breaking of the drought.

One of the principal impediments to a rational solution of the whole problem is a social one—the singular and persistent attachment of the *sertanejo* to his inhospitable home. He is obsessed with an urge to return to the scene of his misfortunes as soon as the news reaches him, wherever he may be in Brazil, that the rains have come again. As a result, much of the emigration which relieves the pressure on the parched area in times of drought is only temporary.

By its own choice this gaunt and austere race, so different from their fellow-Brazilians of the bountiful coastal lands, live always in the imminent presence of tragedy and death. Roger Bastide, the Frenchman, vividly describes the lot of the *flagelado* as he finally yields to the implacable realities of nature and heads for the coast: he

> looks in silence at his house and the motionless landscape. Then he goes away, with his wife and their emaciated children, beneath the blazing sun, over the roads that tear their feet and toward the lands where water flows and the trees are forever green. He traverses, gray with dust and bleeding from the thorns, the inferno of cactus and fire where the bones of dead animals whiten in the sun and followed by the mournful flight of buzzards in the sky.

In 1919 I saw the haggard survivors of this long and painful flight through the scorched wilderness of the backlands, like so many ghosts returned to the living, being fed in the streets of Fortaleza.

In 1950 Brazil had almost 51,944,000 people. Pending returns from the decennial census now in progress the official statistical agency has estimated in advance its population for July 1, 1960, at 65,743,000. Meanwhile, for the immediate practical purposes of this study, a provisional round figure of 65,000,000 can safely be accepted as an approximation to the actual total. It is, accordingly, the eighth country in the world, after China, India, the U.S.S.R., the United States, Japan, Pakistan, and Indonesia.

The Brazilian government has estimated the population density of the country for the middle of 1958 at 28.6 persons per square mile. The estimated density ranged from 2.2 per square mile for the Amazonia, representing 42 per cent of the national area, to 60 per square mile for seven states of the Northeast and 100 per square mile for the four southern states. Of individual states, the lowest density rate was 1.5 for Amazonas and the highest was 248.5 for the state of Rio de Janeiro. The population density of the state of São Paulo was estimated at 173.6 per square mile. The population of Brazil is concentrated in a strip along the coast, widening out in Minas, in whose southeastern section the present center of population of the country is located. Between 1940 and 1950 the population grew by something over 10,000,000, or at a rate of 26 per cent. The normal annual rate of population increase is probably slightly less than the 2.6 per cent indicated. This compares with a rate of about 1.7 per cent for the United States for the period 1950–54. Brazil's gross birth rates and death rates are considerably higher than in the United States, though both vary greatly from one part of the country to another, so that there is little uniformity in the net birth rate for the nation as a whole. The government estimated the birth rate for the country in 1957 at 43 per 1,000 inhabitants. The rate ranged from 25 for the Federal District and 38 for the state of São Paulo to a high of 48 per 1,000 in Ceará and Piauí. For the United States, the birth rate in 1950 was 19.5 per 1,000, or less than half the gross Brazilian rate.

Large families are the rule in Brazil. An official survey of female fecundity, made on the basis of the 1950 census, revealed some startling facts. For example, it was found that 60 per cent of all women over 15 years of age had live-born children. More than 9 per cent of those between 15 and 19 were mothers. For the age group 45–49 years, nearly 84 per cent had children living, and for those over 80 the proportion was more than three out of four. The average number of children for all women over 15 was more than 315 per 100. For those between 50 and 59, each woman had had an average of six children or twice the rate in the United States, where the size of the average household was 3.53 persons. Of the 50-year-old women included in the study, more than 30 per cent had between 10 and 15 children, and over two of each 100 had at least 15 children.

On the basis of the 1950 census figures, it is revealed that 41.7 per cent of the population is in the lowest age group of 14 years and under. If the base is raised to age 19, the percentage of the total population is increased to 52.3 or over half of all Brazilians. Two-thirds of the population are between the ages of five and 39. At the other extreme, less than 4 per cent of the inhabitants are over 60 years of age. These figures compare with percentages of 33 and 12 for the latter two age groups in the United States. In 1950, the median age of Americans was a little over 30 years, and ranged from lows of 23.6 years in South Carolina and 24 years in Mississippi to highs of 32.8 and 32.9 years respectively in Massachusetts and New Jersey. In Brazil, the productive age group of 20–60 years comprises only about 43 per cent of the total population. The result is that a disproportionate share of private income and effort is devoted to the care and support of children. This unbalanced situation is reflected in backward education, premature employment of children, and the financial stresses and strains of harried parenthood. On the other hand, the care of the aged represents a relatively light burden on the productive segment of the population.

The life expectancy for men in Brazil has been estimated at 45 years and for women at 50 years. The corresponding figures for the United States for 1950 were 66.6 and 72.4 years. There is a wide range in average longevity for Brazilian cities. In São Paulo the life-expectancy rate is around 57.6 years; in Natal it is only 36.2 years and in Recife it is 37.7 years.

Brazil has one of the most rural populations in the world. In 1950, 64 per cent of the population was officially classified as rural and 36 per cent as urban and suburban. This was substantially the reverse of the relative situation in the United States at that time. However, for the decade ending in 1950 the rural population increased by only 18 per cent, whereas the urban population increased by almost 50 per cent. The disparate growth of the cities was not due to natural increase but was largely accounted for by migration from rural areas of the country. The essentially rural character of the Brazilian population is a survival of the colonial and imperial periods and represents the predominantly agricultural economy of the nation. The factors which are responsible for the demographic shift now in process are growing industrialization, with its accompanying urbanization, improved transportation facilities between the rural districts and the cities, and the continuing high death rate of the rural population, which tends to counterbalance the greater fertility of its women.

Meanwhile, the heavy movement into the cities is creating serious social problems of slum development, as in the famous *favellas* of Rio and the *mucambos* of Recife, and of food supply, public health, and crime control, with which the municipal governments are not prepared to deal. Eventually much of this migration will probably be filtered off into urban centers along the new highways or help to relieve the labor shortage in areas of new agricultural development. The preparation and utilization of this large and roving body of people, without fixed roots in the land and with low living standards, with a view to the improvement of its own condition and as a potentially valuable resource for the needs of the nation, is probably the major responsibility of Brazil at this stage of its evolution. To correct the traditional maldistribution of the Brazilian population in order to meet the changed requirements of the modern era is a primary concern of those who direct the destinies of the state. The origins of the problem lie in the survival of a pattern of isolated population centers along the coast, like Belém, Salvador, Rio de Janeiro, and Santos–São Paulo, separated from one another by large areas of wilderness and depending on a precarious food supply from the efforts of a nomadic and backward peasant population in their respective hinterlands. The principal feature of this massive program of resettlement is centered about the government's policy of a "march to the west," represented by the construction of Brasilia and by the building of trunk roads into the empty spaces of the interior.

Of the 20 Brazilian states, São Paulo had a population of 9,142,000 in 1950. The figures for the four other most populous states were as follows: Minas Gerais, 7,728,000, Bahia, 4,834,000, Rio Grande do Sul, 4,165,000, and Pernambuco, 3,395,000. Three states, Ceará, Rio de Janeiro, and Paraná, had between 2,000,000 and 3,000,000 inhabitants. Seven, including Alagoas, Goiás, Maranhão, Pará, Paraiba, Piauí, and Santa Catarina, each had a population of between 1,000,000 and 2,000,000. Those with less than 1,000,000 inhabitants included Amazonas and Mato Grosso, the two largest states in the federation, plus Espirito Santo, Rio Grande do Norte, and little Sergipe. The four federal territories on the fringes of the Amazonia had a combined population of only a little over 200,000 people.

The rate of population increase varies greatly from state to state and from one region to another, depending on comparative trends in economic development. On the basis of the 10-year period ending in 1950, the states of the Northeast showed in general the lowest rate of growth. In that part of Brazil, the rate ranged from 15 per cent in Alagoas to 29 per cent in Ceará. It is remarkable that the latter state, located in the very heart of the drought area, exceeded the growth rate of 27 per cent for São Paulo, which is generally accepted as the pacemaker for the country as a whole. In the half-century between 1890 and 1940 the population of the state increased at the phenomenal over-all rate of 523 per cent, or approximately double the rate of the following decade. Of the four southern states, Paraná's rate of 72 per cent for the 10-year period in question was the highest in Brazil. On the other hand, the population of Rio Grande do Sul, which has a relatively settled economy, increased by only 25 per cent, a rate lower than that of Pernambuco in the Northeast. The population of Minas Gerais, the second state in the Union, had an increase rate of only 14.7 per cent, the lowest of any state in the country. During the particular decade under consideration there was relatively little new development in this key state, which became a secondary source of internal migration to other parts of Brazil. However, the expansion of metallurgical and other industries, reflected in the growth of Belo Horizonte, its capital city, may be expected to show a substantial increase in the population of Minas for the decade ending in 1960. Goiás, with the second rate of demographic advance in the nation, can anticipate an even heavier rate of growth for the following decade as the government's program for the new federal capital in the state begins to materialize.

Brazil has two of the 15 major cities of the world. The largest of the two is São Paulo, which prides itself on being "the fastest-growing city on earth." It now has about 3,500,000 inhabitants; by tomorrow night it will have many more. It overtook Rio de Janeiro several years ago, and the gap between them is bound to widen as São Paulo moves inevitably toward its destiny as the first city in Latin America and the metropolis of the southern half of the globe. There are four cities in the 500,000–1,000,000 class. The largest of these is Recife, queen of the north, with close to 800,000 people. Solid Porto Alegre in the far south, historic and unhurried Salvador or Bahia, and bright and bustling Belo Horizonte are also in the 500,000-plus category. Another quartet of cities are in the 200,000–400,000 bracket. They include tropical and somnolent Belém, whose growth is handicapped by its location on an eddy of the Ocean Sea and by the retarded state of the Amazonia, Niteroi, which is a sort of Jersey City to Rio, awaiting an improved ferry service and a tunnel under the bay to realize its population potential, and booming Curitiba, capital of Paraná and most promising of the four.

There are about 20 cities in the 100,000 class. Due to the accepted classification of "cities" and "municipal districts" or *municipios,* and confusion as to "metropolitan areas," the absolute and relative population of cities is often difficult to determine with better than an approximation to statistical realities. In much of Brazil there is a real dearth of cities to serve as centers around which the areas may fulfill their promise of economic and cultural development. For example, Minas Gerais, with a population larger than that of Ohio, has only two cities of over 100,000 as against Ohio's eight. Excluding the state capital and its suburbs, São Paulo has seven cities in the same category.

CHAPTER 2

The Amazonia

POLITICALLY SPEAKING, MOST OF THE AMAZON VALLEY IS a part of Brazil. In every other sense it is a world apart. Its true status is that of a colony. To the average Brazilian it is little more than a "geographical expression," somehow associated with his country but singularly unrelated to his own life. It is not even accessible to him except by air or ancient coastwise steamer. The long road from the south comes to a dead end in Maranhão, and the Belém-Brasilia highway will only link the Atlantic gateway of the Valley with the true Brazil roundabout by way of the Goiás plateau. Its forbidding reputation as an uncomfortable and unhealthy jungle does not promote a closer affinity between the Amazonia and the rest of Brazil.

The total area of the Brazilian portion of the Amazon's drainage basin is about 1,845,500 square miles. Of this, the part officially designated as the "Great Northern region," which is entirely within the confines of the basin, is composed of the two states of Amazonas and Pará and the four federal territories of Acre, Amapà, Rio Branco, and Rondonia. The Brazilian Amazonia also includes some 465,000 squares miles in the states of Goiás and Mato Grosso, and another 12,000 square miles in Maranhão.

As a measure of the magnitude of the Amazonia, the island of Marajó in the mouth of the main river is half again as large as Belgium and larger than Switzerland plus another Delaware. The Ilha do Bananal, or Island of the Banana Grove, in the Araguaya is the largest fresh-water island in the world. It is 200 miles long and 35 miles wide at its broadest point.

In 1950 the population of the "Great Northern region" was reported at about 1,750,000 inhabitants, an over-all rate of approximately five persons to each four square miles of surface. Of these about 250,000 lived in the city of Belém and about 90,000 in Manaus. There are five other towns with a population of between 5,000 and 15,000, the largest of which is Santarém. The portion of the Amazon basin that lies above the watershed of the Paraguay-Paraná system of rivers within Goiás and Mato Grosso is very thinly settled and the inclusion of its scattered inhabitants would add relatively little to the above total. Moreover, due to the wide dispersion and excessive mobility of its river and jungle dwellers, there is probably a considerable margin of error in any estimate of the area's population.

Though the bulk of the Amazonia is in Brazil, much of its upper reaches lie within five contiguous countries, and its drainage basin extends from the edge of the plains of Santa Cruz in Bolivia around by Peru, Ecuador, and Colombia into southwestern Venezuela. Perhaps Amazonia should have been left in one piece, without national frontiers to break its unity, a wilderness empire to be ruled by some *carai-guassú* of the Tupí race from his capital at Santarém, where the Tapajóz meets the Amazon. For the land was not yet ready for the white man—and still is not. The Tupí also came too soon, but at least it was his world and he had learned to live in his own way with its realities and its mysteries. It is still an unfinished cosmos, and men who live in the long-tailored environment of a civilized world find little familiarity or compatibility within its antediluvian depths. The stranger ultimately may resign himself to the chance of meeting a dinosaur in his path or seeing a pterodactyl fly overhead, as Tomlinson did. I remember once a scene, as from the morning of creation, of myriads of migrant birds singing in the trees that overhung a secluded lake in the forest, one of them a lark from my own native land. When a traveler says that he has seen some fantastic vision in the wilderness, one does not laugh and make light of him.

The first authenticated contact of men from the outside with the Amazonia began with Francisco de Orellana in the years 1539–42. Orellana was a lieutenant of Gonzalo, one of the Pizarro brothers who took over the Inca empire for Spain. Gonzalo Pizarro led an ill-fated expedition from Quito down into the Napo country in search of a reported "Land of Cinnamon." Floundering about in the jungle, he sent Orellana with a small party down-river in search of food, but Orellana found something a few days later that made him forget all about his chief and his hunger. That was a huge east-flowing river. Curiosity and the current must have accounted for his decision to follow the stream to its end in the ocean. The banks of the river were then much more heavily populated than they are now, and Orellana had many encounters, hostile and otherwise, with the Indians before he finally reached the Atlantic many months later. Somewhere along the way he fell in with some natives whom he apparently mistook for women, but whose arrows kept him at a distance, so that he could not verify his suspicions. Anyway, it was too good a tale to miss, so to his reporter, versed in Greek mythology, they were "Amazons" and the river had found its name for good and all.

There have been persistent rumors of others who came before the Spanish conquistador. Two of the roving free-lance ship captains who followed in the wake of Columbus very probably sighted the coast of northern Brazil, but went their way without bothering to make a landing. One was the mysterious Vicente

Yanez Pinzón, who had commanded the smallest of Columbus' three ships on his first voyage, and who briefly showed up above the mouth of the Amazon eight years later, a little before Cabral's chance discovery of the coast about Porto Seguro. It is likely that another lone navigator, Diego de Lepe, repeated the same feat in that era of discovery, and in 1532, ten years before Orellana came out to sea from the west, Diego de Ordaz, one of Cortés' captains, who had already ascended the Orinoco, tried to enter the mouth of the Amazon. There is extant a vague tradition of a Norman seaman, named Jean Cousin of Dieppe, who was supposed to have found the Amazon in 1488. The French story is further complicated by the intriguing detail that Pinzón was second officer on Cousin's ship and, later meeting Columbus at Genoa, told him of his discovery and then formed the partnership with him which was to bear fruit four years later.

Of much greater antiquity is the claim of certain European scholars that the ships of Solomon and Hiram of Tyre plied to the Amazon in search of gold and timbers for the Temple. The hypothesis that the Amazonia was actually the site of Ophir and Tarshish is based on the similarity of place names in the upper Amazon Valley with terms from the Hebraic language. The Amazon itself between the mouth of the Negro and the Peruvian border is still known as the Solimões. Among the streams in the upper basin whose names bear a strange resemblance to ancient Semitic terms are those of two gold-bearing streams in Peru, the Parú and Apu-Parú, or "rich Parú," said to be derived from the Hebrew word *Paruim*. It is further adduced as evidence of the theory that the Egyptian word *pa-aru* signified "river." These particular syllables appear frequently in the nomenclature of Amazonian rivers, as do several other suspiciously similar terms. The Arabic sound of the Bolivian rivers, El Bení and Madidi, has frequently raised unanswered questions in the imagination of travelers. In further connection with this intriguing legend is the mystery of the pottery found on the island of Marajó and in the lower Tapajóz, whose designs are peculiarly reminiscent of western Asia. It is not strange that Colonel Fawcett, the famous English engineer, devoted his last years to a search for a city of the Lost Atlantis in the wilds of the Xingú.

After Orellana's voyage to the sea, the Spaniards paid little attention to the Amazon country. A few tapped its edges in quest of El Dorado or the golden city that was supposed to be situated in the Lake of Manoa, which appears on a Hondius map, along with the female warrior and other stock curiosities of the area. But they were daunted by the difficulties of travel and engaged more profitably in other realms. An exception to their general disregard was the bold foray of the notorious Lope de Aguirre. To pacify the troubled land and to be rid of him once for all, the viceroy of Peru sent Aguirre, the first desperado of the New World, and an assorted band of cutthroats into the jungle beyond the Andes in quest of treasure—and death. Aguirre found neither in the Amazonia, but made one of the most extraordinary river voyages in history. After descending the Amazon for most of its length, he seems to have turned up the Negro and eventually to have reached the mouth of the Orinoco by way of the Cassiquiare canal that links the two river systems. His career of infamy ended when the king's men cut him down in 1561 on the island of Margarita off the coast of Venezuela.

For a time the Amazonia was undisturbed by Europeans. Then in the early seventeenth century the Portuguese began to assert their claims to its vast solitudes. Their immediate motive was a desire to expel other European intruders from the region. In 1615 they drove the French from their settlement of São Luíz on the Maranhão coast, and the next year they founded Belém on the southern entrance into the main river. Shortly afterward they expelled the Dutch from their three posts in the lower Amazon and some Englishmen who had established a base on the principal mouth of the river.

Free from the menace of their European rivals, the Portuguese undertook to make good in earnest their rights in the Valley which, above the mouth of the Xingú, was still untouched by them. They displayed remarkable energy in their efforts but, as concerned the native population, a ruthlessness that was to leave a permanent mark on the demographic pattern of the Amazonia. Contrary to their usual humane policy, they slaughtered large numbers of the aborigines and enslaved many more, with the result that most of the surviving Indians moved farther up the side rivers in order to escape from their oppressors. Meanwhile, Pedro Teixeira, one of the Portuguese leaders of the period, not only explored the lower valley of the Tapajóz but, during the years 1637–39, led an expedition up the main river into the Napo, eventually reaching Quito and thus reversing the course of Orellana a century earlier.

In this period the Portuguese established forts at strategic points in the Valley. In addition to armed posts on both sides of the delta, at Macapá and Belém, others were built at the narrows by Obidos, at the mouth of the Tapajóz, at a site where Manaus now stands on the Rio Negro, at Tabatinga, where the river enters Brazil, and at Villa Bella or Beira in the jungle of the Guaporé or Itenes. These archaic relics of the classical age of fortification are one of the few survivals of the pre-rubber era in the Amazonia. In the meantime, the hold of Portugal on her forest empire was further strengthened by the Mameluco *bandeirantes* from far-off São Paulo, who penetrated the upper basin by way of the rivers of the Madeira system. By the middle of the eighteenth century there were nearly 50 small settlements in the Valley, but the Portuguese had clung to the river banks and practically nothing was yet known of the lands between the rivers.

Except for the expedition of Charles de la Condamine, little serious effort was made at a study of the Amazonia until the 1800's, when the great German geographer, Alexander von Humboldt, came out of Venezuela into the middle of the Valley. Condamine spent several years in the Quito country after 1735, chiefly with the object of measuring a meridional arc of the Equator and thereby determining the circumference of the earth. He returned to France by way of the Amazon and later published his valuable observations of the region in the *Mémoires* of the Academy of Sciences. He was preceded in his descent of the Amazon by the wife of one of his associates, the astronomer Louis Godin. Mme. Godin was at first accompanied by her brother, who died early on the voyage, but with the aid of Indians she managed to reach Belém, where she took ship for France.

In the early period of the Brazilian Empire, which began in 1822, there was considerable unrest in the Amazonia. Two years later a separatist movement briefly threatened to set up a "Confederation of the Equator," and in 1835 there broke out, as a protest against political abuses, a widespread uprising known as "the Cabanagem." For several years there was much disorder, bordering sometimes on a state of anarchy, until the movement was finally suppressed by harsh measures of the military. There was still no economic base for development, though the discovery of the hot vulcanizing process by Charles Goodyear between 1839 and 1844 gave promise of a future for the yet sterile region. Ten years later an important step forward was taken by the inauguration of steam navigation on the Amazon, to be followed in 1867 by the opening of the river to the shipping of all nations. Closely related to this event was the transcontinental expedition of William Herndon and Lardner Gibbon, two officers of the United States Navy, whose findings were published in 1854 as a two-volume Senate document.

By now the Amazonia had become the object of the curiosity of foreign scientists, and from the middle of the century a remarkable group of international scholars carried on scientific research and exploration in the region. Among the earliest to continue the activities of Humboldt were the two Germans, Spix and Von Martius, whose *Reise im Brasilien* was published in 1823. The list of others included such distinguished names as Louis Agassiz, the Swiss-American geologist, Alfred Russell Wallace, the English naturalist, and his compatriot, Henry Walter Bates, who passed the years 1848–59 in the Valley and wrote the classic work, *A Naturalist on the Amazon,* Captain Matthew Fontaine Maury, the American hydrographer, Frenchmen like Castelneau, the Abbé Durand, Jules Creveaux, and Henri Coudreau and his heroic wife, who spent many years in exploring the rivers of the province of Pará. The Chandless, the Heath, and the Orton were named for those who explored their course, as the Roosevelt was later to be.

In the present century the serious examination and assessment of the Amazonia has continued. Across the green stage there have since passed many others: Hamilton Rice on his way into the remote Uaupés on the Venezuelan border; Colonel George Church, civil engineer and scientist, who made the initial surveys and did the groundwork for the Madeira–Mamoré Railway; the German-Swiss of the Goeldi Museum in Belém; Paul Lecointe, author of the encyclopedic work, *L'Amazonie Brésilienne;* Konrad Guenther, the German naturalist; anthropologists and sociologists like Charles Wagley; and the joint company of Americans and Brazilians who traveled over 25,000 miles in the Valley in the 1920's on a survey of the Amazonia's potential for the production of rubber. For several years an international commission of the UNESCO has been engaged in a general study of the region's possibilities for the needs of the human race.

Much of the work of uncovering the Amazonia to the world has been done by Brazilians: men like the explorers, Silva Coutinho and Barboza Rodrigues; the famous writer, José Veríssimo, who published his *Escenas da Vida Amazónica* in the last year of the Empire; and the brilliant and unhappy engineer-novelist, Euclydes da Cunha. Greatest of all the moderns of whatever nationality who were associated with the Amazonia was Cándido Mariano da Silva Rondón. An officer of the engineer corps of the Brazilian army, he first won distinction by building the government telegraph lines and land trail to link the upper Paraguay basin in Mato Grosso with Porto Velho on the Madeira, from where there was an old river connection with Manaus. Most of the remainder of his long life was devoted to the vast wilderness and its denizens, whose blood he shared. He was responsible for the creation of the Brazilian Indian Service, whose aim was to protect the forest tribes from exploitation and draw them peaceably into the current of national life. Meanwhile he explored large areas of land that lie about the watershed between the Paraguay and Amazon river systems, and even the little-known zone across the headwaters of the northern tributaries of the main river. In 1913 he accompanied ex-President Theodore Roosevelt on his famous expedition over the divide from Cuiabá into the basin of the Madeira, by way of the Rio da Dúvida or "River of Doubt." In the party were distinguished naturalists like George Cherrie and Leo Miller, whose books, with Roosevelt's *Through the Brazilian Wilderness,* were valuable additions to the rich literature of the Amazonia.

In spite of all that has been done, since Orellana's epic voyage, to open the valley to the knowledge of western man, there still remain substantial residues of *terra incognita* back of the line of the rivers, as in the triangle between the Negro and the Solimões. It is probable that *seringueiros* or rubber gatherers have penetrated most of these recesses in the course of their long wanderings. But they were illiterate men who could not write of the wonders they had seen, so that their stories have remained untold, like the six who crossed the north and south line of the rivers between the Javarý and the Atlantic.

The principal feature of the Amazonia is the river itself. All other rivers—the Mississippi, the Congo, and the rest—are as so many creeks in comparison with this incomparable stream. Except for the tides of the ocean, nothing else on the planet represents such a cosmic force as this relentless flood which drains an area of heavy rainfall the size of the United States. For those who can comprehend the terms of astronomy, some hydrographer has calculated that the Amazon pours between 63,000 and 150,000 cubic feet of water into the Atlantic every second, or at the rate of 5,500,000,000 to 13,000,000,000 cubic feet a year, to discolor the ocean for 200 miles from the coast. To the Tupís it was the

Paranáguassú, or "the Great River." The Portuguese called it Rio-Mar or "River-Sea." To Henry Bates it was "the Mediterranean of South America."

It is too inchoate and disorderly, too immeasurable by any standards that men would apply to it, to be a thing of beauty, as the Ohio is. Those who live with it can feel no sentimental attachment to it, as they might to the Hudson or the Rhine. They only fear and respect its might and make the best terms they can with its impersonal and sinister presence. No one writes odes to it or paints pictures of it or sings its praises.

Like a mangrove-fringed shore, it has no banks for much of its length. In lieu of clearly defined borders, as any settled and well-behaved river would have, it is usually bordered by a marshy and impenetrable zone of matted vegetation. Its tangled plant life is very different from the open *matto* of the *terra firme* or "firm land" above the level of the flood-plain. At its worst, as in the tidal flats of the "Green Hell," as Alberto Rangel called the region of the delta to the west of Marajó, one may encounter in the waterlogged undergrowth tentacular lianas as long as a city block or an impassable maze of fallen trees.

The Amazon is never a benign river where men feel at home. It is, above all, a destroyer on a scale that is beyond comprehension. Where shores are evident, they are liable to be only ephemeral walls against its destructive violence. One of the familiar phenomena of the River-Sea is the *terras caidas* or "falling lands." This is a particularly terrifying experience at night, as the river undermines its own banks, which slide into the stream with a mighty roar, accompanied by the sound of crashing and tangled trees that have been uprooted. On the night of January 29, 1866, nearly 150 miles of the southern shore fell into the river in a continuous line. The vast volume of earth is swept downstream, much of it to be carried out to sea in what Euclydes da Cunha called "a telluric migration." Sometimes the river breaks loose large areas of land and carries them away as floating islands, eventually to be broken up on the way or attached again to the shore. I once saw such an island, several acres in extent, moving seaward, and in one of the cecropia trees that rose from its surface was a frightened monkey.

In the lower reaches of the Amazon, with which the foreigners who go up to Manaus and back to Belém are most familiar, it is only one river at the *Garganta* or "throat" in front of Obidos. Here it has cut transversally through a range of hills that lay across its path. The channel is less than 2,000 yards wide at this point, but it is over 300 feet deep in midstream where the current rolls at six miles an hour. Elsewhere it is a liquid labyrinth.

The flood cycle of the Amazon and its tributaries is largely determined by the annual melting of the vast snow beds in the Andes. In the lower river the waters are at their highest in June and they fall between September and December. The seasonal variation in the level of the river below Parintíns is normally from 20 to 27 feet. At Manaus, where the articulated floating docks were designed to compensate for the differences in the water level, the Negro may rise between 25 and 40 feet. In the upper Madeira the annual rise is generally between 33 and 45 feet, and in the Juruá it may be as much as 55 or 60 feet. The rise or fall of the rivers may come very suddenly, as a veritable wall of water rolls downstream from off the snow fields. Or the flood may pass as quickly, so that during the critical season steamers are accustomed to anchor at night in midstream. Otherwise a boat may find itself marooned on the river bank until the next year's rise.

The lower Valley in all its most typical aspects may be seen to advantage from the remarkable sandy hill which crops out at the water's edge at Monte Alegre. To the north there stretches a country of open grasslands against a background of low mountains that shut off the horizon. On the lowlands to east and west the endless jungle of the flood-plain reaches up and down the wide basin. In front, beyond a maze of *paranás* or side channels and the *furos* or canals that link them in one hydrographic whole, there is visible the wide yellow flood of the Amazon's main channel. At times of low water cattle graze in the lush pasturage of the islands and the inhabitants plant quick-growing food crops in the new layer of silt on strips of *varzea* land. Later, as the river rises, the islands disappear, and where cattle fed there are large lakes. In the far distance to the south only a low line now marks the border of the moving sea.

The tributaries of the Amazon rank among the great rivers of the world. Within Brazil six major rivers flow into it from the south—the Tocantíns-Araguaya, the Xingú, the Tapajóz, the Madeira, the Purús, and the Juruá. The Javarý of ill fame forms the lower boundary with Peru, and farther to the west are the two Peruvian branches of the main river, the Ucayali and the Huallaga. The northern tributaries of the lower Amazon, like the Parú and the Erepecurú, are relatively short rivers that come tumbling down over a series of cataracts and rapids out of the highlands of the *Guiana Brasileira*. In its lower course the Trombetas, the largest of them, is a wide and pleasant stream.

By right of the enormous volume of its black water, the Negro dwarfs all of the other south-flowing rivers. Where it debouches into the Amazon below Manaus its swarthy flood flows side by side with the turbid body of the main river for a long distance before their waters mingle and the Negro loses its identity to the all-devouring monster. Its remote headwaters lie in Colombia and the Venezuelan state of Amazonas where a mulch of tannin-bearing leaves covers the forest floor, to discolor the water that eventually finds its way into the Negro. Above the mouth of the Negro, the Japurá, known in Colombia as the Caquetá, is a little-traveled stream, like the Ica, better known as the Colombian Putumayo.

Some of the tributaries have a distinct personality of their own. The Tapajóz is the favorite river of most travelers. It comes down out of the crystalline highlands of Mato Grosso and flows among hills for much of its way. When it is not in flood, its water is a clear green. There are pleasing vistas and long stretches of white sandy beach. Below the last of the *cachoeiras* or rapids at Itaituba the river spreads out and at Boím it is nearly 10 miles wide. It is also the most salubrious of all the great tributaries of the Amazon. Its gateway at Santarém, which has the best site in the Amazonia, is worthy of the attractive stream that forms a wide lake in front of the little city. The Xingú is similar in some respects, but is generally a much less inviting stream. One enters it from the Amazon by way of the flooded lands about Porto de Moz, and the long series of *cachoeiras* of the Volta Grande or "Great Bend" prevent easy access to its upper reaches, which begin at Altamira.

At the opposite extreme are the Purús and the Juruá, which form an outlet into the Solimões for the distant Acre Territory. They are unfinished and forbidding streams, and their serpentine courses slither across the low country in long oxbows. Their channels are forever shifting and, like the main river, their water is always yellow. Euclydes da Cunha called the Purús, which he knew so well, the *rio enjeitado,* the "forsaken river," from which men fled as from something accursed.

In the gap between the Purús and the Tapajóz, the Madeira is the center of a vast fluvial system of its own that reaches far into Mato Grosso and Bolivia. Among its branches and their ramifications are streams famous in the history of the Amazonia, like the lonely rubber rivers, the Gý-Paraná or Machado and the Abuná, the Guaporé that skirts the border of Brazil for a long distance, the Bolivian Beni and Madre de Dios, and the latter's mysterious affluent, the Manú. Since it is navigable about 800 miles to the formidable rapids which begin at Porto Velho and extend for 220 miles to Guajaramirim on the Mamoré at the southern terminus of the railroad, the Madeira has long been important in the economy and life of the vast region it drains.

Unique among all the rivers is the stygian Negro, where one might well meet Charon himself ferrying the dead. There are other black rivers in the Amazonia, like the Jutaí, but none so awe-inspiring. In the Boiossú Channel it is nearly 20 miles from shore to shore, and its wide course is strewn with islands that are covered with dead forests, as if some cosmic cataclysm had swept over it. Very different is its principal affluent, the Rio Branco, or White River, that is the road to the open Campos Gerais and the picturesque borderlands of the Mountains of the Moon. There are broad *praias* of clean sand, as on the Tapajóz, where cooling breezes blow off the water at night and the traveler finds welcome relief from the mournful atmosphere of the Negro below and from the depressing confinement of flooded jungles.

No serious effort was made to exploit the natural resources of the Amazon Valley until the coming of the rubber era in the last century. A desultory and unorganized search for forest products for which there was a demand in foreign countries had gone on along the lower rivers ever since the Portuguese established their authority over the region. But the population of the area was still very sparse and the volume of this extractive business was restricted and intermittent.

All this changed with the development of a market for crude rubber that followed the invention of the vulcanizing process and the technical improvements made by Thomas Hancock. Two main sources of latex, the *Hevea brasiliensis* and *Castilloa elastica* (or ulei) trees, are native to the Amazonia, though the habitat of the *Castilloa* extends as far north as Mexico. Another variety of *hevea,* known as *benthamiana,* is found largely in the region to the north of the main river. The reserves of wild rubber trees were particularly large in the upper reaches of the southern rivers, and those remote areas early became the center of the industry. The trees nowhere occur in solid stands but are scattered among other species in the forest. As the trade developed its standards of quality, rubber which originated in the Acre Territory and the hill country of northern Mato Grosso was classified as "Up-river Pará" or *fine* rubber, as contrasted with the "weak" rubber from the lowlands and from most of the country north of the Amazon. The annexation of the Acre, formerly a part of Bolivia, by a process of infiltration somewhat similar to that whereby Texas was acquired by the United States, added that favored area to the potential reservoir of latex for the Brazilian industry.

During this initial stage the migration of considerable numbers of refugees from the drought-stricken parts of northeastern Brazil provided a much-needed labor supply. In the meantime the industry gradually assumed the peculiar form which it has preserved with little change to the present. Enterprising individuals or trading firms in Belém or Manaus established claims to large rubber-bearing areas or *seringães* along the rivers. The extent of the properties was reckoned in terms of *estradas,* or the number of trees which a single *seringueiro* could tend or work.

The migrant from Ceará and other states of the Northeast was recruited in either city by agents of the owner or concessionaire of the particular *seringal* where he was destined to serve. He was then transported by river boat to the headquarters of the property to which he was henceforth bound. At this point he was outfitted from his employer's warehouse or *barracão* with the few tools necessary to his work and with other staple merchandise for his own use. The minimum basic equipment generally consisted of a Collins machete, a gross or more of small tin cups for gathering the latex from the tapped trees, a small ax, a Winchester carbine and box of cartridges, a hammock, and a bag of *farinha* or manioc meal. All of these articles were charged against the *seringueiro*'s account at figures usually more than double their cost. The account could only be liquidated by future deliveries of rubber, which generally proved inadequate to cover the worker's accumulated obligations. Pending such an improbable eventuality, he remained in all respects a serf in a feudal system, and his normal fate was eventually to die as a perpetual debtor in the jungle, known only to the major-domo and the bookkeeper at the *barracão* down-river.

Once he reached the site along some river where he was to live and work, perhaps three or four weeks upstream by dugout canoe, he marked out his *estrada* in the forest. This consisted in cutting a path to connect the hundred or more trees which he would tap each morning and whose latex he would collect later in the day. The latex would then be coagulated over a smoky fire of palm nuts and added to the black ball which he slowly built layer by layer. His habitation was a lean-to, roofed with palm fronds to protect his hammock from the rain. The routine of his lonely and isolated existence was relieved only by fishing along the river or by a hunt in the woods around him, but, since bullets were costly, he spent them sparingly and preferred to set improvised traps for the game.

If he were one of the minority of his kind who managed to outlive the multiple hazards of his calling—malaria, accidents in the forest, and the "red ink" on his employer's books—he might collect the balance that was due him and spend it in a few days of roistering in the city. At the end of his spree he would probably return penniless to the *seringal,* with another bag of *farinha* and a new set of entries in the left-hand column of the *patrão*'s ledger. So long as he remained a debtor, escape was difficult. His employer guarded the entrance to the river and the forest behind him was pathless and full of hidden terrors. The authority of the state was against him, and there were agreements between the lords of the rivers that had the force of the fugitive slave laws of our ante-bellum South. So it was safest in the long run just to fall into one's hammock when night came and accept whatever fate each day might bring.

The *seringueiro* was the victim of a system of labor which Euclydes da Cunha called "the most criminal yet conceived by the shameless egotism of men." Euclydes tells of the two islands in the mouth of the Purús and the Juruá that were known as the "Isles of Conscience" because men who were headed up-river abandoned on them their "noblest qualities" before entering "the diabolical paradise of the rubber forests." The evil things that happened in the basins of the Purús and the Madeira and the Xingú could be duplicated in the vast domains of the Suárez brothers in the Beni country of Bolivia, and in Peru in the forests of the Putumayo and the Ucayali. While crossing the watershed between the Huallaga and the Ucayali I came upon the abandoned *barracón* of a former rubber property. The funereal house, that was like something out of Poe, was the haunt of vampire bats, and in the courtyard there were stocks in which the workers had been punished. Sometimes a state of anarchy prevailed on the rivers as men fought one another over the rights to the lands. One day in 1907 eight men were killed in a battle over the ownership of the São Miguel property on the Purús, and when I was in Rio Branco do Acre in 1923 the largest proprietor of the region, who had taken the lands of others at will, was in prison for the murder of a rival. Occasionally the Indians took "the law" into their own hands with interest, as when some 80 *seringueiros* were massacred on the Purús in 1912 in revenge for the murder of one member of a local tribe. Yet in spite of all the crimes and oppression of the rubber boom, the story of the Amazonia during that dramatic period was not one of unmitigated infamy. There were humane proprietors who earned the devotion of their workers and, instead of remaining in Belém or Manaus, shared the solitude of the rivers with their men. And there were *seringueiros* who lived to return to their homes in the Northeast with unbelievable tales of things they had seen in the dark forest by the great rivers.

The rubber boom reached its climax early in 1910. For several years there had been high living in the cities of Amazonia. The large opera house in Manaus still stands as a silent monument to the lavish prodigality of the era, when companies of Italian singers produced a repertoire of Verdi for the delight of the rubber aristocracy. Some crossed the Atlantic and spent their profits in a few weeks of Paris or the resorts of the Riviera. And then in April, 1910, the whole gaudy structure of the jungle bonanza abruptly collapsed about the heads of its beneficiaries. Just before the crash came, the world price of crude rubber had reached a high of 12 shillings or nearly $3.00 a pound. By late 1923 the price of "up-river fine" in Belém and Manaus was between 19 and 21 cents.

Few Brazilians had taken seriously the threat of plantation

rubber. Several years before a quiet Englishman named Henry Wickham succeeded in getting some 70,000 seeds of *Hevea brasiliensis* from the lower Tapajóz into the botanical gardens at Kew near London. Later the young shoots from Kew were transplanted to Ceylon, to form the basis of a plantation industry that later spread to Malaya and Sumatra. By 1913, three years after the break in rubber prices, the production of the Asiatic plantations exceeded the output of the Amazonia, and by 1927 only 6 per cent of the world's rubber supply came from wild trees. This period coincided with the rapid development of the automobile industry, which absorbed the increasing production of the Far East. At the time of the crisis in 1910 the total world consumption of natural rubber was only about 100,000 tons. Thirty years later it exceeded 1,000,000 tons and it is now about twice that figure, while another 40 per cent is produced synthetically.

The chronicle of the Brazilian industry can be told in the statistics of exports, since the domestic consumption of rubber was limited until the establishment of national rubber factories. The first recorded shipments from the province of Pará, amounting to less than 35 tons, were made in 1827. By 1853, as the result of technical improvements in the manufacturing industry in England and the United States, exports had risen to about 2,500 tons. By that time a wide variety of rubber articles, from pencil erasers, for which the raw material, rubber, was named, to over 500,000 pairs of "gum boots" a year, was being turned out in both countries. The first factory was put up at Akron in 1870. By 1908, two years before the end of the boom, Brazilian production amounted to over 35,000 tons. In order to dispose of accumulated stocks and to satisfy previous commitments of the trade, the highest point was not reached until 1912, when the total yield of the Brazilian Amazonia was over 38,000 tons. By 10 years later it had fallen to half that figure. In 1957 the national production of crude rubber had risen again to less than 33,000 tons, or about 1.7 per cent of the total world output, while the national industry consumed another 13,000 tons, which was imported from Asia by way of Dutch ports. In that year nearly 2,000,000 tires and 1,370,000 inner tubes were produced in Brazilian factories.

By the middle of 1910 many of the largest trading houses of Belém and Manaus were ruined. The complex chain of relationships in the business that extended from the actual producers to the exporters had resulted in the overextension of credits which could not be liquidated. In the emergency, the Rio government set up an elaborate program of relief for the region that envisaged radical changes in the whole economy of the Amazonia as well as in its basic industry. However, these impromptu measures had little effect on the general situation, though they eventually led to greater diversification of production in the area and to some minor reforms in the techniques of the traditional industry.

Over the years there had been some sporadic activity in the establishment of rubber plantations, but most of these had fallen into decay. It was not until the 1920's, when the Ford interests built their large plantations on the Tapajóz, that a serious attempt was made to introduce the scientific methods which had been so successful in the Orient. Largely as a result of changed company policies in regard to foreign investments in a field that was outside its main interest, and also probably because of difficulties in creating a stable labor force, the Ford plantations were eventually sold to the Brazilian government. In the meantime, official policies of encouraging the establishment of rubber plantations by foreign manufacturers operating in Brazil has given a new impetus to this phase of the industry. In line with these policies a series of new plantations are now being developed in the state of Pará, including the Brazilian subsidiaries of Goodyear, Goodrich, and Pirelli, while the Firestone interests have initiated extensive plantings in the southern part of the state of Bahia.

The wide variety of other products does not compensate for the failure of the Amazonia's classic industry to hold its proper place in the world. Like the parrots, some of these articles have long been gathered for export; a few are relatively new. The sum of the business is not impressive nor, as conducted at present, is its future promising.

Between 35,000 and 42,000 tons of Brazil nuts or *castanha do Pará* are normally collected each year from the tall black trees in the jungle. They are practically unknown in Rio and São Paulo, and most of the crop goes to New York and English ports. Cacao beans are still collected from about 15,000 acres of the oldest plantations in Brazil. Several varieties of hard fibers, including piassava, tucúm, and guaxima, are produced in considerable quantities, and a large area near Manaus has been planted in jute to provide bagging material for the coffee industry in southern Brazil. There is also a small vegetable-oil industry, which utilizes the nuts of a variety of palms in the lower Amazon. An old industry, localized in the Maués, produces guaraná for bottlers in Rio and São Paulo. The output of "drugs" or medicinals and flavoring materials is small. However, the range of such items is extensive and includes tonka beans, a product of the cumarú tree, balm of copahú, vanilla, rosewood oil, and curare, an Indian arrow poison employed in the treatment of spastic paralysis. Beginning during the Second World War, there was a boom in the extraction of timbó root, the basic ingredient of DDT. Though the Amazon Valley is the largest area of forest on earth, little has been done to develop its timber resources, and the output of its small sawmills is insignificant in comparison with the possibilities of the industry. A veneer plant has recently been established at Porcel in the lower Valley. An innovation in the economics of the area is the cultivation of pepper by Japanese immigrants. The most important development in the Amazonia in recent years is the opening of a large-scale manganese mining industry in the Territory of Amapá to the north of the river's principal mouth. In 1957 this operation produced nearly 700,000 tons of ore, all of which was shipped to the United States.

Most agriculture in the Amazon Valley is devoted to the production of foodstuffs for the ill-fed local population. Though large areas are well suited to the growth of sugar cane, total plantings amount to only about 20,000 acres, whose product is utilized for the production of alcohol and molasses. The sugar consumed in the Valley is brought in from the states farther down the coast. About 50,000 acres are planted to rice, which is an important item in the regional diet. Other staple subsistence crops that are grown in considerable quantities include corn, beans, bananas, and manioc. Some of the world's strongest tobacco is raised in the state of Pará. There are about 1,250,000 cattle in the Amazonia. The largest center of the industry is on the huge island of Marajó, where the animals live in a half-amphibian environment. The hog population of the Valley is estimated at between 800,000 and 900,000.

Generations of little men have nibbled, like mice, at the edges of the Amazonia. In terms of its magnitude, the results are almost imperceptible. Its cities are stagnant or have retrograded. The heart has gone out of them and they are full of ghosts and of mirages that will never materialize. Orellana could travel down the monstrous river today and see little that was new to him. No one knows yet what to do with it all. Its would-be conquerors generally end up shaking their heads in frustration at its impersonal challenge. Those who would solve the problem of its development must be possessed of superhuman imagination and boldness and they must have access to vast stores of capital. They must be willing to forget much that is familiar and to start anew as if on another planet. The man who came nearest to measuring up to these requirements of vision and daring was Percival Farquhar, the American who succeeded in building the famous Madeira-Mamoré Railway after others had failed. The system of docks at Belém is another monument to this extraordinary man, and a rickety little steamer that bears his name on its bow plies up and down the Amazon.

Of the various factors in its development, its climate has been overly maligned. It is uncomfortable for much of the time, but more endurable than the extremes of summer in parts of the United States. There is good air movement, even in the jungle, and the nights are generally quite tolerable and often exhilaratingly cool. People may sweat copiously in the afternoon, but they do not die from the heat. With reasonable precautions in matters of health, outsiders adjust themselves successfully to living in the Amazon Valley and can expect a normal life span. However, the price of ignorance or of contempt for the basic rules of hygiene can be heavy, for the Amazonia belongs to its insects, and all other living creatures live by their sufferance. The Brazilian Public Health Service has greatly expanded its facilities in the area in recent years, particularly for the prevention and treatment of malaria.

The Amazonian soils have definite limitations for purposes of agriculture. The top layer of humus in the forest is generally thin, since there is no autumnal falling of leaves to add to the surface mulch, as in wooded lands of the temperate zones. When the jungle cover is removed the rains soon leach the organic materials out of the soil, so that its fertility is short-lived. Artificial fertilization of exhausted soils is still a thing of the future. A secondary matted growth of hard grasses and other plants quickly takes over a clearing, and the native farmer usually repeats the same process near by as the yield of his crops declines and the difficulties of controlling the new ground cover increase. Beneath the shallow layer of loam or light sandy clay an impermeable hardpan fixes a clear limit to further cultivation of the ground. Large areas of promising soils do exist, but their location and extent have not yet been surveyed as a basis for more extensive farming operations. Moreover, the possibilities of the rich *varzea* lands in the flood-plains of the rivers have only been touched, though their natural fertility has been amply demonstrated. The Amazon Valley could doubtless provide food for a much larger population than it now sustains so inadequately. However, in default of a massive resort to the use of artificial fertilizer, its demographic potential is clearly restricted.

It is in no sense a reserve for the future overflow of the human race. It is not another Ganges or Yangtse valley.

Pending the possible discovery of further sources of mineral wealth, to the casual observer who speculates on its future the Amazonia appears to have little more than trees to offer, uncountable trillions of them. Like so many Lilliputians, lumbermen have hacked away at them as though they were working a wood lot on a New England farm, but without making the least impression on them. The range of species runs the whole gamut of dendrology, from the lightest to the heaviest of woods. To a scientific forester, accustomed to solid stands of oak or pine, the assorted maze of trees is a nightmare. They defy all conventional methods of timbering, and perhaps the ultimate key to their utilization may be a resort to large floating sawmills that would consume every variety of tree in a given area and then move down river to repeat the same process ad infinitum.

For transportation, reliance must still be placed largely on the rivers, which are the natural roads of the Amazonia. Ocean steamers travel the main river to Iquitos in Peru all the year, and H. M. Tomlinson wrote his famous book, *The Sea and the Jungle,* as the result of a freighter's voyage that brought a cargo of steel rails from Cardiff to Porto Velho on the upper Madeira. Most of the main tributaries of the Amazon are navigable for long distances by vessels drawing six to 10 feet of water. Like nearly everything else built by men in the Valley, the fleet of river steamers has greatly deteriorated, but the rivers are as deep and long as ever. Roads are usually difficult to build and maintain in the jungle, but their construction is practicable on the *terra firme* and they can serve a useful purpose as feeder lines for the rivers and for carrying goods around the *cachoeiras* or rapids. Most of the larger rivers are too wide and the water level is too variable for bridging, but ferries may be a practical alternative. The importance of airplanes for long-distance communications is great, and, as throughout Brazil, their possibilities have already been realized in large part in the Amazonia.

Vast stores of potential hydroelectric energy exist wherever the hills cross the line of the rivers. Waterfalls on many smaller streams are convenient to cities and towns. As an example, electricity could easily be generated from the falls of the Arapium for use in Santarém at the mouth of the Tapajóz.

The present labor supply available in the Amazon Valley is inadequate in quantity for the prosecution of large enterprises. Its leaders, the landowners and merchants who lived in Belém and Manaus, wasted and misused its scanty human resources, and the pool of available manpower has not been replenished by a continuing migration from the Northeast, since the Amazonia must now compete on unfavorable terms with the industrialized states of southern Brazil for its traditional source of labor. The addiction of the native population to nomadism, as a form of adjustment to an environment for which it feels little compatibility, constitutes an obstacle to the development of a settled or stationary economy. The circumstance that the river man usually possesses a dugout canoe of his own makes it easy for him to yield to this urge to wander, a habit which he shares in common with the Brazilian *caboclo* wherever he may live. In other respects he is good raw material for the tasks of the Amazonia, to whose natural peculiarities he is physically well adjusted.

Immigration is scarcely the answer to the question of a satisfactory labor force. In 1950 there were only some 16,000 foreigners in Pará and Amazonas and the four territories, and most of these were probably citizens of Peru and other adjoining countries. European emigrants tend to avoid the Amazonia in favor of southern Brazil, whose conditions are more familiar to them, so that little relief can be expected from that direction in the near future. At present the Japanese comprise the only sizable body of foreign immigrants in the Valley, but the difficulty of their integration into the local population makes their presence a controversial issue. The effect of a large movement of foreigners into the Amazonia might well be to weaken Brazil's control and sovereignty over the area, since the normal forces of acculturation which prevail in the south are still weak here. Whatever the problems of their adaptation to conditions of the locale, responsibility for the actual work of developing the Amazonia must largely be left to Brazilians.

The same is not true in the field of investment capital. Brazilians have shown little readiness to invest in enterprises in the Amazonia, and there is little reason to believe that their attitude will change unless the prospect for profit exceeds the opportunities now offered in the southern part of the country. The government is already burdened with heavy commitments in other areas like the Northeast and the new federal capital, and it is unlikely for some time that the national treasury could finance an adequate program for development of the Amazonia. Unless the region is left to vegetate at its present level, with only occasional and minor injections of private capital, the large funds needed for a realistic reform of the Amazonian economy will have to come from the outside. Their investment would, of course, have to be completely divorced from any considerations of political advantage and, with a full understanding to that effect, would have to enjoy the ready acceptance and co-operation of the authorities and of the community at large. Otherwise, any prospect of a major improvement of the regional economy in the early future would be doomed beforehand.

With the exception of a few superior governors of the state of Pará, the Amazonia and its component parts have generally been ruled with little wisdom, efficiency, or disinterest. This has been particularly true in the field of local administration, which has been notoriously corrupt and incompetent. Under the circumstances, a political reorientation of the region is as essential to its fuller evolution as is a radical overhauling of its economics.

The principal impediment to a realization of the Amazonia's great potential is psychological—the perpetuation of a traditional mentality inherited from the rubber boom. Stunned by the catastrophe of 1910, the leaders of the region salvaged what they could of their fortunes and withdrew to the refuge of their homes in Manaus or Belém, or they abandoned the region altogether to live in Rio, the ultimate mecca of discontented Brazilians. The more adventurous went to São Paulo. Since the debacle of the system for which they were responsible, they have done little constructive thinking or planning. They have even lost the boldness and initiative which their predecessors, whatever their ethical standards or business sense, displayed in their far-flung ventures over the Valley.

A phase of the "boom-or-bust" philosophy is an urge for quick and high profits. While this emphasis is common elsewhere in Brazil, it has never appeared on a scale and level comparable to its application in the Amazon Valley. A large proprietor once told me that he considered a return of 100 per cent on all his operations—rubber production and merchandising—as a "Christian profit." Though he was a foreigner, he probably represented the prevailing policy of his kind, whether foreign or native, who dominate the economic life of the Amazon Valley. He may even have been unusually modest in his calculations.

The ruling class of the region is resistant to new ideas and techniques. It has failed to accept the full implications of the Industrial Revolution and of the utilization of modern scientific discoveries. It has refused to recognize that the conquest of the Amazonia is no longer a job for the machete. For the most part, its economic doctrines belong to the sixteenth century. If the economy of the region is still "colonial," it is the fault of its leaders. As in the pre-1800 Hispanic empire, the basis of its development so far has largely been the predatory exploitation of its most apparent resources, with large-scale smuggling activities as a supplementary occupation.

Though frequently tempered by a patriarchal benevolence toward their retainers, the leaders of the Amazonia cling to a class system which offers little outlet to the ambitious or natural talents or energies of the mass of the population. It follows an essentially feudalistic doctrine of economic and social relationships, and resists any educational or managerial innovations which might disturb the present structure of a closed—and inert—society. Of this "gentleman complex" Charles Wagley, in his acute analysis of life in an anonymous town on the lower river, comments as follows: "The bureaucrats, the commercial families, and other members of the local upper class in rural communities are not generally anxious for social change." Advocating "a new economic and social orientation" for the region, he adds: "Brazil is potentially one of the world's richest nations, but it has not as yet made use of its greatest resource, its people."

PART II
THE CHARACTERS

CHAPTER 3

The Indian

THE ORIGINAL BLEND OF PEOPLES THAT WAS TO MAKE UP the Brazilian race was compounded of Indians and Portuguese. As in a coffee blend, the one provided "body"; the other, flavor. A few minor ingredients were introduced as other Europeans early made contact with the receptive Indian women. Then, with the advent of Negro slavery, a large admixture of *robusta* from Africa was added to the blend.

The ethnic formula was never universally applied, nor was its application quantitatively uniform. So whatever the ultimate result may be at some distant time, when the miscegenative process has reached its goal of complete racial saturation, there is still considerable variety in the human product. The extent of diversity depends on the play of taste and chance, such as the exercise of free choice in mating and the momentary availability of the genetic raw materials. When the stirring of the three basic ingredients is over at last, the end result in the pot will be the new *raça brasileira,* as it is envisaged by those who dream of a single people unadulterated by minorities to mar its unity. It holds the promise of a good race.

Since, of the two original components, the Indian was there first, he will be given precedence in this treatment. Relative to the size of his habitat, there were not many of his kind, perhaps about as many as inhabited the land of the Portuguese interlopers. Though, by their very nature, forest Indians are the despair of census takers, there were probably about as many Indians in Brazil in 1500 as there are today; maybe not more than 500,000 in all, but more likely less than more. Even now one seldom encounters more than a handful of them in any one place. There were never "hordes" or "masses" of them, as the Spaniards reported finding in Mexico and the Inca lands. There was no Cuzco or Tenochtitlán around which their collective lives revolved and from which some unity was given to their existence. In fact, this localized world of the Brazilian aborigines was disunited to the point of virtual anarchy, a circumstance which facilitated its absorption by the Portuguese.

Five large linguistic groups lived within the bounds of what is now Brazil. Only two of the five inhabited anything approaching a solid block of territory. Since the Tupí lived in the coastal zone that was the scene of the Portuguese settlements, the colonizers tended to identify all the natives with this widespread stock, whose Guaraní cousins inhabited the River Plate lands to the south and west. The lower Amazon Valley was also Tupí country, and there were even small Tupí enclaves embedded in eastern Peru. The occurrence of the familiar Tupí place names over so much of Brazil is evidence of the wide dispersion of this people. Behind the coastal Tupí and spread over the highlands of the *sertão* were the Tapuya, or Gé-speaking folk. Also the two Indian races whom Columbus encountered in the West Indies had settled large areas of Brazil. Both the Arawaks and the Caribs had moved deep into the Amazonia, and there were clusters of the former south of the divide between the Amazon and Platine river systems. Similarly, an isolated body of Caribs lived inside the Gé world in the Northeast. Finally, projecting up into Mato Grosso from northern Paraguay was a segment of the Guaycurú people. A linguistic map of aboriginal Brazil would probably resemble a political map of medieval Germany.

Brazil consisted of a myriad of small, isolated groups of Indians, mutually unacquainted or hostile. They found no bond of unity even in their linguistic affinities. For groups of the same stock could seldom communicate freely with one another, so different did their speech become as the ingrown tribes developed their own variations of the wider idiom. Each group tended to go its own way and to find its own primitive answers to the elementary problems of survival. By accident or propinquity they often shared the same techniques of hunting or tilling the soil, but beyond the bounds of kinship there was probably no conscious exchange of methodology between these jealous tribesmen.

So the way of life that came out of the pragmatic process had some variety in detail, though the common level of cultural achievement was always low. Whatever the particular environment—rain forest or open grasslands or the desert-like *caatinga* of the *sertão*—they learned to utilize for their purpose the materials they found about them: the fronds and bark and nuts of palm trees, the bones and skins of animals, the arboreal cotton, the sap of plants, the hard rocks of the hills. For food, besides any game or fish within reach of their limited technology, they cultivated both the sweet and poisonous manioc or cassava, corn, several varieties of beans, and other indigenous vegetables, like yams. They also ate whatever fruits grew wild, some of which are yet largely unknown outside Brazil, like the jaboticaba.

The mamão or papaya was native to the country and so was the pineapple, which is still known in civilized circles in Brazil as abacaxí. The Indians had long since learned how to extract the cyanide from the poisonous variety of manioc and to prepare the coarse meal known as *farinha de mandioca,* which is as truly the basic food of the Brazilian countryman as corn or maize is of his Mexican counterpart. In fact, the aborigines fixed the popular diet of Brazil that prevails to the present day.

Like the Aztecs in Mexico, the voracious Pijaos in Colombia, and the far-flung Caribs in general, from whom the term "cannibal" is derived, the Tupí peoples indulged on occasion in cannibalism. Though anthropologists tend to classify the custom as primarily ritualistic or ceremonial, the reports of early European sightseers, like the German Hans Staden, would seem to indicate that the practice also had definite gastronomic overtones bordering on true gourmandise. The object of intertribal wars or raids appears often to have been the capture of victims for veritable orgies of anthropophagy, in which the diners of both sexes apparently participated with real gusto.

An elaborate protocol governed the practice and was evidently designed to mitigate its horrors and to assuage the conscience of its practitioners. The various small groups of the important Tupinambá branch of the Tupís literally decimated each other in these hunting expeditions and thereby made the task of the Portuguese invaders all the easier.

Thus the world of the Tupís and their fellows was scarcely the Arcadia pictured by writers from afar, who were impressed by the absence of avarice and other more sophisticated sins then prevalent in the old civilizations of Europe. Neither, within the circle of the group that was the predominant social unit, was it a perpetual carnival of barbarism. The legend of primeval innocence was cherished by nostalgic, if ill-informed, foreigners well into the last century, and even found its protagonists among the romantics of Brazilian literature, like José de Alencar. One of the earliest apologists for the savages of the New World was the famous Frenchman, Michel de Montaigne, who obtained his data on the subject from secondary sources. Montaigne, who wrote his essay "Of the Cannibals" between 1578 and 1580, was much impressed by what he learned of the simple virtues of a folk as yet unspoiled by contact with his fellow-Europeans, so much more expert in the refinements of inhumanity. "We may call these people barbarous," he wrote, "in respect to the rules of reason, but not in respect to ourselves, who surpass them in every kind of barbarity. . . . Their warfare," he continues, "is wholly noble and generous, and as excusable and beautiful as this human disease can be; its only basis among them is their rivalry in valor."

Other writers have commented on the virtues of the Indian. Alfred Metraux, the modern French anthropologist, has said of the Tupinambás: "Social control over the individual's behavior was very strong. Great stress was put on the smoothness of manners and gentleness, any outburst of anger being looked on with abhorrence. People shunned the company of temperamental persons." Metraux also says, "The Tupinambá were heartbroken to see Europeans mistreat the prisoners they had sold to them. They would come from far away to visit them, and would hide and protect any of their former slaves who escaped."

These were the folk whom the Portuguese found along the coast of Brazil and wherever they were to go beyond the beaches. By virtue of their experience in Africa and the Orient, and by the natural tolerance of their racial attitudes, no other European people of the age were better fitted to deal with the problems of coexistence which suddenly presented themselves. Like the Indians whom they met, they, too, were mostly simple and uncomplex men. Unlike the Spaniards in Mexico and Peru, they did not consider themselves as conquerors. But the Pope had said the land was theirs; so they had come to see about taking it over. They were conscious of their own weakness and hoped that they would not have to fight its occupants. They hoped somehow to find profit in it, but they were not sure whence the profit would come. The men and women who came down to the beaches when the Portuguese landed were naked and had no gold ornaments about them to arouse the covetousness of the newcomers. After their first mutual suspicions were relaxed, both sides "got down to business." Each had something, even if of no great value, that the other wanted. So they bartered brazilwood and strange animals and birds for pieces of cloth and trinkets from the bazaars of Lisbon. They decided that this was better than shooting arrows and musket balls at one another. Later there were to be many armed clashes between bands of Indians and Portuguese, but both sides seem to have decided to live in peace with each other and open hostility was the exception. There was plenty of room for everybody, so that one side seldom got in the way of the other.

If the Portuguese were too oppressive, the Indians in their path might undertake a mass migration into the interior. One large group moved into the montaña country of eastern Peru to escape their tormentors, and several thousand of the Tupinambá left the coastal region of Pernambuco and, after wandering for several years, settled on the large island between the Amazon and the Madeira that still bears their name.

So much for the men. Since the first Portuguese brought no women of their own with them for a long time, and had no convictions as to the virtues of continence, the inevitable happened. The compatibility of the lone Portuguese and the young Indian woman was to have important consequences for the future of Brazil. For out of these unions were to come the new mixed race of *caboclos,* who were to be the instruments of the Portuguese occupation of the backlands. They thus served the immediate purpose of the Portuguese colonial policy by providing a much-needed source of manpower for its imperial designs. The practice was later to scandalize the Jesuit fathers, who assumed the guardianship of the Indian population in Brazil and were much more concerned with the salvation of souls than with the relation between sex and sovereignty.

The two classical examples of large-scale miscegenation in early Brazil were represented by Diogo Alvares Correia and João Ramalho. Both seem to have been seamen on stray ships that carried on mixed exploring and trading operations along the coast, and were either marooned by their captains or chose to "jump ship" and live with the natives, as frequently occurred with the crews of Portuguese ships in India. The scene of Diogo Alvares' adventure was the locality of Bahia, where he quickly became a pillar of local Indian society. The Indians found his superior technology useful to the needs of the tribe, particularly in the making of fire—hence the Tupí name Caramurú, by which he was to be known to history. As chief of the group, he enjoyed the privileges of polygamy reserved for those of his station and in time formed a large personal clan of his own, which was to gain fame as the "first family" of Portuguese Brazil. His favorite wife, Catarina Paraguassú, eventually crossed the Atlantic with him and was made much of at the royal court of France, where she was entertained by the Valois king and the queen mother, Catherine de Medici. When the Portuguese government decided to make a permanent settlement on the Bay of Bahia, the support of Caramurú and his followers proved of great benefit to the success of the enterprise.

When Governor Thomé de Souza arrived at Bahia to lay the first formal foundations of the colony, he found not only Caramurú and his spouse, but over 40 other Portuguese who were living with native women. Many present-day Brazilians are as proud to trace their ancestry to Caramurú and Catarina Paraguassú as there are Americans who claim Pocahontas as a distant grandmother. Gilberto Freyre writes of another marriage between Portuguese and Indian:

> One of the first Brazilian colonists, a man of noble birth, was married to the daughter of an Indian chief. They had many descendants who became outstanding figures among the agrarian aristocracy and in the field of politics, literature, the magistracy, and the colonial clergy, a state of affairs that continued under the Empire and down to our own day. It was one of those descendants who became South America's first Cardinal.

It is significant of the Portuguese respect for the Indian that family names borrowed from the Tupí language have survived the trend of sophistication in Brazil. For example, in the Brazilian section of *Who's Who in Latin America* there appear the names Araripe, Canguçú, Condurú, Itiberé, Oiticica, and Peryassú. A naval officer bears the name Mario Lopes Ypiranga dos Guaranýs, and a Rio businessman is named Mario Tebyriçá. One of the leading authorities on the Brazilian Indians is Nimuendajú, otherwise a German ethnologist named Unkel, who lived among them for 40 years. It is indicative of the lower social status of the Negro that there are no names of African origin in the same catalogue of Brazilians of distinction.

The locale of João Ramalho's activities was in southern Brazil, where Ulrich Schmidel, the garrulous German soldier-of-fortune, on his long peregrination between Paraguay and his home in Bavaria, briefly sojourned in Ramalho's patriarchal domain.

The most famous group of mestizos in the early history of Brazil were the so-called Mamelucos, who were the product of the crossbreeding of Portuguese settlers and Indian women in the vicinity of the Jesuit mission station of São Paulo de Piratininga. Like their Paraguayan counterparts, they were unusually vigorous and enterprising frontiersmen. From their base on the São Paulo plateau, they boldly penetrated deep into the interior of Brazil. Their first expeditions were in the nature of slave raids, in the course of which they reached the Jesuit missions on the borders of Paraguay. Later, as the Bandeirantes, they were the pioneers who opened the vast reaches of Minas and Mato Grosso to the knowledge of the Portuguese and gave some substance to Portugal's claims to the empty backlands. In a search for slaves or gold, or impelled by the *caboclo*'s spirit of restlessness, their bands spent years in long *entradas* to the west, and even over the divide into the basin of the Madeira. Their wanderings as a self-sufficient community formed the model for the open frontier that became a familiar pattern of Brazilian settlement. Sometimes they never returned to the place of their origin, but founded remote villages that were the ultimate outposts of Portuguese—and later, Brazilian—civilization in the wilderness.

When the Portuguese introduced the cultivation of sugar cane into the coastal lands of northern Brazil as the basis for its economic development, they counted on the local Indians as a labor force. However, the aborigines had no taste for the steady and exacting routine of the cane fields or, for that matter, for any kind of regular plantation agriculture. Though their women adapted themselves well enough to domestic labor in the plantation houses, the men proved to be physically and psychologically unsuited to field work. They preferred to migrate farther into the interior rather than to submit to the discipline of the plantation foreman. In order to avoid the breakup of local Indian society, the planters came to employ the Indian men in occupations that were more congenial to them, such as boatmen, hunters, and woodmen, or as a local force of police or militia. Meanwhile, Negro slaves were imported from Africa to fill the important gap in the sugar industry that was to become the mainstay of the colony.

By the end of the first century the basic pattern of racial relationships was well fixed. The Indian's unsuitability as a field hand was generally accepted. With the introduction of Negro slavery, the question of his economic position in colonial society was of little practical concern to his Portuguese overlords, who were satisfied to leave him in the familiar roles that conformed with his independent nature and his past experience.

In the meantime, the Jesuits had taken over the responsibility for his religious training and for inculcating in him the social ideas and habits that were peculiar to the mission system of the Society. In spite of their administrative capacity, the Jesuits were never numerous enough to encompass in their plans for segregating the natives more than a minority of the Indian population. In the dual social order which became the rule in the colony—one largely dominated by idealistic considerations and the other by a profit motive—there was bound to be a conflict of ideas and interests between priests and planters. The stake in the controversy was the labor of the Indian. When in 1759 the Portuguese government of the Marquis of Pombal expelled the Jesuits from the Braganza Empire as members of an international organization, their Indian wards were left to the tender mercies of the civil authorities. Efforts to integrate them into the life of the colony failed, and their natural tendency was to drift off into the forests where they could renew the broken pattern of tribal existence.

It was a long time before anybody championed the Indian in Brazil again. Over most of the country his existence was ignored. The colony became independent and the Empire came and went in two thirds of the last century. But the Indian was no longer a problem or even a subject for serious concern. He was not aware of the literary efforts of romantic writers to glorify his memory or of the scientist-explorers who wrote more realistically of his way of life. It was only when he got in the way of those who would open up the Amazon Valley and exploit its resources that he attracted the national attention to himself. His reaction was either to move farther back between the rivers or, if the odds were not too great, to stand his ground against the intruders and retaliate in his own way. A poisoned trap was set beneath the leaves in a forest path or there was suddenly a long arrow out of nowhere. The Indian wanted no part in the rubber boom, either as laborer or entrepreneur. He effectively closed off certain areas that were rich in hevea—the fierce Assurinís sealed off the right bank of the middle Xingú and the Parintintíns held part of the Madeira basin. He was the implacable foe of the Peruvian *caucheros,* who worked the *castilla* trees on the Brazilian rivers and sometimes abducted Indian women who strayed too far from their encampment. Meanwhile, the disappearance of Colonel Percy Harrison Fawcett, the famous English engineer, in the upper Xingú country made the Brazilian Indian the center of an international mystery that has never been solved.

Finally, the efforts of the Brazilian government to open up lines of communication between the basin of the Paraguay in Mato Grosso and the Madeira brought the Indian into the official ken. Fortunately for the success of the enterprise and the welfare of the Indian, who was disposed by now to consider all outsiders as his enemies, the work was entrusted to Colonel Candido Mariano da Silva Rondón, an able army officer of Indian ancestry. The natural humanity of the Brazilian asserted itself in the labors of Colonel Rondón, which extended over many years and culminated in the establishment of the national Indian Service. Colonel Rondón's objective was not only to protect the Indians against exploitation and mistreatment in general, but to offer them an opportunity to accept whatever in Brazilian civilization might serve their purpose. Little by little he gained the confidence of the suspicious and hostile tribesmen, though sometimes at the cost of his devoted aides. In time friendly relations were established with all the forest peoples, even to the truculent Chavantes in the forest of the upper Araguaya basin.

Of the Chavantes, Helmut Sick, a German naturalist who worked among them in the 1940's with a Brazilian mission, wrote: "These Indians are large in stature, slender in build and powerful. They are, to our eyes, abhorrent in appearance and conduct —the very personification of a fearsome and unpredictable savage."

Though the Indian has been salvaged for the time being as a distinct ethnic entity, his ultimate fate in the future evolution of Brazil remains problematical. With the growth of the nation's population his relative importance as one of its component elements has declined proportionately. He is now a very small minority of the Brazilian people. The conditions that once forced his absorption by the familiar process of miscegenation have lost most of their force. His willingness to accept the responsibilities of fuller participation in the national life is yet to be demonstrated, though devoutly desired by some responsible leaders of the country.

A primitive Tupí or Tapuya tribesman, suddenly confronted with the necessity for spending the rest of his life in Rio or São Paulo, would be as hopelessly disoriented as a pelican marooned in the *mato* of Marajó. A judge in Manaus once told me of his efforts to "civilize" a young orphaned Parintintín whom he had adopted. Brought up in his family and ultimately sent to Europe for a university education, on the young man's return to Brazil he immediately disappeared among his people to live as one of them.

The advance of economic development into the recesses of Brazil will eventually force the issue on the Indian. The alternative would be for him to remain indefinitely a "museum piece" for tourists or a subject for endless analysis by the anthropologists. His years may be numbered. If he should eventually disappear from the stage of history, he would leave behind him no epic memories, no tradition of a Cuauhtemoc or a Tecumseh, or a Lautaro or Tupac Amaru for the greater glory of his race.

Yet, anonymously as he has lived, he has given much to Brazil by which to be remembered. He has left his place names strewn all over the land. A form of the Tupí tongue long survived as the *lingua geral,* or "general language," that was the common medium of communication in the *caboclo* world of the interior, as Guaraní has persisted to this day in Paraguay. Then the Brazilian government, apprehensive of the permanent corruption of the national speech and of the possible social and political consequences of a linguistic dichotomy in the nation, deliberately discouraged its use to the advantage of Portuguese. However, many Indian words have remained embedded in the popular idiom of Brazil, particularly in the nomenclature of natural features, such as flora and fauna and topography. The terminology of plant life includes words like *xuxú* and *xique-xique, capím* and *cipó, caatinga,* and *jacarandá.* Most of the names which the Indian gave to animals have become part of the national vocabulary. An armadillo is still a *tatú,* and an alligator is a *jacaré.* A buzzard is an *urubú,* an anaconda is a *sucurijú,* and an anteater is a *tamanduá.* The word "jaguar" is derived from the Tupí-Guaraní language. Among topographic terms inherited from the Indians are *paraná* and *igapó.*

The *caboclo* is the biological link between the two basic civilizations in Brazil, and much of his mentality and his habits reflect the Indian side of his ancestry. His nomadic instinct, even his urge to return from his wanderings to some familiar and favored locale, his taciturnity, so different from the wordiness of the coastal folk, his hardihood and frugality, his adaptability to the land about him, and his melancholy—all these are of the Indian. So are his food and the manner by which he obtains it, whether from the earth or the forest or the river. Brazilian folklore is deeply permeated with the primitive mythology of the Indian, and the *caboclo*'s Christianity is a compromise with the animism of his Indian ancestors. Whether for good or bad, some of all this has entered into the soul of Brazil.

CHAPTER 4

The Portuguese

BRAZIL WAS PORTUGAL'S GREATEST GIFT TO THE WORLD. Somehow the little kingdom, with a population probably less than that of present-day Lisbon, managed to make good her impudent claim to its magnitude. In Brazil she set up, as Gilberto Freyre has pointed out, the first successful European society in the tropics. And when, after three centuries, her time was up, she let it go without an armed struggle and with a minimum of acrimony to mar the separation. So in the paper currency of the Brazilian republic, the first and the last of the Portuguese—Cabral, the discoverer, and João VI, the king—are honored as though there were no breach in the long relationship.

All this is the more remarkable, because in the Portuguese scheme of empire, Brazil was only an accident and an afterthought. It was hers by right of discovery and the Pope's award, so that she could not abandon it to her rivals. But her prime interest was in the East, and Brazil had to bide its time for her attention until the mother country had exhausted herself in her glamorous ventures in Asia. When Portugal accepted the fact of maturity and turned over the land to its people in 1822, she left it much of herself. She had endowed it with her language and a deep heritage of character and custom. Among the intangibles were racial tolerance, an aversion to violence, a readiness to play with time and talk things out when there were differences, an ability to rise to the occasion when the issue seemed important enough, a shrewd earthiness of outlook, and a certain undertone of melancholy. Beyond the modest churches, like those at Olinda and Ouro Preto, an aqueduct in Rio over which street cars run, some big plantation houses in the north, and a few tiny forts which once guarded the gates to the vast colony, she left few tangibles to remember her by.

Brazil was a by-product of the boldness that made Portugal the greatest maritime power of the world for over a hundred years. During the age when the artistic and intellectual genius of Italy was ripening in the Renaissance, the Portuguese put to sea. The most thalassic of peoples, they got about on the oceans as no other people before or since, and left their mark on many distant shores. The Atlantic is littered with islands which they discovered and named—the Azores, the Cape Verdes, Madeira, St. Helena, Ascension, and Tristan da Cunha. Labrador is Portuguese and Newfoundland is an anglicized version of Terranova. On Newfoundland there is still a town with the original Portuguese name, and the off-shore island of Fógo is another memorial to the sea-going Corte-Reals. To the north of Russia Martím Lopes found and named the large island of Nova Zembla. And far to the south, at the end of the American continent, the Straits of Magellan commemorate the daring of Fernão Magalhães, the greatest navigator in the history of the seas.

Portuguese mariners were the first to round Africa, and the names they left along its coasts tell the story of their voyages of discovery. In addition to those in Angola and Portugal's other African colonies, Portuguese place names on the map include Angra de Cintra, Capes Barba, Palmas, Frio, and Delgado, and many towns like Porto Novo, Lagos, Forçados, and Fernan Vaz.

At the southern end of the continent, the headland which Bartolomeu Dias named Tormentoso for the stormy weather that he encountered in the seas below it was rechristened as Boa Esperança or Good Hope by King João II. Cape Agulhas, the southernmost point of Africa, still bears the name that was first given to it, and Natal, a near-by province of the South African Union, is the Portuguese word for Christmas.

In the Far East, Formosa, otherwise known as Taiwan, is "the beautiful island," and Flores, in the Indonesian archipelago, is "the island of flowers." Beyond the Moluccas or Spice Isles, which the Portuguese held for a time, to the huge island above Australia they transplanted the name of Guinea, which was their first goal on the coast of Africa. The island, then the largest known in the world, was sighted by Antonio de Abreu in 1511 and named by Ortíz de Roda in 1546. In 1606 a Portuguese captain named Luíz Vaez de Torres, who had crossed the Pacific from Peru, sailed his ship through the passage between New Guinea and Australia, to which an Englishman long afterward gave the name of Torres Strait. Torres was second in command of a small squadron which had left the west coast of South America in search of a continent in the South Sea. The real head of the expedition was Pedro Fernandes de Quirós, last of the great Portuguese navigators. At the time Portugal was under the domination of Spain and, like Magellan long before him, Quirós sailed under the Spanish flag. He was obsessed with the idea of finding the continent which he called "Austrialia del Espiritu Santo." Though he found and named the large island of Espiritu Santo, he may never have seen Australia. His lieutenant, Torres, in all probability did sight its low coast off his port bow without suspecting its magnitude.

Portugal did not become a separate nation until well along in the Middle Ages. Her people had meanwhile had the usual experience with the conquering Romans and the wandering Germans, who swarmed over the peninsula after the well-known fall of the Roman Empire. The Romans left behind them the roots of their language and the name of Portus Cale, at the mouth of the Douro, that eventually gave a name to Portugal. The Goths, who were always ill at ease among people of superior culture, left very little in the course of their three centuries' stay beyond some blond genes in the bloodstream of the population. Moslem invaders from Africa came in the 700's and were around on and off for another seven centuries. When they had finally gone, the Portuguese were never again to be the same people.

For a long time Portugal was a dependency of the Spanish kingdom of Galicia, whose people still have a strong linguistic and cultural affinity with their neighbors to the south. Then in 1140 Affonso Henriques, son of a Burgundian count and a princess of León, took the royal title and made of his domains another Iberian kingdom. The centuries that followed were largely devoted to a more-or-less perennial crusade against the Moslem, who were long entrenched in the lands of the Algarves below the Tagus, to strengthening the power of the monarchy against the nobles, and to fighting the Spaniards. Companies of men-at-arms from northern countries occasionally dropped in on Portugal on their way to the Holy Land and found a convenient outlet for their crusading zeal in bouts with the local infidels. The English, who were currently given to martial adventures on the continent, were frequent visitors, and in 1387 the famous John of Gaunt brought valuable aid to the Portuguese in their wars with the Castilians, and initiated the long identification of the House of Lancaster—and of England—with the affairs of Portugal.

The Portuguese kings and queens were a singularly picturesque and forceful lot, both in their personal and public capacities. Their strong heads and hearts were frequently in conflict, to their own mortal, if romantic, distress and the bedevilment of the realm. Most beneficial of the early monarchs was Diniz, known as the "Ré Lavrador" or "farmer king," for his efforts on behalf of the peasantry, who suffered much from the disorders of the times and the greed of the nobles. Most famous of the kings were João, or John, I, known as "the Great," and his grandson, João II, the Perfect. The first of these monarchs of the House of Aviz ruled from 1385 to 1433 and the second from 1481 to 1495. To these may be added Manoel the Fortunate (1557–78).

It was to these men, strong if not always wise, that Portugal owed much of her resplendent if ephemeral glory in that age. For it was they, and above all, Henrique, son of João I and Philippa of Lancaster, who planned and directed the series of ocean voyages which gave Portugal a far-flung empire and imperishable memories of greatness to cherish in the long days of her decline. Henrique, or Henry, known to history as "the Navigator," forsook the royal court to dedicate his life to promoting the maritime interest of the nation. In the observatory which he set up at Sagres on the coast he conducted what was in reality a unique school of the sea. There he gathered about himself the master mariners of the time, cartographers, astronomers, and shipwrights, to train them in the practical lore of the oceans—the play of winds and currents, the improvement of navigational instruments for the determination of position, the drafting of sailing charts, the building of larger and better ships for the long voyages he had in mind, and the problems of water and supplies for the crews. His objective was to find a sea route to the Far East that would break the Venetian-Arab monopoly of the trade in spices and luxury goods from the Orient. As his captains returned from their preliminary voyages, first in the north Atlantic and later from the African coasts, he added their findings to the charts and to the store of other data that would serve the purpose of their successors.

Year after year successive expeditions crept farther down the shores of Africa. In 1434 Gil Eannes sailed around Cape Bojador and two years later Affonso Gonçalves reached the Rio d'Ouro. In the early 1440's the lucrative slave trade was opened and in 1445 Diniz Dias arrived at the Guinea coast. In 1460, the year of Prince Henry's death, Diogo Gomes found the Cape Verde Islands. The Equator was crossed in 1471, and in 1484 Diogo Cam discovered the mouth of the Congo. The next great advance occurred after two more years, when Bartolomeu Dias reached the southern end of the continent. On his return to Lisbon preparations began to be made for the voyage to India that was to be the realization of Dom Henrique's dream. In July, 1497, four ships cleared from the Tagus Roads for Asia under the command of Vasco da Gama, and nearly a year later they reached the city of Calicut on the Malabar Coast. When Vasco da Gama cast anchor at Lisbon in August, 1499, only about one-third of his crews returned with him, as an early omen of the curse that was to haunt the great Portuguese enterprise in the East. But in the profits of the moment the human wastage and its future significance were forgotten.

To follow up the voyage of Vasco da Gama, King Manoel sent out a large fleet of 13 ships the next year under the command of Pedro Alvares Cabral. Its sailing instructions were provided by Vasco da Gama on the basis of his own experience, but after touching at the Cape Verdes, Cabral changed his course to the southwest and on the 22nd of April, 1500, sighted land on his right in about 17 degrees south latitude. He made a landing in a harbor which he named Porto Seguro or "safe port," spent about eight days in its vicinity, set up a wooden cross in token of Portuguese ownership of what he called "the Island of Santa Cruz," and sent one of his ships back to Lisbon to inform the king of his chance discovery. Then he went on his way to what he considered more important business in India. He saw only about 50 miles of the Brazilian coast, so that he could have no idea of the size of the vast country on which he had come so inadvertently. It was not until a few years later, when Gonçalo Coelho and Amerigo Vespucci, the Florentine bank clerk turned navigator, explored the coast to the River Plate that the Portuguese began to have some notion of the extent of their new property.

Before proceeding to India, Cabral left two of his sailors on shore to begin the settlement of the country and to explore their surroundings for the information of future callers from home. He also shanghaied one of the trustful Indians who greeted the newcomers and sent him off to Lisbon to learn Portuguese, so that he could serve as interpreter to subsequent expeditions. There is no further record of either of the three expatriates involved in this exchange of persons. However, the Portuguese were at home anywhere in that age, and the two marooned seamen doubtless went native with gusto. As for the first South American to visit Europe, he probably died of homesickness before completing his language studies.

Pedro Vaz de Caminha, the official chronicler or reporter of Cabral's fleet, commented favorably in his report to the king on the verdant countryside and the primitive innocence of the naked aborigines. But he wrote nothing that might arouse the cupidity or deep interest of the court and so divert its attention from the newly opened spice trade with India.

Any immediate question of Spanish counterclaims to Brazil had apparently been already forestalled by the papal Line of Demarcation of 1493 and its amendment by the Treaty of Tordesillas a year later. The arbitrary division of the unknown world between Spain and Portugal by the Borgian Pope, Alexander VI, was designed to avoid any jurisdictional conflicts between the two Iberian powers. The original line would have excluded Portugal from the New World, but its later extension by negotiation to the meridian bisecting the western hemisphere 370 leagues to the west of the Cape Verde Islands assured to the Portuguese the title to most of the Brazilian coastal lands. At that time the two nations were enjoying a rare interlude of compatibility, and no problem of ownership arose until their interests clashed later in the River Plate area of South America. Roving Spanish ships under one of the Pinzón brothers and Diego de Lepe appear to have cruised along the northeast coast of Brazil in the year of Cabral's discovery, but Spain failed to make an issue of their findings.

During the beginnings of the new colony it was the French

and not the Spaniards who gave concern to the Portuguese. Francis I, the Valois king of France, had greeted the papal award with irreverent contempt, and his views were warmly seconded by the Breton and Norman ship captains, who early began to ply off the Brazilian coast in search of brazilwood and other commodities of the country. Stray Portuguese ships were also engaged in the same traffic, and a common labor-saving device of the time was to capture a cargo already bound for European ports. When the Portuguese made their first efforts to establish themselves in Brazil, they had to uproot the bartering stations of the French, who continued, however, to plague them, first in the Maranhão region of the north, and later—and more seriously—with their attempts to found a settlement on the shores of Rio Bay.

For the first 30 years after 1500 Portugal made only desultory moves to assert her ownership of Brazil. A ship or two customarily made an annual trip across the Atlantic on the royal account. They dumped a few prisoners from the Lisbon jails and socially unacceptable women along the coast to fend for themselves and, incidentally, to help hold the country for Portugal until the government might get around to taking other measures to that end.

Brazil might have become another prison colony, like Australia of the Botany Bay era, if it had not been for the results of private initiative. Whereas the movement to Asia was an affair of state and those who went thither did so as employees of the crown, Brazil was first settled by people who chose to migrate on their own responsibility and with the intention of staying overseas. The effects of this *laissez-faire* policy were a body of colonists devoted to both the land of their birth and of their adoption.

Among those who crossed to Brazil on their own were small farmers who had suffered from the competition of African slaves at home or who only wanted to better their lot in a new and more promising environment. There was land for the taking, and in time some of the settlers became lords of the manor in their own right, as the plantation system struck its roots deeper into the country. Also among those who came were members of the gentry at home who had fallen on bad times. One of the most useful elements in this spontaneous migration was a large number of "new Christians," or Sephardic Jews, who had professed the state religion to avoid expulsion from the country. Their conversion remained suspect to the newly organized Inquisition, which was eager for customers, and to escape from its scrutiny they were glad to find a refuge in Brazil. To the new colony they brought the valuable assets of their capital and business sense and superior intellectual equipment.

For a while an atmosphere of benign anarchy prevailed in the new settlements. There was no organized administration of the state, and in lieu of any constituted authority with coercive powers, the pressure of an incipient public opinion was the only restraint on the individual. The pattern of the hierarchical structure of society that gradually took shape in the north early became evident, as men with natural gifts of leadership or superior wealth came to dominate the inchoate colony. There was little place for refinement of manners or mind in its rough frontier way of life, and the moral influence of the clergy was almost totally lacking until the arrival of the Jesuits. Those who suffered most from this loose state of affairs were the Indians, who refused to live up to the expectations of the settlers for a ready and cheap labor supply. As the Tupí's ingenuous dream of friendly coexistence with the white strangers faded, outbreaks of violence between the two races became increasingly common, until the Indians moved inland to avoid contact with their persecutors.

The sovereignty of Portugal in Brazil was definitely established in the half century that began with 1530. Until then Asia still held a high priority in Portuguese policy, and Brazil had to await her turn. Meanwhile, the big carracks lumbered out farther and farther into eastern seas to the very edge of the Pacific. Diogo Lopes de Sequeira reached Malacca and Sumatra in 1509, and Francisco Serrão found the coveted Moluccas three years later. In 1516 Duarte Coelho, who was to be one of the pioneers in Brazil, penetrated into the interior of Cochin China and Siam. The next year Fernão Peres de Andrade arrived at Canton in China and four years later traveled inland to Peking. In 1557 the Portuguese established themselves at Macao on the river below Canton, where they have remained for over 400 years. Fernão Mendes Pinto, who went to the East in 1537, founded a trading post in Japan in 1548. He had spent the years between in China and other lands in a series of adventures so incredible that, like Count Benyowsky and Baron Munchausen, he gained wide fame as a teller of tall tales.

Soon after the opening of the trade with India, efforts were made to establish the political framework of the commercial and maritime empire that eventually reached from the Persian Gulf to the China Sea. Largely responsible for its consummation were the two viceroys, Francisco de Almcida and the great Affonso de Albuquerque, who made Goa on the Malabar coast of India the capital of the Portuguese East. Goa, which was to be the center of the missionary activities of the famous Jesuit, Francisco Xavier, is still a colony of Portugal, as are also Daman and Diu farther up the coast. Though the Oriental trade continued to be profitable for a time, the costs in terms of men and money steadily rose until the balance became so small as to discourage its continuation. Other factors that contributed to its decline were the economic policies of the Portuguese crown, which was the sole beneficiary of the trade, and the growing competition of the Dutch and English. After a century there was little left of Portugal's mighty venture into the *Ultramar* except Goa and Macao and the memories of past glories enshrined in the Hieronymite convent at Belém, and the *Lusiads,* the epic poem of Luíz Vaz de Camoëns.

Now it was the turn of Brazil. The government at Lisbon had at last recognized the danger of leaving the unorganized colony at the mercy of the French or other aggressors. The measures which it began to put into effect in 1530 were carried out with remarkable wisdom and tenacity by a few men of extraordinary skill. The first instrument of the crown in its new policy was Martim Affonso de Souza, a seasoned seaman and leader. He surveyed and charted the Brazilian coast for almost its entire length, stopping at the young settlements that were scattered at long intervals along the way, where he won the confidence of the colonists. He waged a ruthless warfare against French interlopers in the north country. Later, as a center for future development in the empty south, he laid the foundations of a village at São Vicente near the present site of Santos and another on the near-by plateau at Pirantininga, which was eventually to become the great city of São Paulo.

He made no move to disturb the existing free-and-easy system of home rule, which served the function of local government well enough at this embryonic stage of the colony's evolution. However, he saw the need for some consolidation of the nuclei of settlement as he found them and for extending the area of Portuguese occupation. The device which was adopted was one already utilized in settling the Azores and Madeira. The same system was later resorted to by the Dutch in the Hudson Valley, by the French along the lower St. Lawrence, and by the English in the southern colonies. This involved the feudal principle whereby an individual was granted extensive jurisdiction, with compensatory privileges and powers, over an area which he agreed to settle and develop. As eventually put into practice in Brazil the plan resulted in the partition of the country into 10 so-called *capitanías,* each of which was granted to a *donatario,* who was commonly a nobleman or other person of means or influence at court. The "captaincies" had an ocean frontage of 50 leagues and in theory extended to the line of demarcation in the interior of the colony.

The plan as applied in Brazil had mixed results, depending on a number of circumstances, but especially on the character of the individual *donatario.* The most successful were those which centered in Pernambuco on the northern coast and São Vicente in the south. The grantee of the first of these concessions was Duarte Coelho Pereira, one of the veterans in the opening of the Portuguese empire in Asia. Some of the other *capitanías* were failures, and their lands continued to lie fallow as before.

In 1549 the king, convinced by experience of the defects inherent in the system, limited the prerogatives of the *donatarios* and laid the foundations for a central government of the colony. As his agent, Thomé de Souza was sent out with the commission of governor-general of all Brazil and with instructions to establish his capital at Bahia or São Salvador. Beyond integrating the authority of the realm over the colony, he interfered little with local practices except where they clearly contravened the larger purposes of the crown.

By now the economy of the colony was no longer dependent on the export of dyewood, monkeys, and parrots. Sugar cane had been introduced from Madeira and the slave trade had been opened with Africa, so that the future was well assured. Further progress was made during the long governorship of Mem de Sá between 1554 and 1572, by the end of which Brazil was solidly established in its primacy in the Portuguese empire.

So was the civilization that Freyre has described in detail as "an agrarian, slave-holding, and hybrid society." The foundations of the system were large plantations, a servile labor force, and an unrestrained genetic urge. It was a patriarchal order, whose masters were long to be the real rulers of the colony. They were lords of the vast lands they held and of all the men and women, white, black, and brown, who lived on them. As planters, they had restored in Brazil the traditional basis of Portuguese life, which had been displaced by the dominance of commercial interests that began with the overseas enterprises of the fifteenth century. Occupied with the cultivation of the soil, they were again in their natural element, even though the land and its crops were strange to them. The tropical habitat, devoted to the pursuit of agriculture, quickly became home to them and they experienced no "culture shock" in their adjustment to its strangeness. To the Negro slaves, too, it was home, and while it was not for them "the best of all possible worlds," in some respects they fared better than they had in their native Africa. Racial crossbreeding had long been a habit of the Portuguese. They had practiced it freely with the Moslems who shared their country throughout the Middle Ages, with the Negresses in Guinea or in Portugal itself, and later with the assorted women of the East —Aryan, Malay, Mongol, or Melanesian. In Brazil the same sexual catholicity was to continue unabated. The earlier settlers, few of whom brought their own women with them, were often greeted on the beaches by naked Tupí girls. Later there were too many compliant or subservient females, Indian or Negroid, all about them. The easygoing clergy, who ministered to the religious needs of the planters and of their families and dependents, were generally inclined to be indulgent in the matter of carnal sin. The state, whose purpose was served by the added population that resulted, closed its official eyes to the widespread custom.

The colony still had two and a half centuries of time to run before the Brazilians took it over for themselves. For 60 years—from 1580 to 1640—Spain ruled over Portugal and, indirectly, over all its realms, wherever they were. But for Spain, too, this was the period of her *decadencia,* and she was too full of troubles of her own to interfere seriously with the Portuguese order of things in Brazil. The *conquista* was over, and after the defeat of the Armada in 1588 her sprawling empire was the object of attacks by the other maritime powers of Europe. Her enemies became the enemies of Portugal, and in the years between 1624 and 1654 the Dutch came and went in northern Brazil. If it had not been for the Brazilians themselves, the Dutch might have stayed, for it was the colonists who finally drove them out of Pernambuco and reclaimed the north for the mother country.

In the 1600's the Luso-Brazilians began in earnest to move away from the settlements in the *marinha* and into the back country. The movement had begun earlier with the establishment of cattle ranches in the valley of the São Francisco, which remained isolated from the sugar economy of the rich coastal lands. The main rivers of the Amazon system were explored, and at least points of bearing were fixed for the future, when there might be more time and men for the development of the region. Meanwhile, the Jesuits had undertaken the task of protecting the Indians from exploitation and converting them to Christianity, and in their wanderings they, too, contributed much to opening up the interior to knowledge, if not to the settlement and development of its vast spaces.

Much more important than any of these phases of penetration was the cycle of the long expeditions that originated in São Paulo and constituted a veritable epic in the history of Brazil. At first these *entradas* were largely slave-hunting raids by the Mamelucos or mestizo products of the union of Portuguese settlers and Indian women. The nomadic *bandeirantes,* as these hardy and enterprising pioneers were known, were in the habit of descending the Tieté from their starting point on the Paulista plateau to the line of the Paraná. From the intersection of the rivers, they turned south to the confines of Paraguay, where they raided the Jesuit missions and enslaved their Guaraní charges. In the process they came into contact with the Spanish dominions, as they also did in the Uruguay lands farther to the south, and thereby laid the foundations for border disputes in later years.

After a time they turned their attention toward the far west of Brazil. Crossing the line of the Paraná, they moved into the open lands of Mato Grosso and then over the divide into the basin of the north-flowing Madeira. Antonio Raposo, one of the most famous of the *bandeirantes,* raided the Jesuit missions in the Guayrá region of Paraguay in 1628 and brought back thousands of Indian slaves to São Paulo. Several years later he crossed the body of Brazil in a northwesterly direction, climbed the Andes, and reached the Pacific Ocean, into which he waded, like Balboa, with uplifted sword. When he returned to São Paulo long afterward, by way of the Amazon and the Brazilian coast, it was as a stranger, but he was to belong with Marco Polo and Cabeza de Vaca to the company of the great wanderers of all history.

Aware of the riches which the Spaniards had found in Peru, the *bandeirantes,* in their treks into the highlands of Minas and Goiás, eventually found the treasure they were always seeking. One of the legendary figures of the backlands was Fernão Dias de Paes Leme who, like a pied piper of the *sertão,* had led a whole tribe into slavery in São Paulo in 1661. Later, in the course of a seven-year *bandeira,* he found unmistakable evidence of gold in Minas, and also green tourmalines, which the Portuguese mistook for emeralds. His aide, Borba Gato, discovered the gold field of Sabará, and later lost its location. In the course of his comings and goings among the hills of Minas Borba Gato fell afoul of the royal agent of mines, who had assumed control of the area for the account of the crown, and lived as a fugitive of justice among the Indians for 20 years. He was then pardoned on condition that he disclose the site of his findings and died piously in bed at the age of 90. Another of the famous *bandeirante*-prospectors was Bartolomeu Bueno da Silva, who discovered gold in Goiás in 1682 after burning "firewater" before the Indians and threatening to dry up all their rivers unless they revealed the source of their golden ornaments. He and his son were known to the Indians as Anhanguera Sr. and Jr., or the old and the young devil, for the fear with which their magic was held.

In the meantime, the *bandeirantes* had played out the acts of their mighty drama, as a different breed of men took over the stage. They had explored on their own initiative an enormous wilderness, and they had given some substance to the claims of Portugal to the lands that reached from the settlements along the coast to the Paraná and the Paraguay and the far Itenes. They had found the gold that was to result in the reorientation of the whole economy of Brazil. And centuries later the task which they left unfinished was to be resumed as the new "march to the west" that is represented by Brasilia and the long roads which reach from São Paulo and Rio, and from Bahia and Belém, cut deep into the open spaces beyond the great rivers of the *sertão*.

There had been too few of them, as there always were in the opening-up of the interior of Brazil, to leave many permanent marks of their passage or their stay in the vast green desert which they explored in their aimless wanderings. They moved across the open grasslands and over the *Serras* and through the bush country as a self-sufficient pioneer community, complete with slaves, planting and harvesting in the seasonal stages of their long migrations. Sometimes they drifted back to São Paulo after many years of absence; sometimes, as the memories of their beginnings faded with time and space, they remained where they happened to be and built a lonely settlement, to be lost in its isolation in the outer edges of the open frontier.

The gold rush in Minas and the discovery of diamonds in 1728 shifted the economic center of gravity from the north to the south of the country. The sugar industry in Pernambuco and elsewhere in the Northeast had long prospered, but increased plantings in the West Indies and the growing ineptness of the Portuguese commercial system had dealt it a heavy blow. So when gold was found in the highlands to the northwest of Rio, many planters migrated with their slaves to the new Golconda. During the same period the beginnings of mixed farming in the province of São Paulo reflected the basic transition in wealth and influence that was taking place, and that was the forerunner of the coffee era in the same region. The change was officially recognized in 1763 by the transfer of the seat of government from Bahia to Rio and the creation of a vice-royalty to rule all Brazil.

As the mother country declined in the eighteenth century, the colony grew in stature and in confidence in its own destiny. Portugal was involved in dynastic and other struggles between the European powers that were beyond her dwindling strength and prestige, and in any alliances which she made she was always a junior partner. Internationally, she became increasingly a ward of England, a state of commercial and maritime dependence that was sealed by treaties with the Stuart governments of Charles II and Anne. Meanwhile, England learned to drink heady Port wine instead of Bordeaux and received, in exchange for the concession, Bombay and Tangier and extensive commercial privileges that made "the Portugal trade" a lucrative monopoly of her merchants.

In spite of the Marquis of Pombal's efforts to tighten control of the colony in the second half of the century, the Portuguese rule of Brazil was never downright oppressive, as that of Spain sometimes was, though clumsy it might be on occasion. But time was running out for Portugal, and the colony had become an anachronism. Though the royal officials were often bumbling and even grasping, the colonial regime was generally easygoing, and the majority of Brazilians were probably still willing to accept things as they were rather than resort to violence to change them. However, the authority of the crown had been exercised with particular harshness in the mining areas of Minas Gerais, with the result that a group of young intellectuals of the province formed a conspiracy to overthrow the colonial government. They had been impressed by the success of the United States in gaining its independence and had read the usual works of the French philosophers, but their plot was badly managed and lacked wide popular support. The conspirators were captured, and one of their leaders, Joaquím José da Silva Xavier, better known as "Tiradentes," was executed in 1792 after a long trial. Public opinion was eventually aroused by the proceedings and Tiradentes became the first national hero of Brazil, though the immediate political effects were nil.

The occasion for liberation was providentially supplied by Napoleon Bonaparte. Late in November, 1807, a victorious French army marched down the valley of the Tagus out of Spain. As it neared the outskirts of Lisbon, the Portuguese royal family and a few thousand courtiers and officials hurriedly boarded an English fleet in the harbor and sailed off to Brazil.

After a most unhygienic voyage, they arrived at Rio with their finery and treasure and created, among many other problems, a major housing shortage in the overcrowded city of some 130,000 people. The King, Dom João VI, set up his government and court and presumed to rule Portugal and its empire from Rio for 13 years, or six years after the Congress of Vienna. Brazil now had the status of another "realm," like the mother country, and was no longer a colony, so that the new regime was not in the nature of a government-in-exile. Instead, it represented an overseas transfer of the Portuguese capital which anticipated the move of the Brazilian capital from Rio to Brasilia by almost a century and a half.

The sudden introduction of so many high-toned and supercilious Portuguese into the provincial atmosphere of the tropical city was not accomplished without a multitude of stresses and strains on both sides. The hospitable natives resented the superiority complex of their demanding guests, though the Cariocas, natives of Rio de Janeiro, enjoyed the sensation of having a royal court in their midst instead of a mere viceroy. However, Rio, which was then almost devoid of any organized intellectual life, underwent a veritable cultural revolution during the stay of the visiting elite from Lisbon. Among the innovations were the first printing press, a national library, an academy and museum of fine arts, a botanical garden, and a number of institutions of higher learning.

Of the newcomers, the King probably adjusted himself most readily and successfully to the new milieu. He formed a deep and genuine attachment for his Brazilian capital and its warmhearted denizens, sentiments that were reciprocated by his local subjects. A kindly and uncomplicated man, he found relief in this mutual compatibility from the harrying demands of public business, foreign and domestic. It also provided a form of escape from an uncongenial relationship with his strong-minded and brazilophobe Spanish queen, who maintained a separate establishment of her own in another part of the city. He avoided as long as possible the pressures to return to Lisbon, and when he finally yielded he departed from Brazil with great reluctance. He shrewdly sensed the inevitability of an early and definitive break between the two "kingdoms" over which he ruled so benignly and lackadaisically, and wisely advised his son, whom he left behind as regent, to join the movement whenever it might come.

It came swiftly the next year. When the Lisbon government, which was of a different mind in the matter from its nonchalant head, ordered the young prince to come home, he raised his sword in a grandiloquent gesture at Ipirangá near São Paulo and shouted, "Independence or death!" That was on September 7, 1822. The result was the freedom of Brazil and the creation of the Brazilian Empire, which the able but harum-scarum Dom Pedro I ruled until his abdication and return to Portugal nine years later. Thereafter, the Portuguese who came to Brazil were to come as foreigners, though as favored immigrants in a hospitable land where their predecessors had left many more good memories than bad.

CHAPTER 5

The Man of Color

THE IMPERIAL CENSUS OF 1872 CLASSIFIED THE POPULATION of Brazil as 38 per cent white, 20 per cent black, and 42 per cent mixed (*pardos*). According to the census of 1950 the corresponding ratios were 61.6 per cent, 10.9 per cent, and 26.5 per cent. The balance of 1 per cent was accounted for by the Indians, by 320,000 members of the yellow race, and by persons who refused to declare their color. However wide the margin of error, the comparative figures are indicative of the progressive trend toward the whitening of the Brazilian population. Foreigners who have resided in Brazil for 40 or 50 years are quick to substantiate by their own observations the changes which have taken place in the coloration of the Brazilian people.

While the official category of "mixed" or "colored" (*gente de cor*) includes many of exclusively Portuguese-Indian ancestry, the most important ingredient in the demographic blend has been the African. By 1700 the Negroes not only outnumbered the Indians, but they generally lived in much closer proximity with the whites, so that the process of admixture was thereby facilitated and encouraged.

In view of the circumstance that miscegenation in Brazil continues to be unrestrained by law, moral considerations, or racial prejudice, it is impossible to apply any "scientific" standards of classification in the field of color. The average Brazilian of mixed race is of light complexion, and since the tropical sun is likely to be an important factor in facial pigmentation, the "benefit of the doubt" is always on the side of the white element in his background. Moreover, it is left to the individual to declare his own color, and since the national philosophy is opposed to all "racist" ideologies, its tolerance is reflected in the official statistics. This tacit acceptance of biological and genetic realities is only a recognition or rationalization of the obvious facts of Brazilian life. However, since the national goal of a "Brazilian race" is associated with the idea of whiteness, or *brancura,* additional motivation is provided for the miscegenative process. Thus colored women may desire to have children who are whiter than themselves, not because dark color is a social stigma in itself, but because the major rewards of life in Brazil seem to go to those of lighter complexion. The relative "backwardness" of the Negro population is a heritage of slavery and is largely a matter of economic status. Except for the more fortunate or enterprising minority among them, the Negro or dark mulatto has not yet caught up with the "time lag" in his evolution, and he is eager to overcome the social handicaps that result from his late entry into the modern economy of Brazil. One of the consequences of a lower social and economic status is inferior health conditions. As Roger Bastide has pointed out, due to their higher death rate the darker part of the colored population are losing ground to the whites and light mulattoes, a larger proportion of whose children are able to survive the hazards of infancy.

The colored comprise over half the population in the old colonial regions of northern Brazil. Wherever there was sugar cane, there were Negro slaves, and the "sugar civilization" of the colony was built by the labor of black men. The Indian was temperamentally unsuited to work on the plantations, and it was the Negro who took his place in the cane fields and made possible the continued hold of Portugal on the vast colony that otherwise offered so little to its founders. In the state of Bahia which, over four centuries ago, received the first Negroes to come to Brazil, nearly three of every four persons are Negroes or mulattoes. In no other part of the country is the African so much in evidence. Nowhere else has he or she so deeply influenced every phase of life—garb and food and talk, religion and the arts and the tempo of all effort. No other large city in the world is at heart so much his as is Salvador.

In the south the story of color is different. Except in Rio de Janeiro and where the Paraiba's valley spreads out in the lowlands about Campos and also in the narrow coastal plain of Santos–São Vicente where cane was cultivated, there were no large concentrations of Negro slaves in the early period of the colony. The Negroes who were taken into Minas at the time of the gold rush in the 1700's have been absorbed into the population, as have those who came later to the coffee plantations of São Paulo. As miscegenation has proceeded in these areas, the migration of Bahianos and other colored people from the north has tended to replenish the volume of the Negroid population in the industrialized states of the south. In Rio, whose population has always had a heavy base of colored blood, even though progressively whitened until its presence was scarcely evident to the casual observer, the growing slums or *favellas* of the city are largely populated by mulattoes, most of whom are latecomers out of the north. In São Paulo and Paraná probably about one person in eight has at least a trace of Negro blood in his veins. In Santa Catarina the proportion falls to about one in 18, which is the lowest in Brazil.

Antonio Gonçalves brought the first Negro slaves into Lisbon in about 1442, a half century before the discovery of America by Columbus. Shortly afterward the Lagos Company was formed for the purpose of importing slaves from the Gold Coast, and by 1450 the trade was well established.

It is not known when the first slaves were introduced into Brazil, but it is clear that they came from Lisbon, where there was already a large store of the human commodity. The initial consignment of slaves to be shipped directly from Africa arrived in 1538. The early settlers tried to make the most of native manpower, and it was only after the sugar industry was well under way that any considerable numbers of Negroes were introduced into the colony. Even as late as 1585, according to Father Anchieta, the famous Jesuit, there were only 14,000 Negro slaves in a total population of 57,000. Of the slaves at this time, probably 4,000 were in the region of Bahia.

The slave trade continued with little interruption until it was stopped by an imperial decree of September, 1850, nearly 40 years before the final act of emancipation. Since the records of the trade were destroyed at the beginning of the republic, the total volume of the trade is unknown, but according to Arthur Ramos, the leading Brazilian authority on the subject, it probably did not exceed 5,000,000. According to Johan Von Spix, the German naturalist who was in Brazil between 1817 and 1820, about 50,000 a year were then imported into the country, of whom some 15,000 were introduced through Bahia. Imports of slaves were very heavy between 1817 and the last year of the trade in 1850. Figures from official and other sources of the relative proportion of free and slave at the beginning of that period vary so greatly that they have little value. However, at the end of the Empire when the remaining slaves were freed, there were about 723,000 of them.

The Negro slaves in Brazil came from a wide variety of African stocks who differed physically, temperamentally, and culturally from each other. The principal slave stations on the west coast of Africa were Lagos and São João de Ajuda (Whydah) on the Gulf of Benin to the west of the Niger delta, and the Portuguese islands of Forte de el Mina and São Thomé. The Guinea coast and Angola were always important sources of slaves as, for much of the three centuries of the trade, was the lower basin of the

Congo. Toward the end of the commerce in the last century, most of the slaves who were destined to be field hands in Brazil were of the tractable Bantu peoples from the lands below the Congo. For domestic service and to man the more skilled occupations in the city and in the sugar mills in the plantations, the Bahianos came to prefer the more northerly tribes, most of whom were Islamized. These folk included the Yorubas, Fulahs, Mandingos, Ashantis, and the ardently Moslem Haussas. Many of these Negroes were haughty and unpredictable, literate of mind and statuesque of body, and in every respect but political and social status some of them were superior to the generality of their masters. One may still see on the streets of Salvador the proud and unsmiling descendants of those extraordinary Negroes.

On the passage between the west coast of Africa and Brazil, all of which was in tropical waters, a loss of 20 per cent of the human cargo was considered normal; sometimes the rate rose to 30 and even 40 per cent. On arrival at Rio or Bahia, the survivors were first put "in condition" before being sold. It was customary then to expose them naked to prospective customers in the slave market, as Spix saw them displayed at Rio. Some of the leading slavers were Brazilian mulattoes, like Felix de Sousa, better known as "Chacha," who flourished in the early part of the last century.

Once settled as a hand on some plantation or in the retinue of a town house, the lot of the slave was better than that of his fellows in other lands. "The negro slave seems very happy in Brazil," wrote Lieutenant Lardner Gibbon of the United States Navy, who was in the Amazon Valley in the middle of the last century. "This is remarked by all foreigners." Mrs. Martha Graham, the Englishwoman who was in Brazil in the early 1820's observed that "The negroes, whether free blacks or slaves, look cheerful and happy at their labour." Of slavery in Brazil, Richard Burton, the famous British orientalist, who lived and traveled extensively in the country for several years, said that "Nowhere, even in oriental countries, has the 'bitter draught' so little of gall in it; In the present day the Brazilian negro need not envy the starving liberty of the poor in most parts of the civilized world." Donald Pierson, the American scholar who has made a study of the Negro in northern Brazil, concluded that "humane and intimate relations between master and slave were —in all likelihood—the general rule."

The Brazilian slave was well fed and his diet was more nourishing than the fancier food of his owner. There were no problems of adjustment to a warm climate that was so like his own. In fact, his new physical environment was probably superior to that of most parts of Africa from which he had come.

The master-and-slave relationship in Brazil was unusually benign, as many foreign observers have pointed out. The Portuguese planter was an easygoing taskmaster and his instincts were rather humane than otherwise. In normal times there was probably little harshness in his treatment of his slaves, and cases of outright sadism were rare, though crimes of passion were sometimes committed under the impulse of sexual jealousy. Foreign visitors frequently testified to the atmosphere of kindness that appeared to characterize the dealings between the lords of the plantations and their black dependents.

Spix comments on the lightness of the slave's burden of labor. "They are rarely overworked," he says. In addition to the 52 Sundays, there were 35 saints' days in the year that were his own, and up to a total of 18 holidays declared by the government, or a possible maximum of 105 days. And he concludes: "Here he enjoys life."

A paternalistic Church and, at its behest, the state, assumed the role of the slave's protectors. The Church always emphasized his status as a human being, possessed of an immortal soul, and not as an ephemeral chattel. The slave who was cruelly treated might appeal to the authorities for redress of his wrongs, and in practice this was not an empty provision of the legal code of the colony. The integrity of the slave family was respected and it could only be transferred as a unit. Man and woman could not

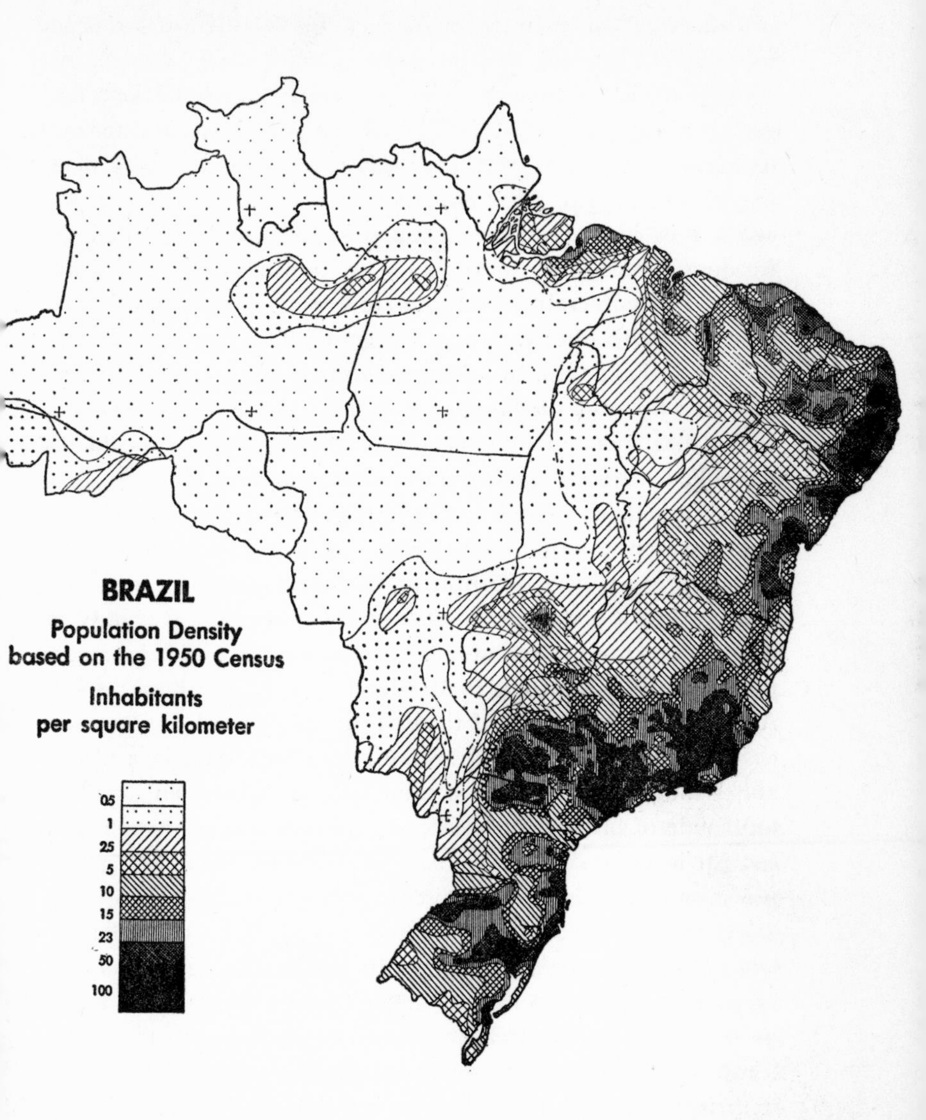
BRAZIL
Population Density
based on the 1950 Census
Inhabitants
per square kilometer
05
1
25
5
10
15
23
50
100

be separated by sale, nor could their young children be taken from them.

Emancipation was accepted as a concurrent phase of slavery itself, and the process of individual manumission operated coterminously with the very institution. There were many occasions for the freeing of slaves. A slave who offered his owner the amount of his original purchase price had to be granted his freedom. It was always possible for an industrious slave who was skilled in some craft to accumulate enough money in his free time to buy his liberty, though frequently he first bought that of his wife and children. In time there grew up associations of freedmen who financed the liberation of their fellows still in bondage. It was also common for a benevolent master to free one of his slaves at Christmas or on the occasion of a christening, a birthday, or a marriage in his own family.

There seem always to have been slave owners who questioned the basic morality of the institution. Occasionally one freed all his slaves in a body. Abolitionist sentiment increased greatly in the latter eighteenth century, and during the Empire it became a powerful and vocal force in Brazilian society. José Bonifacio de Andrada, first statesman of the early Empire, asked the question that then disturbed many Brazilians: "How can there be a liberal and lasting constitution in a country inhabited by an immense multitude of brutal and hostile slaves?" He saw, as many of his compatriots did, slavery as a barrier to the creation of an "homogeneous nation" free from "discordant elements."

There were eight slave revolts in the province of Bahia between 1807 and 1830, which culminated in a more serious outbreak in 1835. These were largely the work of the proud and independent Haussas and other Sudanese Negroes. In the seventeenth century renegade slaves had formed a remarkable Negro state in the backlands of northern Brazil. Known as the "Republic of Palmares," it resisted for many years all efforts of the government to destroy it, and it only succumbed when an armed force of Paulista frontiersmen was brought up from the south and turned loose against its defenders. As an epic of the *sertão,* the heroic defense of Palmares ranks with the siege of Canudos immortalized long afterward by Euclydes da Cunha. It was the resurgence of open rebellion by the slaves in the last century that accelerated the movement toward inevitable and total emancipation.

The final stages of emancipation were gradual, and when the final decree was issued in 1888, most of the work was already done. Half the slaves in Brazil had previously been freed in a period of 12 years. Though the further importation of slaves was prohibited in 1831, the law remained inoperative until 1850, when it was put into effect at the insistence of the British government. At that time the slave population was probably around 3,000,000. In the meantime, Lincoln's emancipation proclamation in 1863 gave a further impulse to the abolitionist cause in Brazil. A law of 1871 freed all children born to slave mothers, and another of 1885 declared all slaves over 60 to be free. Slavery was thus being cut off at both ends of the life cycle, so that it was now only a matter of time until the institution died a natural death. However, the pressures of abolitionist sentiment in high places forced the issue on the imperial government. Matters came to a head in May, 1888, during the absence of Emperor Pedro II in Europe, when his daughter, the Princess Isabel, approved the law passed by the imperial parliament. At the time there remained only about 700,000 slaves to benefit from its provisions. The next year the Empire ended with the forced abdication of the Emperor and the founding of the republic.

The ultimate consummation of the abolition movement was unattended by violence or by a prolonged aftermath of bitterness as in the United States. The economy of the northern states was seriously disrupted for a time by the fundamental change in the traditional pattern of its labor force. Slaveowners were not compensated for their losses, and some were unable to make the shift successfully to a free labor system. Some of the former slaves, usually the older ones, tended to remain where they were and to work for wages. Thousands moved into the towns and cities to enjoy the newly won fruits of freedom. In the old slave areas there was a general letdown of effort that persisted until the new freedman accepted the changed pattern of employment. Meanwhile, as the Industrial Revolution reached Brazil and gradually changed the tempo and dynamics of the economic order, the Negro had to begin a long and difficult apprenticeship in its responsibilities. The alternative was to resign himself indefinitely to the old familiar and unhurried ways while he watched the new Brazil go by.

In time the stigmata of his former condition would disappear from his body and soul. He would be only another Brazilian, undistinguishable from his fellows. Even his color, the mark of Africa, would disappear, too, for he is caught in the genetic revolution that began with the first mating of Portuguese and woman of color.

In spite of his initial handicaps, there was much in his favor. Above all, the deep humanity of Brazil was on his side in his struggle to incorporate himself into the life of the nation. He would not have to contend with any "segregation" policies or racist philosophies. He would not be told where he would have to live or with whom he might associate or marry. Enough of his kind had already demonstrated their capacity for high accomplishment that he need suffer from no inferiority complex by reason of his color or his servile background. If he would find no open prejudice of race or color in his way, he might encounter social barriers that had their roots in differences of economic status. Because he was poor and unlettered, certain doors might be closed against him, as they would be against any European immigrant whose only assets were the clothes on his back. He was starting at the bottom of the economic ladder, but at least no one on the higher rungs would trample on his fingers, and they might even reach down and give him a helpful lift. There was an immense fund of good will for him to draw on, and if he were willing to make the effort, the future could hold the same rewards as for any other Brazilian.

For the mulatto things are different. By the very circumstance of his ancestry, he has already broken through most of whatever obstacles might stand in his path, so that the field is open for him. He might even become president of the republic, as at least one of his kind has been. Brazil's most famous novelist was the son of a Portuguese and a Negress, and several of her finest poets have been "men of color." Many of her leaders in the professions, the arts, the press, the army, and in political life have been mulattoes. They provide a rich pool of talent for the needs of the nation and the enrichment of its culture. Their natural facility and grace of expression have given them a special place in the fields of writing and public expression, and the good manners that are a *sine qua non* for advancement in Brazil come easily to them. The attractiveness of the quadroon or octoroon woman in Brazil is legendary, and as the *moreninha* of song and story, she provides the ultimate link in the creation of a white Brazilian race.

CHAPTER 6

The Native

THE BRAZILIANS, LIKE MOST PEOPLES, ARE THE END-PRODUCT of racial admixture, physical environment, and the special circumstances of their history. As might be expected in so large a country, the human resultant of the process is far from uniform. It is only natural that there should be regional types as varied as in the United States, though continued migration within the country will gradually temper the force of regional differences, as the mobility of the American people has done in the United States. The influence of ethnic composition, climate and topography, geographical isolation, and economic development has traditionally accounted for the division of Brazil into six major and distinct cultural areas. They are, in the Northeast, the coast from Bahia to Belém and the *sertão* or backlands, the states of Minas Gerais and São Paulo, the city of Rio de Janeiro, and the state of Rio Grande do Sul. There are several out-regions or intermediate areas that are without a definite personality of their own but are within the sphere of influence of adjoining regions. Among these are the large state of

Mato Grosso, the states of Espirito Santo and Rio de Janeiro, and the economically important state of Paraná. Perhaps the state of Goiás, in which Brasilia is located, will ultimately become a melting-pot for all the various folk of Brazil and eventually produce a new Brazilian type. While certain qualities are common to the majority of Brazilians wherever they live, the local variables remain striking and important.*

The *Nordestino* or man of the old north-coast country, best exemplified by the Bahiano on its southern fringe, is warm-hearted and sentimental, given to fluid speech and endowed with a lyric imagination. The *Sertanejo,* who lives inland to the west of him, is austere and laconic, nomadic and physically hardy. The Mineiro, a true mountaineer, is much like the New Englander before the Irish, the French-Canadians, and the New York commuters and summer residents moved into his hilly preserves—conservative and cautious, sober and prudent, reserved and undemonstrative, and with a deep fund of common sense and passive strength. The Carioca of Rio is volatile and voluble, irreverent and cynical, sybaritic and devil-may-care. The Paulista is practical-minded and dynamic, adventurous and energetic. The Gaucho of Rio Grande do Sul is frank and unemotional, a rugged horseman with a yen for the open spaces, and more like his Spanish-speaking neighbors than his cousins of the other Rio Grande.

Though Brazil is a political democracy, no one pretends that it is a classless society. It is still too close to the Empire to be otherwise. Nobility under the Empire was a lifetime privilege and titles were not inherited. Many of the imperial nobles are perpetuated in street names in Rio, but the only living nobles in Brazil are papal counts, generally Italians. An imperial pretender still holds court of a sort in Petropolis, Dom Pedro's city, but to the generality of Brazilians he is a harmless anachronism.

* For a fuller discussion of regional differences, the reader is referred to Chapter X, "The Brazilian," in my book, *This New World: The Civilization of Latin America* (New York: E. P. Dutton & Co., Inc., 1954).

It is an open society in a state of flux. Class distinctions are meanwhile accepted as part of a natural system of rewards and chances. If success is largely an affair of luck, it does no good to rebel against the system, but it is better to await another turn of the wheel. While there are wide differences in social position and wealth, there is very little sign of the "exploitation of the masses" that the professional agitators talk about. So there has been no social revolutionary movement, as in some of the Spanish-American countries. Only the Communists talk about "proletariats" and "bourgeoisies," dogmatic terms incomprehensible in the flexible society of Brazil.

The criteria of upper class are birth, wealth, and distinction, either in the public service, the professions, or the arts. There are families that by right of age are of the aristocracy. Some have been identified with the life of Brazil for four centuries. Wealth in itself is not a prerequisite, but its possession helps by providing the air of leisure and the impedimenta of living associated with gentility. Traditionally, wealth for social purposes is reckoned in terms of land, and a million acres of *caatinga* may be worth more than a million dollars in securities stored in a strong box in a Rio bank. Above all, one of the great Paulista coffee fazendas is a proper setting for "persons of quality." Some persons, generally of foreign origin, in spite of fortunes made in business, remain outside the pale. For all their wealth, the taint of the "adventurer" may be on them.

High achievement in one's chosen field of activity, whether it be as a writer or an artist, a doctor or a scholar, is recognized by all but the most snobbish members of the aristocracy as a condition for entry into the national elite. Of the following notables of the republic—Ruy Barboza, orator and jurist, Marshall Rondón, the explorer, Santos Dumont, the pioneer of aviation, Portinari, the painter, Villa-Lobos, the composer, Oswaldo Cruz, the physician, Rio Branco, the diplomat, and Euclydes da Cunha, the writer—only two were of the aristocracy.

Good manners—the behavior complex of the continental gentleman—are an indispensable mark of the Brazilian aristocrat, and it is only in the past 30 years that the "roughneck" has become a feature of Brazilian political life. The *cavalleiro* is generally well educated and traveled and is at ease in any situation. He is not likely to indulge in conspicuous display of his wealth. Diamonds have always been widely distributed in Brazil, Parisian gowns are no monopoly of his womenfolk, and in the modern carriage trade, a Cadillac may carry some immigrant who has struck it rich in São Paulo. Even the city's Arenida Paulista is no longer a residential preserve of the aristocracy. In Rio, the *granfinos* are no longer distinguishable by their apparel or bearing.

The middle class in Brazil is an inchoate body. It is more numerous by the year and its economic significance is very great. It has no feeling of class solidarity and is too busy with its affairs to exert the influence in politics that is justified by its growing numbers and superior education. Its lack of cohesion is probably due in part to the circumstance that a large part of its membership is made up of elements of foreign origin which are mutually isolated from each other by their cultural background.

The family names of most Brazilians are conventional enough. There are hordes of Costas and Carvalhos and Silvas and Machados and people of other cognomens out of Portugal. There are 218 José Silvas in the Rio telephone book, of whom 37 have no middle name, and 178 María Silvas, 26 of whom are apparently without any other name. But their first or Christian names are probably the most unconventional on earth. The result is that except for myriads of Joãos and Josés, or Johns and Joes, a Brazilian is liable to be known by his first name. Families often try to find so unusual a name for a newborn child that there is little likelihood of its being duplicated in the city. A man is frequently listed in the telephone book according to his Christian name. For example President Vargas, the famous Brazilian dictator, was universally known as "O Getulio," or "The Getulio." Brazilians ransack the classics and the Bible and history and the dictionary for distinctive names for their children. They even resort to numerals, as the prominant Rosado family in Maranhão did, to designate their 21 offspring. In this case the numerals were French and not Portuguese, and the children were called Un, Deux, Trois, Quatre, Cinq, and so on up to Vingt-un. Number 18, or Diezhuit, was elected to the National Congress, and one day a Rio newspaper carried the headline, "Diezhuit was met at the airport by his brother, Vingt." One Mineiro mother hopefully christened her child "Ultimo," or "the last," and lived to see him a member of the Chamber of Deputies in Rio. In 1959 among the 326 members of that body were the following: Epilogo or "Epilogue" de Campos, Expédito Machado, Bonaparte Maia, Philadelpho García, and Ferro, or Iron, Costa, besides a sprinkling of such un-Portuguese names as Yukishigue Tamura, Rachid Named, Wilson Fadul, Antonio Baby, and Alberto Hoffmann.

The variety of Christian names of the large Oliveira clan in Rio, as listed in the local telephone directory, is probably typical. Besides a Septimo, or Seventh, and Trece, or Thirteen, 13 of them bear classical Greek names that range from Alcibiades to Pericles, and include, among others, an Amphilophio, an Apollinario, a Diogenes, and a Euripedes. Four of them are named Caesar, Cicero, Tacitus, and Diocletian. Six of the local Oliveiras are named Gladstone, Jefferson, Milton, Nelson, Newton, and Washington. Among others are a cosmopolitan assortment which includes namesakes of Atahualpa and Napoleon, Hammurabi, the Babylonian king, and Kropotkine, a princely Russian anarchist, and out of the Dark Ages, a Carloman and a Dagobert. There are also a Bonanza and a Rockefeller Chrysostomo. The biblical influence in Brazil is further represented by Ananias Matta in Rio and Methuselah Wanderley in Recife.

Contrary to the usual impression, by no means all Brazilian women are named Maria. The diversity of feminine names is illustrated by women of the large Silva family who are listed in the Rio telephone directory. They are generally melodious names, sometimes derived from Indian legend, and include an Alzira, an Aurea (Golden), Ayrosa, Belleza (Beauty), Dulce (Sweet) and Dulcina, Belmira, Djalma, and Iracy. Among the Oliveiras, Greek mythology was drawn on for the names of Eurydice and Mnemosyne.

The salutations used in addressing persons in Brazil depend on such considerations as age, social position, education, occupation, but mostly on the degree of intimacy in the relationship. Brazilians dislike formulas where people are involved, and things like forms of address are likely to be subjective. Foreigners learn only by trial and *faux pas* the correct thing to say. For example, a married woman who has reached matronage may be hailed by her first name, preceded by "Dona," as "Dona Elena." If she is a servant, the "Dona" is omitted. There is no equivalent for the Spanish "Don," and the term "Dom" is applied only to certain members of the clergy. The nearest approach to the Spanish "usted" or formal "you" is "O senhor," which means literally "the mister." The next step toward complete informality is the use of the word *"você."* Friends and members of the family address one another by their first name and use the familiar "tu" in conversation. Brazilians are much given to the use of diminutives which are composed by affixing an "nho" or "nha" to the person's name or appelation, as "Mariozinho." They are an expression of endearment or familiarity, as when a child addresses its grandmother as *"avozinha."*

Since the doctorate is the mark of the educated man in Brazil, Brazilians are liable to take no chances of offending one who wears an air of learning and so address him as *"doutor."* If the one addressed is not a doctor, he is pleased by the compliment anyway, so that nothing is lost by the error and some good will may be gained. The degree is rather liberally dispensed, so that more realistic, though well informed, natives do not take it very seriously. Thus a cartoonist shows a Carioca saluting a doctoral friend from a taxi on the Avenida Rio Branco as every face in the block turns about to answer the greeting. One with no claim to intellectual distinction, but with "status" in the community, may become a "colonel" by acclamation, as in Kentucky. Most of the honorary "colonels" in Brazilian life seem to come from the state of Minas. It is still possible to hear the old-fashioned and courtly form of address, *"vossa Excellencia,"* applied to important personages, but well below the level of presidency. Also, a judge may be addressed by the ponderous Portugueseism, *"Desembargador,"* and a lawyer as *"Licenciado"* or "licensed one."

Food in Brazil ranges from the savage to the sophisticated. It all started with manioc meal or *farinha de mandioca* which the Tupí had been eating long before the hungry Portuguese appeared. Hans Staden, the German soldier of fortune, who lived in Brazil in the sixteenth century, where he narrowly escaped being devoured by the local Indians, said, "It is the custom of the Portuguese to send ships which are well armed into the country of their enemies to trade with them, giving them knives and sickles in exchange for mandioca meal, which the savages have in great quantities. The Portuguese have many slaves employed in the sugar plantations and require the meal for their food." The last word on manioc meal was spoken by two Spanish naval officers, Jorge Juan and Antonio de Ulloa, over 200 years ago, when they wrote, "The common food of the inhabitants of all ranks is the *farina de pau* or wood-meal, which is universally eaten instead of bread." And they added that "it is little more than sawdust, both with regard to taste and smell." Henry Bates, the English naturalist who lived in the Amazon in the first half of the last century, wrote that he once spent two years without tasting wheat bread. "Manioc meal," he commented, "is a poor, weak substitute for bread." While the consumption of *farinha* seems to be decreasing as that of rice is increasing, only a larger weight of bananas is eaten by the average Brazilian.

The prime soup of Brazil is *canja,* made with chicken and rice, which Theodore Roosevelt called "the finest soup in the world." Another good *potage* is the thick vegetable soup of Minas, which used to be served at the old Rio Barcellos Restaurant in Rio, along with most of the other dishes typical of Brazil.

Fish do not occupy the place they deserve in the Brazilian diet. Some of the rivers team with them, but one seldom sees a fisherman sitting on the bank of a stream. The lack of refrigeration in a warm climate is partly responsible for the failure of Brazil to make the most of its fish resources. Much commercial fishing goes on along the coast, but the fish is eaten locally in the cities, and away from the seacoast fresh fish are a rarity. Along the northeast coast fishing is a subject of romance rather than economics. The romantic fishermen go out to the horizon from places like Fortaleza in seagoing rafts or *jangadas* and return to shore in the evening with the day's catch. The hardy *jangadeiros,* their skin browned by the sun and beaten by the salt spray of the sea, are as much a part of the local scene in northern Brazil as are the coco palms along the beaches. Of late, unromantic Japanese trawlers work the deep waters out beyond the range of the *jangadas* and bring in lobster and tuna for the select trade in Recife and other cities of the north coast.

The Portuguese brought with them to Brazil an obsession for codfish or *bacalhau,* which their bold fisherman brought into Portugal from the Newfoundland Banks. So *bacalhau* has ever since been the image of fish to most Brazilians, and it is one of the country's principal imports. The mammoth pirarucú of the Amazon is salted and sold locally, but wherever the Portuguese influence on the kitchens of Brazil has survived, the cod is fish. Richard Burton wrote in the last century of São Romão, a village on the São Francisco, "An idea of the popular apathy may be found from the fact that whilst the river flowing before their doors produces the best of fish, the townspeople eat the hard, dry 'bacalhau' or codfish, brought in driblets from Newfoundland." In the coast country, farm workers, before going out to the field in the morning, would put a chunk of *bacalhau* in their hip pocket to munch at midday.

The classic meat of Brazil is *carne secca* or *xarque* (pronounced "sharkey"). Slabs of meat were hung over a wire, to dry and harden in the sun, to make the jerked beef or *charqui* of the Incas. The art was widely known among the Indian peoples of the New World, and the French "buccaneers" acquired their name from the *boucan* or smoked meat of the Arawak natives of Haiti, who had a large body of relatives in the middle of Brazil. *Xarque* has the great merit of keeping well in a hot climate, and, re-hydrated, it is a common ingredient of country dishes.

The Brazilians eat large quantities of meat, both beef and pork, in other than its dried forms. *Bifes* of various cuts are an important item on restaurant and household menus, and there is excellent ham that comes from the packing houses in the south. Also, roast pork or *lombo de porco assado,* usually with trimmings, can be a succulent dish in Brazil.

Brazilian cookery runs to elaborate stews and other elaborate concoctions that often have an African origin in the sense that the cooks who devised and prepared them were Negro women, generally of Bahia. There used to be a saying in Brazil that "the blacker the cook, the better the food." While the base of a particular dish is usually the same, the rest of its components may depend on the array of ingredients at hand. The *vatapá* of Bahia is a case in point. Its preparation is usually an all-day exercise. It may start with shrimps, or *camarrões,* and a pitcher of coconut milk. The meat used may be fish, chicken, or lean pork. It will probably contain crushed chili peppers and other seasoning, plus a dash of cashew nuts, and the resulting mixture will be thick-ened with rice, corn meal, or *farinha.* Once on the table, its eating is not to be undertaken lightly.

Proclaimed as "the national dish of Brazil" is *feijoada,* or more properly *feijoada completa.* An all-out *feijoada* is truly a work of culinary engineering. It is built around black beans, or *feijão preto.* Before the cook is through with its assembly, it may con-tain, *inter alia, xarque,* smoked sausage, smoked pork, smoked tongue, bacon, pig's feet, a pig's ear and tail, *farinha,* onions—and much of the pantry's other contents. Full *feijoada* procedure calls for a glass of *cachaça* or strong rum as a primer. A heavy and soporific dish, it is likely to be served at the beginning of a long week-end. The Brown family, who lived in Brazil for many years and wrote the *South American Cookbook,* called it "the best bean dish of all time." *Ropa velha com tutú,* or "old clothes with tutú," is a sort of aftermath of a *feijoada* Friday, *tutú* being the left-over beans.

A more modest Brazilian specialty is *churrasco,* whose native habitat is the state of Rio Grande do Sul. It is a local phase of a meat dish common to the River Plate lands, where it was the *gaucho*'s original manner of preparing his evening meal in the open. It is simply an affair of hunks of beef roasted on a spit. A restaurant in the Botafogo section of Rio serves an excellent *churrasco* with vegetables and Rio Grande wine. Incidentally, in addition to white and sweet potatoes, onions, and other cooking vegetables familiar to Americans, there is *xuxu* (pronounced shoo-shoo) or the squash-like chayote.

For desserts, Brazilians have long been addicted to "sweets" or heavy, calorific pastries, such as are displayed in the popular *confitarías* like the Colombo in Rio. These delicious *doces* are saturated with soft Brazilian sugar and popular folklore. Among them are *beijinhos de moça* or "maiden's kisses," *beijos de cabocla* or "the *cabocla*'s kisses," *olho de sogra,* "the mother-in-law's eye," and *sonhos* or "dreams," a puff served with the morning coffee. In a *sorvetería* or refreshment shop in Salvador I found, along with ice creams and sherbets, "milk shacks" (shakes), "dusty millers," and *"beijos frios"* or "cold kisses."

Marmalades and jellies are popular with Brazilians. Excellent orange marmalade is made in Rio Grande do Sul. *Goiabada,* or guava paste, served with yellow Minas cheese, is the inevitable dessert in restaurants unless the diner specifies otherwise when ordering his meal.

Fruit is an increasingly important part of the Brazilian diet. No better oranges, tangerines, and bananas are found anywhere, and enormous quantities of them are eaten. Japanese farmers now supply the São Paulo market with good strawberries. Among other fruits which I found exhibited in a market in Recife were mango, *cajá* and *cajú,* the yellow fruit to which the cashew nut is attached, *carambola, mangaba, mamão* or papaya, *jambo, abacaxí* or pineapple, *fruta do conde,* and avocado. Brazilians make a favorite ice cream of avocado, but a common way of eating it is as an iced purée with sugar and lime juice. One who has tried this treat will never face an avocado again in any other dress. Canned fruits are also common, and among them are Argentine peaches, pears, and cherries, canned in Rio.

Coffee is the staff of life in Brazil. The native begins his day with it, perhaps before he is out of bed, and during the day he is never far from the steaming coffee urn. The coffee is freshly ground and roasted every day, and the strong dark powder is served either with heaps of sugar in a small cup of hot water or in a large cup with warm milk. The public coffee shops are an indispensable feature of Brazilian life, and all day long their high counters are lined with men and women having another *cafezinho.*

In the southern part of the country, much herva matte, or Paraguay tea, is drunk, often as an alternative to coffee. This is a standard drink of the River Plate countries and is produced in Paraná. Also considerable China tea, grown in Brazil, is consumed in the cities. A drink that is native to the country is *guaraná.* It is made from the seeds of a tree that grows in the Maués valley in the state of Pará. In its primitive form it is sold in round, chocolate-colored sticks, which the denizens of the Amazonia, using the rough tongue-bone of the pirarucú fish, file into a cup full of water. The potion is then sweetened and flavored before partaking. It is a very popular beverage in the cities of the south, where the powder forms the basis of a variety of hot and cold drinks. A large assortment of fruit juices is sold in drink stands and by street vendors. Catering to the same market are American cola drinks bottled in the country. There is also a long-established business in bottled waters, including non-carbonated spring water, which is popular with foreigners uninitiated in the mysteries of local drinking water.

Beer has long had a great vogue in Brazil. Burton even found beer, "everywhere the test of civilization," in a town on the São Francisco. The domestic brews are generally of excellent quality. The good wines of Rio Grande do Sul have cut deeply into imports of French wines, and Brazil, which was once a major market for champagne, now drinks very little of it. Of the stronger distilled liquors, rum has been produced since the early days of the colony. Little of it is of first-rate quality, and a green variety, known as *pinga,* is particularly lethal. Brazilians are very temperate in their drinking habits, and except among the lower class, drunkenness is extremely rare. The Reverend Kidder, who traveled extensively in Brazil during the Empire, remarked that "the contrast between the general sobriety of all classes of Brazilians and the steady drinking of some foreigners and the regular 'blow-out' of others is painful in the extreme."

The literate third of Brazil read newspapers. There are dailies, like the *Estado de São Paulo,* that rank with the best, and there are shabby sheets that live by devious devices. There are too many papers, particularly in Rio, and the circulation of even the largest is low by New York or London standards. Advertising revenues are likely to be low, and so is the pay of reporters and writers. Yet in spite of apparently precarious economics, many newspapers are long-lived. The more substantial of them have considerable influence on popular opinion, and some of the signed articles that are so important a feature of Brazilian journalism are read avidly by a wide public. Sensational tabloids, with headlines in red, and complete with gossip columns, sob stories, and gruesome accounts of crimes, represent another angle of the press.

For all its low economic status, the journalistic profession never lacks recruits. An unusual proportion of the leaders of Brazil, especially those from the north, have written for the papers at some stage of their lives, and nearly all the writers of mark have served their time with the press. The collective prestige of the profession is great, as reflected in the building of the Brazilian Press Association in Rio.

Large-format pictorial weeklies like *Cruzeiro* and *Manchete* are popular reading. Other magazines that have a large circulation are *Selecções,* the Portuguese edition of *Reader's Digest,* and *Visão,* a news commentary weekly, published in São Paulo but part of a hemispheric chain.

Sections of a Brazilian newsstand may appear very familiar to Americans. A random array of magazines, with covers flashy and fleshy, bear names like *Hollywood, Cinderela, Intimidade, Sedução, Sentimento, Confidencial, Capricho, Meia Noite* (midnight), *Noturno,* and *Querida* (sweetheart). Comic strips, mostly of American origin, appear in newspapers and in periodical form on the newsstands. Among translations or adaptions of familiar "comic books" that have a large public, one may find *Superman, Popeye, Tarzan, Flash Gordon, Felix the Cat, "Bill-Kid," Luluzinha, Pato Donald* and *Pato Dizzy, Terror Negro,* and *Jeronimo, Heroe do Sertão.*

The Brazilian who can afford the luxury of books buys—and reads—them. Among cultivated persons of means there are many bibliophiles who have large private collections. Good bookstores are abundant, but good public libraries are not. However, São Paulo has a large and well-administered library that should become a model for other urban centers. For those who read there is a rich and varied literature in both fiction and non-fiction, as described in the literary histories of Samuel Putnam and Erico Verissimo.

There was a time when French books were almost as common in bookstores as those in the language of the country, and French cultural influence was so strong that it had the effect of delaying the full development of a national literature. Many French books are still sold, but Brazilians no longer have an inferiority complex about their own literature. They are cosmopolitan in their reading tastes, and their bookstores and libraries will contain a large sampling of American and European works, often in the original language.

Several *livrarías* in Rio and São Paulo carry an extensive line of American and British books, and large collections are available in the cultural center libraries of both countries. As an index of current reader interest, translations of the following books were among those displayed in bookstores in 1959: *Lolita* and *Peyton Place,* Hemingway's *The Old Man and the Sea,* Budd Schulberg's *What Makes Sammy Run?,* Richard Armour's *It All Started with Eve,* Gunther's *Inside Russia,* Caryl Chessman's *The Law Wants Me To Die,* and *Is the United States a Second-Class Power?,* by Drew Pearson and Jack Anderson. A new phase of Brazilian reading habits and moods was represented by the writings in Portuguese translation of Dale Carnegie and the Reverend Norman Vincent Peale, along with Oliver's *How To Make More Money without Capital* and Dr. Fink's book, *Release from Nervous Tension,* translated as *Domine O Seu Sistema Nervioso.* Also, among old favorites, there were *Moby Dick,* Poe's Tales, *The Last of the Mohicans,* and Willa Cather's *My Antonía.*

No Brazilian would be bored by an interval of leisure. He would always know what to do with any spare time that came his way, if only to do nothing. He might just loaf contentedly and gracefully. But he would not fuss and fume, restlessly gnaw his fingernails, or feel conscience-stricken because he was not working. He will work long hours, in two jobs if necessary, to "make ends meet" in an inflated economy, but he will not glorify his toil. He holds no brief for work for its own sake, but accepts it realistically as an important element in the economic system. He is not lazy by nature, but he knows how to fill in the gaps between working to his own satisfaction.

Early visitors from self-consciously bustling lands used to comment disparagingly on what they called the native's "apathy" when they found him lying unconcernedly in a hammock at midmorning in some remote village. As a matter of fact, he probably preferred to do his work in the cool of the evening, or he may have risen at dawn and already finished half a day's work and was only taking an early siesta. Maybe he was ill with malaria or some other debilitating disease, as I have seen half the inhabitants of a village in the Amazonia.

The middle-class urban Brazilian, who works in an office from nine to five, may go to the movies in the evening. There is usually an American picture and either a national film or one from France or Italy. Brazilian films, like *Cangaceiro* and *Black Orpheus,* which was produced by a French director in the *favellas* of Rio, have had a good reception in New York. However, the national motion picture industry has not realized the full possibilities of the history of adventure in the Brazilian west as represented, for example, by the long *boiadas* or cattle drives. The legitimate theater, which formerly featured comedies, like *Where the Sabia Sings,* has declined in recent years, but efforts are being made to revive it in the entertainment field. The Municipal Opera House in Rio generally offers a series of musical programs in the winter, and perhaps a few weeks of opera as well as a dramatic company from Europe. Most of the devotees of the indifferent night clubs are likely to be foreigners. There are many radio and television stations throughout the country, and the number of listeners is very large, as is also the phonograph-owning public.

The idea of public entertainment in Brazil is generally associated with the Rio Carnival. This annual Saturnalia of song and dance is essentially a popular festival and as such has had difficulty in adjusting itself to changes in the life of the city. Most of the revelers in the streets have always been drawn from the lower classes, who are organized in "carnival clubs" that prepare their floats and costumes months in advance of the celebration. Also new songs are written for the occasion by local bards, often from the *favellas* or slums. Formerly the jubilant street crowds were noisy but otherwise orderly. However, in recent years criminal elements from the north have made their appearance in the hurly-burly, with a disturbing rise in crimes of violence. As a result, "better-class" families that used to look upon the proceedings as essentially a plebeian affair and only participated on its fringes as decorous Pierrots and Columbines have tended increasingly to boycott the somewhat orgiastic goings-on.

There is nationwide enthusiasm for sports, most popular of which is soccer football. Games are staged before multitudes of spectators in vast Roman amphitheaters. When a Brazilian team won the world soccer championship in Europe a few years ago, it was a high point in the history of the republic. Tennis and water sports are also popular, and in 1959 Maria Ester Bueno, a Brazilian, won the world championship for women at Wimbledon.

The strongest organization in Brazil is the family. It is stronger than state or church, or any of the organs or instrumentalities thereof. It is stronger than any formal association or collectivity of which the individual may be a member. In fact, the strength of the family may be a deterrent to impersonal collective action in the community. The Brazilian is not an "organization man," and he feels that if he became a "joiner" he might partition his personality among the various entities until only his name were left to him.

Maria Graham wrote in the last century: "The family attachments here are quite beautiful. They are as close and as intimate as those of clanship in Scotland." Indeed, the traditional Brazilian family has much of the self-sufficiency of a clan, with subjective elements that are peculiar to the nation. The Brazilian family provides for its members affection, companionship, entertainment, comfort in time of trouble. It is a social-security system and an employment agency. It is a private court of justice that disciplines its erring members. It can be a formidable political machine in local elections.

In its typical form it is large and may embrace hundreds of relatives—sons and daughters, brothers and sisters and their children, hosts of cousins of various degrees, and a large scattering of aunts and uncles. It may include an illegitimate branch of the family. And, to complete the rolls, it probably comprises a sizable company of godchildren. A family reunion, as on the "patriarch's" birthday, can be an impressive gathering. The natural seat of the Brazilian family is the large fazenda or a town in which the family is long established. The family needs space for its full expression and does not flourish in crowded and impersonal cities. The uniformity and anonymity of rabbit-warren apartment houses is incompatible with its spreading habits. Also, modern transportation and the call of economic opportunity in the cities is menacing its solidarity and its place in Brazilian society.

Nineteenth-century travelers in Brazil had much to say about the status of women. Their comments were generally unfavorable. They stressed her inferior place in society and particularly the seclusion in which she was kept by her jealous but philandering menfolk. This they ascribed to the survival of half-Moslemized Portuguese customs that forbade women their proper role in Brazilian life. Some travelers also noted that as relations with the outside world increased, the old restrictions on women tended to disappear. Allowance must be made for the circumstance that people usually show less understanding of the family mores of another people than of any other phase of human conduct. Also, on the other side of the social ledger it must be recognized that the woman of the old regime had much authority and prestige within the home. It is true that she married too young and had too many children. And although she spoiled her sons, both sons and daughters returned her affection with lifelong devotion.

Mrs. Louis Agassiz from New England, who admired the Brazilian woman, lamented her lot in these words, "Life is one of repression and restraint. She cannot go out of her house except under certain conditions, without awakening scandal. Her education leaves her wholly ignorant of the most common topics of a wide interest. . . . Among my own sex, I have never seen such sad lives." However, she observed much improvement in Rio, where many Brazilian men of her acquaintance expressed their agreement with her views. Lieutenant Herndon, the American naval officer, after a visit to Belém, wrote that "The Brazilians, as a general rule, do not like to introduce foreigners to their families, and their wives lead a monotonous and somewhat secluded life. . . . An intelligent and spirited lady friend" told him that she hoped her husband would take her abroad to live "where she might see something, learn something, and be somebody." The Reverend Kidder, after reporting that it was the habit of the Portuguese in colonial times to "incarcerate" their wives in a convent when they made a business trip to Portugal, commented that "The manners and address of Brazilian ladies are good and their carriage is graceful. . . . They have no fund of general knowledge, . . . but they chatter nothings in a pleasant way. . . . Wives in Brazil," he said, "do not suffer from drunken husbands, but many of the old Moorish prejudices make them the objects of much jealousy." And he concludes that "the lives of the Brazilian women are dull and monotonous to a degree that would render melancholy a European or an American lady."

In no other respect has Brazil changed more than in the situation of its women. The change has not come about through the agitation of feminists or of foreign women set on the "liberation" of their sisters from masculine bondage. It has come about naturally, without manifestoes and *pronunciamentos,* as things are inclined to do in Brazil, and both men and women have decided that it is best for everybody that way.

The woman goes out when she wishes. She teaches in the schools and works in offices and factories. In some university classes there are more women students than men, and some of the best professors are women. Women are in the professions and the diplomatic service. Middle-aged women with grown children hold important positions in business and professional life. The

Brazilian woman's great strength of character now has a wider field in which to play, and her enormous fund of wisdom and devotion has been freely placed at the service of the nation.

Meanwhile, the basic relationships between men and women have not suffered from the changes. A woman now chooses the man she will marry. She is no less a woman for her new condition in Brazilian society, and she is still infinitely feminine. Aside from the influence of the constitutional ban on divorce, marriage has a greater stability than in the United States, and though legal separation is permissible, it is seldom resorted to. As Brazilians have a flair for "talking out" their differences, married couples tend to live out their common problems. Sex has long since been accepted for what it is. People do not write treatises on it or fill the magazines with articles about it as if, like space travel, it were something new.

No other Latin American people have analyzed themselves so frankly and honestly as have the Brazilians. None have been more critical of national faults than writers like Fernando Azevedo, Gilberto Freyre, Afranio Peixoto, Paulo Prado, Alceu Amaroso Lima, and Hernane Tavares de Sá. The picture they draw of their own people is not always uniform, but certain common characteristics are likely to appear in all of them. To a foreigner who has lived in Brazil their agreement with his own observations is usually striking.

The basic quality of Brazilians is humanity. This takes the various forms of respect for the lives and personalities of others. It is expressed in the Brazilian's strong aversion to violence, whether between nations or individuals. The crime rate in the cities is probably "normal," but little of it is calculated or premeditated. Murders are generally prompted by sudden outbursts of passion, except among the *caboclos* of the *sertão,* where the vendetta is common. There the hand of revenge can reach far, as it did for the former Kentucky feudist who killed a man in southern Brazil and later found a brief security as employee of an American engineering firm in the interior of Ceará. Then one day a stranger interrupted his lunch hour to close the vendetta, and he never returned to his place at the construction camp table.

But the law runs thin in the backlands, as it always does in an open frontier. And much of Brazil is still frontier. When it is present, authority is liable to be capricious, exercised by some local chieftain, ignorant or contemptuous of codes and courts. Where the formal panoply of authority and the restraints of civilized society are absent, each man tends to be a law unto himself, restrained only by individual conscience or whatever elemental concepts of justice and mercy he may harbor—or by the primitive fear of personal vengeance. So men may kill for greed or because their blood runs hot in them.

In the rest of the country there are accepted rules that govern personal relationships and mitigate the clashes of personality. These rules are dictated by good taste or good sense. For example, one does not mix in another's affairs. A foreigner, traveling at night along a dark street in Rio, comes upon a man beating a woman, who is presumably his wife. He goes to the woman's rescue, only to have both turn on him for interfering in something that was not his concern, and he learns quickly that there is no place for would-be Galahads in Brazil. Two open streetcars or *bondes* meet at a switch on the line. The motormen, obviously enemies, alight and begin to belabor each other with their iron switch rods. Meanwhile, the Brazilian passengers remain outwardly unconcerned, though a woman faints. But when a foreigner makes a move as if to break up the fight, his neighbor seizes his coattail and pulls him back into his seat.

In their dealings with others, Brazilians would rather please than hurt, but the formalized courtesy that marks relationships is more sincere than otherwise. At least it very seldom is a cover for ill-will. In the structure of human relations, there are four distinct levels. The first, and closest, is the sector of the family, within which the ordinary guards of privacy are down and the heart has full play. The second is the privileged area of friendship. The third is that of regular acquaintances, with whom no sentimental ties are involved. The fourth is that of the stranger, toward whom there are certain impersonal responsibilities. Thus the manner of address and the degree of warmth in communication are determined by a code of natural good breeding that may have little to do with social position.

Life in Brazil is tempered by a rich sense of humor that is typical of the country. Though it is most commonly exemplified by the Carioca and is expressed in quips and wisecracks, there is a deep fund of it in most Brazilians that tends to relieve many of the inevitable tensions of daily living. It has nothing to do with the extremes of joviality or hilarity. The Brazilians are not a gay people, but their ability to laugh at the funny side of a situation is a valuable counterpoise to feelings of anxiety and worry. Their writers have often stressed the element of melancholy in the national temper, which may be a heritage from the Portuguese but is sometimes aggravated by local or individual circumstances, economic or otherwise. The Negro gave the Brazilian's ancestor the gift of laughter to help him forget the melancholy of the *fadas* and the forest.

Sometimes there is a barb in Brazilian humor—maybe a deflating gibe that leaves its object in midair. For example, during the revolt of the Copacabana fort in 1922, an agitator addressed an improvised gathering in Rio's Praça Tiradentes. After a tirade against the government, which was warmly approved by his casual audience, the speaker wound up in a burst of oratory in which he invited his hearers to overthrow the republic the next morning. At this point a wag on the edge of the crowd took advantage of a lull in the harangue to shout, "And what if it rains?" So, since Brazilians like to stay indoors when it rains, the republic was given a new lease of life.

CHAPTER 7

The Stranger

ONE OF THE LEADING GEOGRAPHERS OF BRAZIL IS NAMED Hilgard O'Reilly Sternberg. A maternal ancestor of Juscelino Kubitschek, president from 1956 to 1961, came in the last century from what is now Czechoslovakia. The head of the largest business organization is Francisco Matarazzo, whose Italian grandfather settled in Sorocaba in the interior of the state of São Paulo in the 1880's. He later moved into the Paulista capital, where he built an industrial empire whose provinces included textile manufacturing, shipping, sugar refining, flour milling, grain brokerage, and the production of vegetable oils. For many years the largest coffee *fazendeiro* in Brazil was a German immigrant named Francisco Schmidt. The world-famous Brazilian pioneer in aviation was Albert Santos-Dumont. The Minister of Foreign Affairs is Horacio Lafer, and among Brazilian diplomats are Oswaldo Furst, Donatello Grieco, José Jobím, Mario Savard de Saint Brisson Marqués, and Frederico de Castelo Branco Clark. Walter Burle Marx, musician and composer, was founder and conductor of Rio's philharmonic orchestra. Elsa Houston, a well-known Brazilian singer, was a descendant of Sam Houston. Brazil's first architect is Oscar Niemeyer. One of the justices of the Brazilian Supreme Court is Octavio Kelly. All these un-Portuguese names are representative of one of the world's great melting-pots.

The first foreigners came early into the void that was then Brazil. In the first century of the colony, Brazil was to all intents and purposes a no-man's land. Navigators from western Europe who occasionally touched on its shores were aware of Portuguese claims to the empty land but seldom took them seriously. To them it was open country, and whatever it held that might minister to their profit or pleasure was theirs for the taking. The risks of a landing were small, for the coast was too long to be effectively policed by the slender resources of Portugal, already overextended by her great man-consuming enterprises in the East.

The crews of foreign vessels were liable to be a cosmopolitan lot, and a French ship out of St. Malo, for instance, might have on board Germans, Flemish, Englishmen, and Italians as well as its nucleus of Bretons. The Portuguese themselves were too mixed a people to harbor anti-foreign feelings as a general rule of conduct. As a result of their early contacts with African Negroes, the Moslems of the lands about the Arabian Sea, the peoples of India, the Malays of the archipelagoes, and the Chinese and Japanese of the Far East, they were the most international-minded folk of the age. They were incapable of xenophobia for its own sake, and so long as their basic interests were not threatened, they were inclined to follow a policy of live and let live where foreigners were concerned. In Brazil their only condition of acceptance, beyond a display of friendly intention, was the stranger's profession of the Catholic faith. Even that test was sometimes waived, as when Woodes Rogers' Anglican privateers were merrily entertained by laymen and clerics alike at Angra dos Reis. Much earlier, according to Hakluyt, Italians, like members of the Genoese families of Adorno and Doria, the Englishman, John Whithal, and a few stray Germans resided peaceably in the Portuguese community at Santos, near São Vicente.

Since then about 6,000,000 in all have come. Many of these later moved into other countries in South America or returned to their land of origin. But enough remained to leave a deep impress on the life of the nation.

The first organized immigration into Brazil began with the arrival of about 1,680 Swiss in 1820. Only two years were left of the colonial regime, and the Portuguese king, who then ruled his realms from Rio, ordered the immigrants to settle in the locality of Cantagallo on the lower Paraiba River. During the Empire about 7,000 Germans entered Brazil in the period between 1828 and 1850. Most of them established themselves in colonies in the province of Rio de Janeiro and in the southern part of the country. However, nearly 10 times as many Portuguese entered Brazil in the 1860's. In the 10 years 1881–90, which overlapped the republic by two years, over 500,000 immigrants of different nationalities arrived, and during the following two decades nearly half of all the immigrants who have entered Brazil since its beginning poured into the country. The principal impulse behind this massive movement was the need to replace as a labor force the Negro slaves who had been freed in 1888 and to provide the necessary manpower for the expansion of the coffee industry in the state of São Paulo.

Not since 1910 has the current of immigration again reached such heights, though in the decade between the wars (1921–30) the total rose to 840,000. The average for the three years that ended in 1957 was 75,000 a year, but the next year only 7,610 immigrants entered Brazil from Europe, and in 1959 fewer than 10,000 came. During the period 1954–56 only four nations, Syria, Spain, Yugoslavia, and Jordan, in that order, furnished more than 10,000 of the total entries, and of these the majority came from Syria.

The reasons for the decline were the interruption of normal communications between Brazil and Europe during the two World Wars; the attitude of the Axis powers, which discouraged emigration of their nationals and ordered the repatriation of large numbers of Italians and Germans for military service; and radical changes in the immigration policies of the Brazilian government. In 1934 a quota system was adopted which limited annual entries to 2 per cent of the total immigration from each nation since 1883. In the meantime the liberal subsidization of immigrants, which included free ocean passage, was suspended. In addition to these restrictive factors, official Brazilian policy became more selective. The entry of unskilled laborers was made difficult, and preference was given to industrial technicians and to farmers who could help to raise the level of agricultural production.

Other factors responsible for the decline in immigration have been the improved economic conditions in Europe in recent years, restrictive emigration policies of certain governments, and reports of mistreatment by Brazilian immigration officials, particularly in connection with the entry of personal baggage and other belongings. Also, Brazilian desires for larger immigration from its traditional sources of manpower have been thwarted by ignorance of the opportunities offered by Brazil to foreigners.

During the same period a program of state colonization was introduced. Nearly 5,000,000 acres of public lands were set aside as sites for these agricultural colonies or *nucleos coloniais*. Each of these tracts was divided into farms of between 25 and 75 acres, the nominal cost of which could be spread in annual payments over a period of 10 years. Other forms of aid, including loans by the Bank of Brazil, were offered to the immigrant farmer pending the time when he could be self-sufficient. In order to avoid the recurrence of early experience, whereby isolated immigrant centers resisted incorporation into the national life, it was stipulated that 30 per cent of the farmers in these colonies must be Brazilians. The full potential of the program, which provided for the settlement of over 500,000 persons, has been slow of realization, and the attainment of the goal is still distant. Among groups of other nationalities, agricultural colonies have been founded by Japanese, Dutch, and several Slavic peoples.

Since Independence in 1822, Brazil has received more people from the mother country than from any other source. Moreover, the nearly 2,000,000 immigrants of Lusitanian origin represent a disproportionately large share of the population of a small nation. While this migratory tide from Portugal began late, it has been steadier than the movement from other countries, and a larger percentage of the migrants have remained in Brazil. Portuguese immigration has been favored by their exemption from the quota system and by the circumstance that Portuguese were able to cross the Atlantic during the Second World War when immigration from other sources was cut off. Though the butt of much Brazilian humor, the Portuguese have been welcomed because of the ease of their assimilation and because of their reputation for hard work. They have made a very solid contribution to the development of Brazil and fill an important place in its commercial life, whether as corner grocers or as the heads of large wholesale trading firms. Even if somewhat patronizing, the Brazilians have a deep sentimental attachment for "the old country" and its citizens. They made much of the two Portuguese aviators, Sacadura Cabral and Gago Coutinho, who were the first to fly from Europe to Brazil, and gave an enthusiastic reception to the presidents of Portugal on their visits to Rio. In 1959 they held a congress of Luso-Brazilian studies in Salvador to celebrate the cultural and literary ties between the two peoples, and Brazilians who travel to Europe for pleasure are likely to include Lisbon in their itinerary.

Of non-Lusitanian peoples, the Italians are easily first in the population of Brazil. One of them, Filippo Cavalcanti, a Florentine, arrived in the sixteenth century, and his numerous descendants comprise one of "the first families" of the country. Also, during the early period of the colony, the three Adorno brothers from Genoa were pioneers in the sugar industry that was to become the principal support of the colonial economy for more than a century. Since the middle 1880's over 1,500,000 Italians have come to Brazil, over two-thirds of whom arrived in the 20 years that ended in 1903. In the meantime Italian immigration has followed no regular rhythm, and its volume has declined greatly in recent years. In 1951 only 10,000 came, and in the period 1954–57 more Spaniards than Italians entered Brazil. In 1959 there were fewer than 400 entries from Italy, though the Brazilian goal is 20,000 Italian immigrants a year.

Most of the original immigrants, on landing at Santos, were assigned to the coffee fazendas in the state of São Paulo, though some settled in Rio Grande do Sul, where they were to give an impulse to the grape and wine industry. Many of them drifted into the city of São Paulo, to whose growth they made a major contribution. Some of them managed to acquire farms of their own or to establish businesses in the towns of the interior. Many of them prospered and became great names in the Paulista economy, as did Francesco Matarazzo and Giuseppe Martinelli, the man from Lucca who made a fortune in shipping, banking, and coal mining, and built the tallest building in South America. Others in the same category were the Crespis and the Lunardellis, the Gambas and Puglisis, and, more recently in metallurgical manufacturing, Francisco Pignatari.

Adjustment to life in Brazil presented few problems to the Italian immigrant. Usually his working capital consisted of little more than a strong back and a fund of good will, so that at first he was not too exigent where "the extras" of living were concerned. The two languages had enough of the Latin in them to be mutually comprehensible. There were no religious barriers. The Brazilians of his own station in life were friendly enough and he easily established a satisfactory *rapprochement* with them. He felt no particular urge to live apart in a "Little Italy" in the city, unlike some of the more incompatible foreign groups. He was generally well disposed toward the land of his adoption and wanted only a chance to make the most of the opportunities. If he succeeded and claimed the place in the larger community that was his due, he was likely to collide with the vested social and political interests of the local aristocracy. But there were too many of his kind and there was too much vitality and promise in them to be kept back for long. In time the opposition to his advancement was relaxed and there was little left beyond his name and the remains of his native accent to set him apart. His sons considered themselves for all intents and purposes as Brazilians and were as liable to marry Brazilian women as the daughters of fellow-immigrants. In the process of integration that came so naturally to the Italian, he gave much to Brazil beyond the labor of his hands, for there was a lighter touch to the land for his presence in it.

Approximately 750,000 Spaniards have migrated to Brazil, of whom by far the largest number arrived in the period between the Spanish-American War and the First World War. While it is easy for the Spaniard to adapt himself to life in Brazil and the two Hispanic languages are similar enough to present no barrier to communication, an unusual proportion of Spanish immigrants have later moved on into the River Plate countries, where they feel more at home than among their Lusitanian cousins. Those who have remained have merged quite effortlessly into the general community and soon lose their identity in the population, though they are not inclined to give up their Spanish citizenship. A few have prospered beyond the common run of their countrymen, as did Francisco Serrador, who arrived at Santos in 1892. He became the leading pioneer in the motion-picture business in Brazil, in which field he is commemorated by the Cinelandia district in downtown Rio where most of the city's larger movie theaters are concentrated. He also built several skyscrapers in Rio, including the hotel that bears his name.

There are relatively few Brazilians of French ancestry. Since the early period of the colony there has been no concerted immigration from France, and those who have settled in Brazil in this century have done so as individuals.

Yet French mariners appeared in Brazilian waters only four years after the discovery of the country by Cabral in 1500, and continued to plague the Portuguese for over a century. Ships from Honfleur, St. Malo, and other Breton and Norman ports visited Brazil yearly in search of dyewood and other commodities. The French set up small trading and provisioning stations at convenient places along the open coast, where they cultivated the good will of the local aborigines. Though the Portuguese made desultory raids on these posts from time to time, they were not able to expel the French interlopers altogether until the next century.

In the meantime a short-lived colony was established in Brazil under the auspices of the French government. The founder of the colony was a well-known figure of the era of religious wars named Nicolas Durand de Villegaignon, who, among other feats, had rescued Mary, Queen of Scots, from her Presbyterian subjects and brought her to France. Villegaignon, himself currently a Calvinist, proposed to settle his fellow-Huguenots in the primitive and pagan atmosphere of Guanabara Bay, now the site of Rio de Janeiro. He obtained for his project the endorsement and blessing of the famous Admiral Coligny, who was responsible for Laudonnière's ill-fated colony in Florida.

The first Protestant settlers arrived in 1555 in what was still, save for the Indians, a demographic void, since the Portuguese were unimpressed by scenery. The colonists, who could expect no support from Paris, soon began to quarrel among themselves in a manner reminiscent of their homeland, and their leader, again a Catholic, returned to France. The French colony at least had the effect of calling the attention of the Portuguese to the advantages of its site, and in 1565 they founded the city of Saint Sebastian of Rio de Janeiro on the shores of the bay. Two years later they drove the last of the French colonists from the islands where they had settled and put an end to the dream of "Antarctic France." Long afterward, in 1711 and 1712, the French privateers, Leclerc and Du Guay Trouin, raided the city of Rio de Janeiro but made no effort to re-establish the authority of France in the locality.

After the collapse of Villegaignon's scheme, the French transferred the field of their activities to the unpopulated coast to the north of Pernambuco, where they continued their earlier trading and piratical enterprises. They made only one attempt at permanent settlement, the founding of São Luiz or Saint-Louis in Maranhão, where they remained from 1594 until 1615. In the end all they had to show for their halfhearted ventures in Brazil was the sterile colony of Cayenne or French Guiana.

Except for some stray soldiers of fortune, like Hans Staden and Ulrich Schmidel, both of whom wrote entertaining accounts of their wanderings and experiences in the sixteenth century, very few Germans ventured into Brazil before the period of the Empire. The first group of immigrants entered the country in 1828, and by the middle of the century about 7,000 Germans had arrived. Altogether some 250,000 have settled more or less permanently in Brazil. Almost a quarter of these came in the fateful inter-war decade 1924–33. During the four years ending in 1957 German immigration fell to a low of less than 5,000.

Of the first-comers, some established themselves in Petropolis and other hill towns of the province of Rio de Janeiro, but the majority settled in the wooded zone of the Serra da Mar that lies between the coast and the central plateau of Santa Catarina and northern Rio Grande do Sul. Since the Portuguese tended to avoid the forests in favor of open country, this part of southern Brazil was then relatively unpopulated, so that the isolation of the German immigrants laid the foundations of the political problems which were to arise much later.

Most of the early immigrants were peasant farmers who brought their womenfolk with them. They had little contact with the Brazilians who lived on either side of them or with the instruments of public authority. They were largely left to their own devices, with the inevitable result that they developed a society whose basic elements were peculiarly Germanic. As if by default, they created a virtual state within a state, to rationalize whose autonomy they invoked the concept of federalism in the theory that their self-contained communities merited equality with similar Brazilian entities within the country. They continued to speak their native tongue. They built in the wilderness rude replicas of the familiar institutions of the homeland—churches and schools and social clubs. They worked very hard, and for a time their standard of living was lower than that which they had left behind them. Sometimes it was as low as that of the *caboclo,* who knew nothing better than his accepted lot in life.

But by their grim efforts they established themselves solidly in the land. They were prolific, and their sons made farms of their own or moved up over the plateau into Paraná or out into the open country of Rio Grande do Sul. Some of them crossed into Paraguay, where they founded neat settlements like Colonia Hohenau, or into the Argentine Misiones. Eventually they built big towns that flourished, like Blumenau and Joinville in Santa Catarina or São Leopoldo and Novo Hamburgo in the south. In time they dominated the life of Santa Catarina and were a great power in Rio Grande do Sul, even in its capital city. Meanwhile, new immigrants from Germany had settled in São Paulo and in the coffee lands beyond, where the pressures for assimilation were stronger and where they shared with other immigrant stocks the great opportunities for advancement which existed there. In Rio Grande the old Brazilians finally accepted the German immigrants as part of the local scene, even if with some reservations as to their full membership in the national family. To the minority who were Catholics a sense of belonging came easier, for they found in the Church a common tie with the Brazilians. Little by little their feeling of superiority disappeared and they began to feel a strong attachment to the nation, though they preserved a certain nostalgia for the fatherland, and wherever they were in the majority, the mark of Germany was all about them. In time some of them made fortunes for themselves, as the Schmidts did in the coffee industry of São Paulo, the Konder brothers in paper manufacturing, and Abraham Eberle in a variety of enterprises in Rio Grande do Sul.

Many years after their first arrival in the new land of Canaan that Graça Aranha wrote of, but especially after the unification of the Reich in 1871, the Teutonic enclave in southern Brazil attracted the attention of imperialistic-minded leaders at home. To them this overseas *Deutschtum* was a ready-made nucleus for the realization of their dreams of a colonial empire in South America. By World War I the dreams had taken shape in the minds of those who made German foreign policy. A complex of the instrumentalities of power, headed by the embassy in Rio and comprising steamship lines, banks, and large trading houses, served consciously or indirectly the designs of Berlin. When Brazil finally entered the war on the side of the Western allies, there was a significant touch of irony in the circumstance that her Minister of Foreign Affairs bore the name of Lauro Müller.

Not only were the plans of the German imperialists frustrated, but the loyalty of German-Brazilians was put to a severe test. The descendants of the early settlers, to whom Brazil was now home, generally refused to answer the call of a common blood that was invoked by German propaganda. However, enough of the latecomers served the purpose of the German war effort to give grave concern to the Brazilian government. For its part, the Brazilians identified the survivals of the German way of life in the southern states with the enemy cause and struck at its roots in schools, churches, societies, newspapers, and other organs of Germanic culture. They discouraged the use of the German language, and names like Hans and Ludwig were changed to João and Luíz. Brazilian children were mixed with German-speaking children in the schools in the hope that the young *kinder* would learn Portuguese from them, but the result was that the Brazilian children acquired a fluency in spoken German. The eleventh-hour crash program to brazilianize the Germanic segment of the national population had only limited success in its immediate objectives. However, it did result in greater awareness by the Brazilian authorities of the risks implicit in their easygoing attitude toward foreign blocs within the nation. This awareness eventually led to a general tightening of controls over immigration and to a more intensive effort to assimilate minorities of foreign ancestry into the national community. After all, this policy was in line with the basic Brazilian philosophy of racial integration, and it was, therefore, certain to prevail in the long run.

The rise of Nazism in Germany was later to present Brazil with a renewal of the problem in an aggravated form. As the power of the Hitler regime grew, it made plans to utilize the German Brazilian population in its monstrous schemes. To its earlier apparatus of penetration it added the airplanes of the Condor Airlines, which charted the Amazon Valley and, as part of a system designed to circle South America, covered the length of the Brazilian *marinha*. It also sent fanatical Nazi agents into Brazil to stir up all those who had a German background, however distant or diluted, and to organize a supply and warning service for Nazi submarines. Its propaganda aimed to convince the Brazilians of German invincibility.

But it was all too late. The results for Germany were not in proportion to the magnitude of the endeavor. Except for a few diehards and some of the latecomers, the German-Brazilians lent less aid to the Nazi war effort than they had in the First World War. Though the Vargas government did not enter the war against Germany until late, it permitted the Allied air forces and navies to make use of invaluable bases on the Brazilian coast, like Natal and Belém. When Brazil finally entered the war, she took an active and creditable part in the hostilities by sending a force to Italy and by patrolling her long coastline against the menace of German submarines. Also, the loyalty of the great body of her citizens of German blood had amply demonstrated the folly of foreign attempts to divide her people in a time of crisis.

The only foreign people who have ever been a serious threat to Brazil were the Dutch, who occupied much of the northern part of the country in the seventeenth century. The Dutch had traded extensively with Brazil for a long time, either directly or through intermediaries in Portugal, but their territorial ambitions did not develop until the creation of the Dutch West India Company in 1621. Three years later a Dutch fleet captured Bahia and began Brazil's "Thirty Years War" that ended in 1654.

The struggle with the Dutch in Brazil overlapped in time the Thirty Years War in Europe. It was a miniature—if anything in Brazil can be miniature—of the first of "world wars." On one side it directly involved only the United Provinces, and on the other, Portugal and Spain, but the defenders included not only Portuguese and colonials of Portuguese descent, but Indians and Negroes. The Indians, Tupí and Tapuya from the backlands, fought on both sides, as did the Negroes, slave and free. One of the Tapuya bands in the service of the Dutch was commanded by a German-Jew named Jacob Rabbe, who was married to an Indian woman. The Portuguese brought into Brazil a company of Neapolitan mercenaries under one Giovanni Vincenzo de San Felice, Count of Bagnuoli, that proved to be of dubious military value. One of the ablest officers on the Dutch side was a Polish officer named Arciszewski. Another was General Sigismund von Schoppe, a stout German soldier of fortune. Also, a Colonel Henderson and a company of English adventurers served with the Dutch for a while.

In the seventeenth century international relationships in Europe probably sank to their lowest level in all history. Statecraft was satanic in its immorality. There was no faith between nations or their agents, and their wars degenerated into a savagery that even the Brazilian Tapuyas would scarcely have condoned in their less inhibited moments. Meanwhile, the normal force of antagonism was aggravated by the bitterness of religious differences between Catholics and Protestants, while the Jews were caught in the middle of the universal fray. It was in this general atmosphere of barbarism that the conflict between Dutch and Portuguese was waged in Brazil, a circumstance which rendered the humanity of the Dutch governor-general, Maurice of Nassau, all the more remarkable.

The chain of events that led to the Dutch occupation of much of Brazil included the long Spanish domination of Portugal, which ended in 1640, midway in the period of the Dutch regime in the great Portuguese colony. Since Spain was the hated arch-enemy of the Dutch, the Portuguese empire was open to the aggressive designs of the Hollanders. Portugal had become a minor power, both on land and sea, and the principal concern of her government was to avoid embroilment in the current chaos of European rivalries, while seeking alliances for her protection. She even maintained an alliance with the Dutch in Europe while they were openly engaged in the dismemberment of her empire overseas! She, moreover, long considered making an offer to buy back Pernambuco from the Dutch. Though Portugal had fallen so low from her once high estate, the nation possessed reserves of vitality and resolution that she could invoke in an emergency, as she did in throwing off the Spanish yoke in 1640, and which she eventually called into action in the war against the Dutch in Brazil.

In May, 1624, Bahia, the capital of Portuguese Brazil, surrendered to a Dutch fleet under Jacob Willekens and the famous Piet Heyn, who later captured the Spanish silver galleons in Cuban waters. When the news reached Europe it produced a furor in Lisbon and Madrid, where Lope de Vega hastily composed a play entitled *El Brasil Restituido,* and Velazquez' Count-Duke Olivares began to organize a counterstroke against the Hollanders. The next year an impressive Hispanic armada under the high command of the grandee, Don Fadrique de Toledo y Osorio, retook the city of Bahia. In 1627 Piet Heyn raided the shipping in the Bay of All Saints, after which the colony had a three-year breathing spell.

In the meantime, the directors of the West India Company resolved to direct their future efforts against Pernambuco, the center of the rich sugar industry. In February, 1630, a force of 67 ships with more than 7,000 men attacked Recife and gained a foothold in the city and in Olinda, a few miles up the coast. The place was energetically defended by the colonists under the command of Mathias de Albuquerque in the beginning of a long guerrilla war that continued intermittently until the expulsion of the invaders 24 years later. The Dutch, unable to cope with the unconventional tactics of the Portuguese, were shut up inside the city, until a mulatto deserter, Domingos Fernandes Calabar, instructed them in the same methods of warfare, thereby turning the tide of the rebellion for a time.

The arrival in 1637 of Johan Maurits as Dutch governor-general changed for the seven years of his rule the whole situation in northern Brazil. This extraordinary prince of the house of Orange, known to Brazilians as Maurice of Nassau, ranks, with Francisco de Toledo, Stamford Raffles, and Marshall Louis Lyautey, among the great colonial administrators of all time. Conciliatory and tolerant, humane and enlightened, he treated Dutch and Portuguese with equal justice and consideration. In the words of Charles R. Boxer, author of *The Dutch in Brazil 1624–1654,* "He fell in love with Brazil from the moment he stepped ashore." In his first letter to the directors of the Company he called it "one of the most beautiful countries in the world," and he said of it, "I do not think a milder and more temperate climate can be found anywhere." He expressed the perpetual problem of Brazil in these words: "The soil needs nothing but inhabitants and cries out for colonists to till and people this solitude." Of those whom he ruled so benignly he said, "I know by experience that the Portuguese are a people who value courtesy and consideration more highly than they do money and goods." With their usual irreverence, the common Brazilians came to refer to him as "Santo Antonio," and when he returned home from his *"beau pays de Brésil,"* his fellow-Hollanders nicknamed him "Maurits the Brazilian." It is no wonder that his memory is still honored in Brazil, as though he were of the country. The principal bridge over the river at Recife is "the Bridge of Maurice of Nassau," and his face appears on the paper currency of Brazil. Even the savage Tapuyas revered him, and a group of them insisted on accompanying him to Holland, where they lived on his estates and would dance naked for the entertainment of his guests, though to the great scandal of the Calvinist clergy.

In Recife he lived with pomp and circumstance, like a Renaissance prince. He invited to Brazil a large company of artists, scholars, and scientists, who graced his court and left for posterity a pictorial and written record of the land and its people. They studied tropical diseases, made collections of the fauna and flora of the country, and founded the first meteorological station in the New World. It was one of them, the brilliant young German naturalist, Georg Marcgraf, who said of his scientific methods, "I will not write about anything which I have not actually seen and observed."

But Johan Maurits also extended the area of Dutch rule in northern Brazil as far as the Maranhão country. He was not able to retake Bahia, where the Portuguese held out through the remainder of the Dutch occupation, though the Dutch laid waste the rich Reconcavo district across the bay from the old city.

Due to the special temper of his rule, there was a respite in open hostilities in the locality of Pernambuco during the period of his governorship. To the despair of the West India Company, he was little concerned with profits, and his accounts must have rivaled those of that legendary foe of comptrollers, Gonzalo de Córdoba, "the Great Captain" of Spain. Dutch and Portuguese lived in relative harmony in Recife, though they never learned to speak each other's languages more than haltingly and disagreed on social matters like drinking and the proper place of women in society. Also, the Dutch showed little inclination for rural life and tended to remain inside the towns. Many of them married local women and thereby often formed ties of sentiment and interest that proved stronger than loyalty to the country of their birth.

One of those who renounced his Dutch citizenship, became a Catholic, and chose to adopt the land of his Brazilian wife was a cavalry officer named Jasper van der Ley, who was the founder of the important Wanderley clan in northern Brazil. One of his descendants is Gilberto Freyre, the leading social historian of the colonial period. Vergniaud Wanderley is a federal senator from the state of Paraiba, and among other Wanderleys in Recife are Abelardo, Matusalem or Methuselah, Wandenkolk, and Wilson. The Lintz family became the Lins, another well-known name in the northern states. Etelvino Lins de Albuquerque is a senator from Pernambuco and João Alberto Lins de Barros was a prominent national figure during the Vargas regime.

After the recall of Johan Maurits and the reduction of the Dutch garrison for reasons of economy, the Brazilian war of liberation was resumed in earnest. Since the resistance movement was largely the work of colonials, its leaders are ranked among the heroes of Brazilian history. Among Portuguese and Creoles they included André Vidal de Negreiros, João Fernandes Vieira, a well-to-do planter, and Francisco Barreto. Others were the Negro, Henrique Dias, and the Indian chieftain known as Felipe Camarão. The rebels gradually drew a tight ring around Recife and defeated the Dutch in a couple of pitched battles, in one of which the Dutch suffered over 1,000 casualties. Of their enemies, the governing council in Recife reported:

> The Portuguese have become so experienced in this war that they can face the most veteran soldiers. . . . They hold their ground after receiving a volley, and then fall on our men. They also know how to take full advantage of the ground, and to lay ambushes, charging out of the woods on our men and inflicting heavy losses on them. . . . In bodily strength, self-control and character, they are the equals of our veteran soldiers.

The beleaguered city was temporarily relieved by the arrival of reinforcements in 1646, but a much more serious obstacle to the plans for liberation was the heavy damage inflicted on Portuguese shipping by Dutch privateers, which threatened for a time to sever completely all connections between Brazil and the mother country. Meanwhile, the war steadily became more destructive of men and property, and the important sugar-producing areas were laid waste.

In spite of the timid king's halfhearted policies, a large fleet was eventually assembled at Lisbon. Early in 1654 it appeared before Recife and, in conjunction with the rebel forces on land, forced the surrender of the Dutch garrison, and New Holland was at an end. Barreto, the commander of the victorious soldiery, treated the defeated with consideration, but expelled most of the large Jewish community as collaborators. One body of Jewish exiles migrated to New Amsterdam, to become the first of their religion to enter the present confines of the United States.

In later centuries the Dutch showed little interest in migrating to Brazil until recent times. Then in 1951–52 about 1,000 settled in two agricultural colonies, one near Campinas in the state of São Paulo and the other in Paraná. Most of the Hollanders had formerly resided in Indonesia, and probably no foreign colony in Brazil has been so successful in so short a time as have these Dutch farmers.

Of the various Slavic peoples who have settled in Brazil, and who were formerly designated as either "Russians" or "Austro-Hungarians," the best-known contingent consists of the Poles. Polish immigrants, largely peasant farmers, tended to locate in the Paraná highlands, where they are much in evidence in the vicinity of Curitiba. Their principal distinguishing marks are their frame farmhouses and their covered wagons, which one is likely to meet on the road between the airport and the center of the city. The Communist government of Poland has made persistent efforts to propagandize the local inhabitants of Polish stock, but with indifferent success. Though only about 42,000 still unnaturalized Poles lived in Brazil in 1940, subsequent immigration has been insignificant in quantity, and in three years 1955–57 only 153 entered the country. By 1959 the total of Polish-born in Brazil had risen to only about 48,000, of whom 87 per cent retained their original nationality.

Typical of the economic and social problems of foreign agricultural colonization in Brazil is the Latvian colony at Varpa in the "pioneer fringe" of western São Paulo. The original immigrants were mostly religious dissidents who came from the Baltic lands in the early 1920's. There were about 2,000 of them, and a disproportionate number of them were non-productive. They had little working capital and the soil of the colony was inferior. The colonists were forced to live on a communal basis until they established themselves firmly enough on their separate farms to make their way independently. For a time they followed the usual Brazilian system of changing land use according to shifting prices for their products in the São Paulo market. However, they finally arrived at a pattern of combined mixed-crop farming and poultry raising that provided them with a satisfactory operating and living basis. For many years they preserved their native language and customs and resisted whatever Brazilian influences impinged on the colony, but as the younger colonists tended to move into the city of São Paulo, they quickly lost their Latvian character and accepted the assimilative pressures of the metropolis.

The Japanese are the most controversial foreign element in Brazil. The first large group of 800 arrived at Santos in 1908. Since then something over 200,000 have entered the country legally, of whom about half came in the 10-year period 1914–23. In no other country outside the home islands are there so many people of Japanese blood. In no other has so little progress been made toward their integration into the body of the nation.

The mechanics of Japanese immigration into Brazil differ from those of other nationalities in that it has been organized and directed by large colonization societies of a semi-official nature. The costs of even third-class passage from Japanese ports are too high for the average peasant farmer, particularly as he is generally accompanied by his family. The first contingents were welcomed by the coffee interests of São Paulo, who provided immediate employment for them on their fazendas. During the civil war of 1932, in which the state of São Paulo rebelled against the federal government, the only ship given clearance to enter the port of Santos was a Japanese steamer that was carrying a large passenger list of immigrants.

As the pattern of Japanese immigration developed, it became more diversified. Some of the original laborers on the coffee plantations drifted into São Paulo, where they started small businesses of their own or entered the local labor market. Others grouped themselves in agricultural colonies like that of Bastos in western São Paulo, where they grew rice, vegetables, and fruits or produced natural silk. The best known of these ventures is the large Agricultural Co-operative of Cotia, which originally began its operations with 83 members and now does a gross annual business of over 6,000,000,000 cruzeiros in poultry products, tomatoes, sweet potatoes, and other truck-farming crops, cereals, and a variety of fruits. Meanwhile, many Japanese have pushed out into the zone of the new coffee frontier in southwestern São Paulo and the contiguous areas of Paraná. There they are more liable to be found as entrepreneurs than as farm workers. For example, the largest skyscraper in the new city of Londrina bears the title of Edifiço Tokyo, and throughout the booming town so many shops are operated by Japanese that store signs are frequently in both Japanese and Portuguese.

Another scene of Japanese enterprise is the ocean waters off the northeast coast, a province until recently reserved for the seagoing rafts of the famous *jangadeiros.* Efficient Japanese trawlers now fish for tuna and shellfish out beyond the limits of the picturesque *jangadas.* Whereas Brazilian tables have gained, just as São Paulo and Rio eat better for the produce of Cotia, one of the sentimental traditions of the old Brazil stands to lose by the changes.

It is over 30 years since the Japanese made their first large-scale efforts at colonization of the Amazon Valley. In the late 1920's a mission composed of technicians and government agents made a survey of the region to study its suitability for Japanese immigration. In 1930 the governor of the state of Amazonas granted a concession to the immigration company organized for the purpose. The concession provided for a grant of 1,000,000 hectares or nearly 2,500,000 acres of public lands on the condition that 20,000 families be introduced within a specified time. The leading promoter of the vast scheme was Dr. Tsukasa Uyetsuka, a high official of the Tokyo government, who for more than 20 years continued to be the moving spirit in Japanese designs for penetration of the Amazonia. The original scheme made little headway in its early years, and by 1936 only 200 families had settled in the region. It was in this year that opponents of the project in the Federal Senate at Rio succeeded in canceling the state concession as contrary to the national interest. Fifteen years later Dr. Uyetsuka renewed his attempts to settle a large number of Japanese in the Valley. He planned to locate 5,000 families in the area. They would, he assured the Brazilian authorities, free the country from its dependence on foreign sources of jute. While the quota was not realized, a considerable number of Japanese immigrants settled in the Amazon Valley, where they devoted themselves to the production of jute and to the cultivation of rice, pepper, and tea. The best known of the Japanese colonies was located on the island of Tome Assú in the lower Amazon, where the colonists specialize in the growing of pepper. Another colony was established on the Rio Negro near Manaus.

A later development has been the formation of a steel company, known as Usiminas, with joint Japanese and Brazilian capital on a ratio of 40–60 per cent. The company plans to establish mills near the rich iron deposits in the state of Minas Gerais, with an ultimate capacity of 2,000,000 tons of steel. The Japanese participation in the enterprise is being financed by the three largest steel-producing firms of Japan. The state of Minas is a large shareholder in the company, and the balance of Brazilian capital is contributed by a number of banks and government development agencies as well as by private investors. Of the initial foreign capital of $116,000,000, some 10 per cent is supplied by American interests.

Some Brazilian authorities continue to talk in terms of a goal of 500,000 Japanese immigrants. Because of Japanese success in developing certain lines of agriculture hitherto neglected in Brazil, such as the cultivation of truck gardens, there is strong local pressure to relax the restrictions on Japanese immigration. Persistent efforts of the Japanese government, including the visit of the Premier Kishi in 1959, have been made to obtain concessions to that end from the government of Brazil. Though not on the scale of the pre-World War II years, Japanese immigrants continue to come to Brazil. For example, one ship brought about 500 in June, 1959. One of the features of the campaign to increase immigration from Japan has been the personal efforts of Den Obinata, a famous Japanese movie star who has a large farm in the state of São Paulo, to encourage his compatriots to settle in Brazil.

In spite of the magnitude of the Japanese movement into Brazil, many Brazilians still have misgivings as to its wisdom. They point out in support of their views the tendency of the Japanese to isolate themselves from the body of the national population. The Japanese seldom marry outside their own nationality, and in São Paulo, for example, it is rare to see young Japanese in the company of Brazilians of the same age group. It is argued, therefore, that their tendency to aloofness is not in accord with the basic Brazilian philosophy of racial assimilation. They are suspected of continuing their loyalty to their homeland and of secretly depreciating the inhabitants of their adopted country. Whatever progress may have been made in integrating the Japanese into the life of Brazil, there is little doubt that these charges were formerly true. During the 1920's my visit to a large coffee fazenda in the state of São Paulo happened to coincide with the arrival from Santos of the officers and crews of a Japanese naval squadron, accompanied by the Consul-General from São Paulo and a Shinto priest. The several hundred Japanese laborers on the plantation spent the day in a round of festivities and ceremonies that was evidently designed to help perpetuate their ties with the country of their origin.

During the Second World War the Japanese colonies in the state of São Paulo gave much concern to the Brazilian authorities. Japanese were suspected of giving information to and otherwise assisting German submarines along the shipping lanes off the coast. At the end of the war against Japan, the members of a Japanese terrorist society, Shinto Remmei, refused to recognize the defeat of Japan. After they had assassinated several colonists who disagreed with them, the Brazilian government endeavored to convince these diehards of their error. However, when copies of the famous photographs of the surrender on the battleship *Missouri* were displayed in the Japanese settlements, the local extremists contended that the photographs only portrayed the allied surrender to the Japanese warlords. Other evidence failed to shake their attitude, until copies of the imperial rescript of surrender were circulated. Even then, some of the most fanatical leaders of the secret society sent a representative to Japan to ascertain the truth and report back to his associates. After the end of the war a group of the various sects delivered the following message to the security police in São Paulo: "Waking up from a dream which lasted a year, we declare that we accept and recognize the truth about the situation of our country, which was unfortunately beaten in war. We regret our past faults and we promise to make all efforts to explain the real situation to those who still have illusions."

The importance of immigration from the Middle East has been out of proportion to its numbers, which were never great until the 1950's. As the influence of the Japanese has largely been in agriculture, the impact of the Levantines has been particularly felt in retail trade. Before the breakup of the Ottoman Empire at the time of World War I, immigrants from that part of the world were generally grouped together in Brazilian statistics and parlance as "Turks," as was also done in the rest of Latin

America. They are now differentiated according to the nationality of their origins as Egyptians, Jordanians, Lebanese, Syrians, and Turks. In the three years 1955–57, 6,800 persons entered Brazil from five Middle-Eastern countries. Over half of these were Lebanese. The second largest group came from Jordan, followed by some 800 Syrians in third place. Typical of this immigration is the influx from Syria, over 21,000 of whom arrived by 1940, and 68,000 in the three-year period 1954–56.

A large proportion of the Middle Easterners in Brazil started as small shopkeepers, often in drygoods and notions, or as peddlers. By dint of shrewd trading many of them prospered and came to own and operate large merchandising businesses of their own, and some of them entered the manufacturing field. Their progress was aided by the strong family solidarity that characterized them. As they grew in wealth and culture, their standing in the general community rose, and a few of them in São Paulo attained the social goal of a residence on the Avenida Paulista and even of marriage into the local aristocracy. Among the more prominent and successful families are those of the Abdalas and the Jafets, one of whom became president of the Bank of Brazil. They were particularly active in the Amazon Valley, where one of their number, Francisco Chamie, a Syrian, became a leading trader and exporter, and for a time dominated the export business in Brazil nuts.

Most of the immigrants classified as "Israelites" are persons of Jewish background, but of various national origins. A number of Sephardic Jews from Portugal settled in northern Brazil in the early period of the colony, where they prospered as sugar merchants and financiers. A group of them ran afoul of the Inquisition and migrated to what was then New Amsterdam, where they were well received by the Dutch authorities. A small cemetery in lower Manhattan is a memorial to this early immigration from Brazil. A limited number of Jewish immigrants entered Brazil from Russia, the former Austro-Hungarian Empire, and other European countries, and directly from Palestine, during the Empire and early republic. A later contingent of refugees from Nazi persecution arrived during and after the Second World War. By the three-year period, 1955–57, average entries amounted to about 600 annually. A few of them brought considerable capital with them, which they invested in a variety of enterprises, mostly in construction, manufacturing, and mercantile lines. The absence of anti-Semitism in Brazil has eased their way and generally facilitated their adjustment to local conditions.

An interesting phase of recent Jewish immigration has been from North Africa. This movement has been sponsored and largely financed by a colonization society in the United States. By special arrangement with the Brazilian government nearly 3,000 Egyptian Jews were admitted in 1957–59 following the Suez crisis. By an earlier agreement, under which 1,000 Jewish families were to be admitted from Morocco, Algeria, and Tunis over a two-year period, a considerable number of other Jews were settled in Brazil.

Most of the Americans who live in Brazil are businessmen and missionaries and their families. According to the eight American consular offices, a total of about 12,000 resided in the country in 1959. This figure included about 260 employees of the United States government. The largest number of Americans, 4,572, lived in the district of the Consulate-General of Rio, and another 4,537 were in that of the São Paulo consular office. The others were scattered among the other consular jurisdictions as follows: Belém, 730, Salvador, 610, Recife, 390, Belo Horizonte, 349, Curitiba, 179, Santos, 166, Porto Alegre, 182. In 1959 it was estimated that about 9,000 Americans visited Rio each year as tourists. Other Americans living in Brazil include teachers and doctors and engineers, technicians and scientists, who are either employed by American firms or by agencies of the Brazilian government, such as Petrobras.

In 1957, a typical postwar year, 1,361 Americans entered Brazil with "immigrant" visas. Of these, nearly 800 were wives and children. Of the men, 187 were classified as "technicians," 77 as engaged in foreign trade, 69 as factory "operatives," five as farmers or stockmen, and 230 as belonging to other occupations or professions. Only six Americans became naturalized Brazilian citizens in that year.

Many Americans have resided in Brazil for long periods, during which they have identified themselves with the life of the country. Lieutenant Lardner Gibbon of the United States Navy, who explored the Amazon Valley in the early 1850's, encountered one at Barra or Manaus. He was a New Englander named Marcus Williams, and in partnership with Enrico Antonil, an Italian, he traded up and down the Amazonian rivers. Gibbon wrote:

> He told me that although the trade on the river was attended with hardships, exposure and privation, there was a certain charm attending the wild life, and its freedom from restraint, that would always prevent any desire on his part to return to his native country. I heard that he carried this feeling so far as to complain bitterly, when he visited Norris, the consul at Pará, of the restraints of society that compelled him to wear trousers at dinner.

Soon after the Civil War two groups of "unreconstructed" southerners—about 3,000 persons in all—migrated to Brazil. One contingent of them settled in the region of Santarém at the junction of the Tapajóz and Amazon Rivers. Though the site is one of the best in the Amazon Valley, the tropical colony did not prosper, and the bulk of the settlers returned to the United States. Of those who went to southern Brazil, the largest number became farmers in the locality that became known as Villa Americana, now a station on the Paulista Railway. Some settled at Iguapé on the coast near Santos and still others around Lake Juparana in Espirito Santo. Eventually many members of the southern group moved into São Paulo and Rio de Janeiro, where some of them gained fame as doctors and dentists. Among the former were Dr. Job Lane, who founded the Samaritano Hospital in São Paulo, and Dr. Franklin Pyle, who was associated for many years with the Strangers' Hospital in Rio. For a long time the most popular dentists in Brazil were named Coachman, Hentz, Keyes, Shaw, and Yancey.

Among the hundreds of other Americans who have contributed to the improvement of health conditions and education, to economic development, and to other phases of the national life of Brazil are: the doctors of the Rockefeller Foundation; the geologists, Orville Derby and John Casper Branner, later president of Stanford University; Benjamin Hunnicutt, president of Mackenzie College in São Paulo; Asa K. W. Billings, the engineer; Herbert Moses, the newspaperman; Percival Farquhar, builder of railroads and port works, sawmills, and cattle ranches and leading spirit in the foundation of the Brazilian steel industry; Hugh C. Tucker, representative of the American Bible Society, who died in 1956 at 99, after 70 years in Brazil; and Edwin V. Morgan, American Ambassador to Brazil for 21 years.

Like the French, the English early sailed to the coast of Brazil. Sometimes their ships, bound for the River Plate or the South Sea on long marauding voyages, put into Brazilian ports for water and "victuals," as Thomas Cavendish did on his way around the world in 1591. Thwarted in his quest by the people of Santos, he burned the near-by town of São Vicente "to the ground." The famous William Hawkins had made three trading voyages to Brazil 60 years before, which was "a thing in those dayes very rare." Hawkins was careful not to antagonize either the Portuguese or the aborigines, with whom "he behaved himself so wisely . . . that he grew into great familiarity and friendship with them." When he took one of the local chiefs to England with him, he left behind as hostage Martin Cockeram, also of his home port of Plymouth. Though the Indian, after being presented to Henry the Eighth and his court, died as a result of "the change of aire and alteration of diet," Cockeram was permitted to return unharmed to England, where he lived long as an authority on Tupí culture.

A few years later, several "substantial and wealthie merchants of Southampton," including Robert Reniger and Thomas Borey, were in the habit of making "this commodious and gainefull voyage to Brasil." They were followed shortly afterward by "one Pudsey," another Southampton merchant and "a man of good skill and resolution in marine matters," who traded in Bahia in 1542.

Hakluyt gives in some detail the story of John Whithal, who settled in Santos in the 1570's and in his own words found there "honour and plentifulnesse of all things" as a "free denizen" of Brazil. Whithal married a daughter of the Genoese, Giuseppe della Doria, who was one of the leading citizens of the locality, and received as dowry part of his father-in-law's sugar mill. He urged some of his friends to undertake trading voyages to Brazil, on which he assured them a goodly profit of 300 per cent. He sent the new company of "Adventurers for Brazil" an initial order for a large assortment of hardware, textiles, and clothing and a variety of other miscellaneous items such as soap, writing paper, spices, and guitar strings. When their ship, the *Minion of London,* arrived at Santos with the cargo as ordered, plus a bedstead for Whithal and his wife as a gift from the merchants, the Englishmen were "well received and intertained of the Captaine [of the port], the Kings officers, and all the people."

The welcome which the Portuguese at Santos gave to the London merchants was representative of the good relations which generally prevailed between the two nations during that age. Even the depredations of Captain James Lancaster, who sacked Pernambuco in 1594 with the collaboration of Dutch and French ships in the harbor, did not entirely destroy the confidence of the Portuguese in the good faith of the English. At that time Portugal and her colonies were a part of the Spanish empire, and the enemies of Spain were not likely to discriminate between the two.

The Methuen Treaty of 1703 cemented the commercial relations between England and Portugal and only confirmed the growing political and economic dependence of the smaller nation on English sea power and wealth. As a result, Englishmen continued to enjoy a privileged position in the foreign trade of Brazil until the end of the colony and during the Empire.

The British who came to Brazil after the beginning of the republic generally did so in connection with the formation and management of their business enterprises in the country. These included railroads like the Leopoldina, the Great Western of Pernambuco, and the famous line between Santos and São Paulo-Jundiaí, known to the British as the "San Paulo Railway." They also included the St. John del Rey gold mines, a complex of banks, steamship agencies, utilities, and trading companies, and a variety of manufacturing industries. Among the latter were flour mills, cigarette factories, and the cotton textile mills that were founded by Manchester spinners.

CHAPTER 8

The Animals

BRAZIL LACKS THE SPECTACULAR FAUNA OF AFRICA. IT HAS no elephants or lions, no gorillas or hippopotami. Its leading rhinoceros, Cacareco, an immigrant in the São Paulo zoo, was elected to the city council in 1959 in a display of typical Brazilian irony. There are no large herds or packs of anything. But if Brazil has no aardvarks or impalas, no wart hogs or wildebeest, it has plenty of anacondas and armadillos and howler monkeys and marmosets. It has the biggest bugs on earth, and probably the most.

As might be expected, the heaviest concentration of animals in Brazil is in the rain forest of the Amazon Valley. The Valley is not a fit haunt for hunters, except for those primitive men who are familiar with its antediluvian ways. For any others it is too confusing and uncomfortable by day and too frightening by night. It is only a "paradise" for naturalists. Since the Amazonia is one vast animal preserve, there is nothing in it comparable to the Krueger National Park in Africa. Nor are there any "game laws" to protect men and animals from each other. While the zoo at Belém is the city's principal tourist attraction, neither it nor the zoological gardens at Rio are worthy displays of the nation's animal life.

The Brazilian has a peculiar affinity for animals. This is especially true of the Indian, who sometimes must feel more akin to the animals about him than to the civilized white man. His simple mythology is built around animals or monstrous forms of them. In his cosmogony he does not differentiate between himself and the beasts of his acquaintance. In his imagination he may be descended from an animal and on his death he may become a jaguar or a deer. Unlike the *caboclo* or *mameluco* in whose body his blood is mingled with that of the white man, he does not kill for the pleasure of killing but only for food, or rarely to protect himself, for it is very rare that he is attacked. His hut is often a veritable menagerie. Among the pets there may be a toucan or a couple of parrots, a monkey, a peccary, a playful coati, and a big curassow bird that he has brought down from the treetops and tamed to serve as a ratter. There might even be a boa constrictor in the thatch of the roof. The animals wander in and out of the house at will and sleep on the dirt floor at night. Sometimes an animal will follow him on his comings and goings in the forest, and the Indian may let one of them sleep in his hammock with him to keep him warm at night. The parrots may sit on his shoulder and talk to him or the toucan may search for bugs in his hair. Sometimes his woman may nurse a young animal at her breast. If he keeps a few chickens he will not kill the roosters, because he likes to hear them crow in the early morning. A feature of an Indian fiesta is the mimicry of familiar animals in their dances and processions.

People in the towns and cities are also addicted to pets. There is generally a parrot or a songbird in the house, and there may be a marmoset or monkey or other small animal about the home. I remember a telegraph operator who had a pet troupial, an amusing bird that would sit on his shoulder and chatter to him as he worked his key. It would forage about the town, where it was a familiar figure, but would always return in the evening to roost in the telegrapher's office. I also knew a man at Porto Velho on the Madeira whose pet puma accompanied him about the town, where the big cat was accepted as an important denizen if not exactly as a citizen. Lieutenant Lardner Gibbon, who descended the Amazon from Peru in the early 1850's, wrote that "Many gentlemen had tigers [jaguars] about their establishments." He said that "They were docile and playful in their intercourse with acquaintances, but they were generally kept chained for fear of injury to strangers."

Foreigners easily become as zoophilous as the native Brazilians. When our Brazilian-American survey party came down the Amazon after several months on the upper rivers, our collection consisted of the following: four ocelots, including a black one, one capybara or water hog, one coati, 11 monkeys of five different species, four araras or macaws, nine parrots and parakeets, 10 other miscellaneous birds including songsters and game birds like the *mutúm* and *jacamín,* and a wild dog. I had thrown our boa constrictor overboard after I had stepped on it in the shower. It had had the run of the steamer and was as friendly as any of our animals. One of the ocelots and the coati slept together on the foot of my bunk. The wild dog was a very rare creature. It had a pointed head, small ears, and coarse reddish hair. It had webbed feet and was half amphibious, and delighted to stand on its head in a bucket of water. It did not bark but squealed like a pig. In other respects it was like a dog. I later gave it to the Washington Zoo where, as the only one of its kind in captivity, it became a major attraction.

Because of their earlier attachment to other pets, Brazilians do not have the dog complex of Americans. A dog is only a dog, and the mongrels of ancient and uncertain lineage that one sees about the Indian huts in the Amazon country are kept for hunting. The kennel clubs in the big cities of the south are generally the work of foreigners. Poodles have appeared as a mark of sophistication and status, and have even penetrated into Belém along with the Cadillacs.

Though the animal life of the Amazonia is rich and varied, the casual traveler in the forest may see little of it. He is, nevertheless, always aware of its presence and propinquity, either because he expects to find wild animals living in such an environment or because he hears the sounds they make about him. The jungle animals are timid and avoid man. The only danger *on the ground* is from poisonous serpents. Many animals hide during the day and only appear at night. One of the characteristic features of the Amazonian fauna is the unusual number of species that live in the treetops. This separate arboreal world teems not only with birds but with mammals that seldom or never descend to the ground. These include monkeys and sloths and a multitude of other geophobic creatures. For their water supply there are ponds in the sky—small pools in the depressions in the tops of palm trees or in the calyxes of large flowering plants. Frogs, insects, and even small shellfish may spend their lives in these aerial puddles. No animal anywhere is probably so well adapted to this style of living as the spider monkey, the world's first flying trapeze artist. Equipped with four hands that are ideally suited for grasping and a long and powerful prehensile tail, this natural acrobat leaps across incredible spaces with the greatest of ease. The Indian who wishes to capture a tree-dwelling animal shoots it from its perch with a poisoned dart from a blowgun and then injects a neutralizing salt into its wound while it is still stunned from the effects of the poison.

Except for an occasional glimpse of some creature of extraordinary beauty or ugliness, the sounds of the tropical forest are much more impressive than its sights. The ensemble varies greatly from one time of day to another and between different parts of the country. Sometimes, in the suffocating heat of mid-afternoon the buzzing of insects may be the only noise to break the heavy silence. But the din of dawn or dusk may be a veritable cosmic cacophony. Henry Bates, the English naturalist, who lived along the Amazon for 11 years, wrote repeatedly of what he called "the sounds of multifarious life," "the audible expression of the teeming profusion of Nature," "the almost deafening din," and "this uproar of life that almost never wholly ceased." Only one initiated into its mysteries by a lifetime within the dark precincts of the forest could identify the sources of all the notes in the diapason of discord. The general tone may be set by the unearthly roar of the *guaribas* or howling monkeys. But there are bellowing birds, too, like the umbrella bird that roars like a bull. And according to Konrad Guenther, the German naturalist, there are Brazilian frogs that "roar, hammer, grunt, trill, rattle, and whistle" as well as croak. There are birds and beetles that hiss, and other birds that moan and screech, that laugh crazily, or that utter an eerie and melancholy cry sufficient to chill even the most unimpressionable person. To add to the sonic confusion, there are birds that mimic so skillfully the sounds of ground animals that their mockeries have the effect of ventriloquism.

When a tropical tempest is added to the normal terrors of a novice's night in the gloom of the jungle, the experience is unforgettable. The customary tempo of the nocturnal din rises suddenly as the wind sweeps through the forest felling trees and crashing branches to the ground. With the wind comes a deluge of drenching rain that drowns out all but the loudest cries of the panic-stricken animals. The lightning flashes are sometimes almost continuous, and in the sharp blazes of light one may see animals seeking a cover that does not exist. I remember one such night on the banks of a river in the remote Acre country. Out of deference to his age we had given our only tent to the oldest member of our party. The rest of us lay in our hammocks under the usual improvised lean-tos of palm fronds when the storm broke in all its fury. Though we were soaked to the skin, the tent stakes held until, in a sudden burst of lightning, we saw a big tapir dash through our camp in the direction of the river. He hit the tent amidship and carried it with him into the river, from where we never recovered it.

The most formidable of Brazilian animals is the jaguar or *onça,* the big spotted cat that is found as far north as Mexico and occasionally crosses the border into our southwestern states. The more sinister-looking black variety is probably not a separate species but only a genetic variation of the more common *onça pintada*. The jaguar does not attack man without provocation, but when provoked, its great bulk and strength make it a terrible adversary. Out of curiosity, it sometimes hovers about the edges of a camp on the banks of a river, though it usually keeps a safe distance. It is much more common in the region of the upper Paraguay in Mato Grosso than it is in the Amazonia. A Latvian hunter named Sacha Siemel, author of *Tigrero,* has gained fame by killing over 300 beef-eating *tigres* or jaguars among the cattle ranches of the swampy Xarayes country, where the Paraguay spreads out over the lowlands between Corumbá and Cuiabá.

The haunting-eyed puma, which is known to the Indians as *sussuarana,* is rarer than the larger jaguar. Though hunted nearly everywhere in the western hemisphere as a carnivorous "predator," it probably feels a strong compulsion to associate with man. In early Spanish America it was known as the *amigo del cristiano,* and Konrad Guenther says of it that it is "easily tamed, and of all the carnivora it is one of the fittest to become the graceful domestic companion of the animal-lover."

The biggest land animal in Brazil is the pachydermous tapir or *anta,* which may weigh over 400 pounds. It has the general hang of a hog, but with certain evolutionary modifications in the past 10,000,000 years it might have wound up as an elephant. However, it is now too late to do anything about this, and zoologists consider it more akin to the rhinoceros anyway.

On the other hand, the anteater is a good example of the results of long planning for functional specialization. He is a myrmecophagous beast, and so far as has been ascertained, he has never had any other ideas in life than to eat ants—and termites. The *tamanduá bandeira,* largest of the three Brazilian species, is a sizable animal with a body up to six or seven feet long and an enormous panache-like tail that serves as a blanket on cold nights.

The principal tools of his trade are a long tongue and powerful claws. With his claws he can tear open the concrete-like termite nests or, sitting back on his haunches, rip to shreds any jaguar—or man—who comes within reach of his iron grasp. The smallest of the three varieties of anteater is only about 10 inches long and lives in the trees.

A catalogue of secondary Brazilian mammalia would be very extensive. Certain species might be confined to a limited area in the Amazon Valley; others could be found almost anywhere in the country. The list would include, among others, about 10 varieties of monkey plus an assortment of tiny marmosets, five species of armadillo, six of deer, five of the smaller cats, two of sloth, and as many of the wild boar, in addition to many odds and ends like cutías and coatis, capybaras and kinkajous.

The simians of Brazil range in size from the pygmy marmoset, *Midas Leoninus,* of the Solimões, which is only six or seven inches long, to the burly barrigudo monkey or *macaco-assú,* and the howler or *guariba.* There is nothing comparable to the anthropoid apes of the Old World. In disposition or temperament Brazilian monkeys vary from the gentle and quiet barrigudo to the nervous and disorderly *macaco de prego* or "nail monkey" and surly and intractable howler, which even the Indian cannot tame.

Besides a long-established position as an affectionate or amusing pet, the monkey's flesh is an important—and tasty—item of diet in parts of the Amazonia. However, the practice has psychological limitations, for a deep-seated feeling of man-and-monkey empathy may raise qualms of anthropophagy in both primitive Indian and civilized city dweller. Another aspect of monkeydom in the Amazon country is the destructive habits of certain breeds which raid the fruit plantings of the natives along the rivers.

Anyone who enters the forest is sure to encounter before long the typical signs of monkey business above him—the wild gymnastics in the treetops, the pandemonium of chatter, calls, and shrill cries, and perhaps even twigs or other objects tossed at him.

In the gloom of dusk the howlers suddenly take over the carnival of noise and contribute a deafening note to the discordant cadence of the jungle. Their deep roar from the topmost trees drowns out all other sounds for miles around until the infernal racket ends, as abruptly as it began, with a sharp bark from the cheerleader of the pack. "The rest is silence," at least for a time, and all other noises of the night are minor chord by comparison. Fortunately for the nerves of the novice, it is only a sunset serenade to whatever spirits bedevil the forest night. However, once in the middle of the night on the Xingú I heard three groups of *guaribas* bellowing at one another from as many different directions. No sound from the living world of nature is quite so blood-curdling, and for his satanic overtones science has appropriately named the howler *Mycetes Beelzebub.*

The most interesting—and unprepossessing—of smaller Brazilian animals is the sloth, otherwise known as the *preguiça* or "laziness" and in the *lingua geral* of the Indians as *Ay*. This outlandish creature, with its expressionless face and unsocial temper, is an antediluvian relic. It has a bleating sheeplike cry and its flesh tastes like mutton. It lives in the trees, about which it climbs with slow and deliberate but unerring movements and feeds on the tender leaves of the cecropias. Its hind legs are extraordinarily powerful.

A roundup of the same general category of fauna might yield, among others, such discrepant creatures as the armadillo, armored digger of the open country, the largest of whose family, the *tatú-assú,* may be five feet long and weigh 100 pounds; the riverine capybara, biggest of the world's rodents, that looks like an overgrown muskrat and has the habits of a hippo, even frolicking in the water with Indian children; a pygmy deer of the *campinas* lands, like something out of a fairy tale; and the reddish spotted paca, favorite game of the forest hunter.

Most of the natural dangers to man in Brazil do not come from the ground or the air but from the water—the wild life of the rivers. There is danger from fish like the piranha, barbed rays on the bottom of streams, electric eels, alligators, and, to a lesser degree, from the anaconda. Some of the perils are very real, like the bite of the ravenous piranha; others may be illusory or magnified by the imagination. The alligator or *caimán* is a case in point. The *jacaré-assú,* largest of Brazilian saurians, is a monstrous beast that may grow to a length of 20 feet. Its bulk, its ugliness, its formidable teeth-lined jaws, its evil eye and baleful stare give it a diabolical reputation that is hardly borne out by the facts. It can be very lethal, it has a mean disposition and large appetite, and its reactions are unpredictable. The very suspicion of its presence scares people out of the water. The native who wishes to take a swim in the river may first go down to the shore and call the *caimáns.* He makes a loud grunting noise that is evidently audible and intelligible to any alligator lying beneath the surface, who thereupon rises to locate the source of the call. But the *jacaré* is stupid and cowardly, and it is responsible for relatively few casualties among the riparian population of the Amazonia.

On the other hand, it is the object of a relentless campaign of extermination. It has no friends, not even the Indian, and nobody is interested in a crusade for "conservation of wild life." Only the high cost of cartridges prolongs the term of its ultimate extinction. Hundreds and even thousands of them sometimes lie on the mud-flats of the lakes that connect with the Amazon, where wholesale *razzias* are conducted against them with ax and gun.

To illustrate his thesis of the "cruelty of nature," Paul Lecointe once told me of a three-way encounter of animals which he witnessed on the shores of the Trombetas. He had come out of the woods to the edge of a low bluff that fell down to the *varzea* flats along the river. Directly below him was a huge jaguar, intently watching the water, as the *caimán* crawled out onto the beach. The jaguar suddenly sprang on the reptile, flipped him over with a paw, and proceeded to feast on the soft under side of its neck. He then turned his victim over again, whereupon the alligator returned to the water. The blood from his wound quickly attracted a school of piranhas, which clung to the open gap in his body as he painfully tried to drag himself back onto the land.

By no means is all the water life malign. The rivers are rich in fish, over 500 varieties of them. They range from the curious fishlets that one finds in collectors' aquariums to the huge pirarucú that is six feet long and the even larger paraiba, biggest of all fresh-water fish. They are important to the Amazonian diet though, except for the salting of the pirarucú, there is virtually no commercial fishing industry in the Amazon Valley, as there is along the Brazilian coast. Fishing is a catch-as-catch-can business, and there is a dearth of refrigeration facilities and efficient gear.

Of other large water animals, the most prominent are the big mammalian manatee or sea-cow and three varieties of river porpoises or *botos*. Of the latter Bates said: "On the Amazon they are always heard rolling, blowing, and snorting, especially at night, and these noises contribute much to the impression of sea-wide vastness and desolation which haunts the traveller." One of the familiar local legends about the *boto* is that it has the habit of emerging from the waters disguised as a young man to account for the pregnancy of the riparian maidens. There are millions of big turtles, and their flesh and eggs have long constituted a staple food for the river people. On the wide sandy *praias* of the Rio Branco large numbers of turtles are kept in pens, from which they are shipped to the markets of Manaus. Of the bactracians, Konrad Guenther called Brazil "the land of frogs" and remarked that "almost half the species of the order live here." Helmut Sick, his compatriot, described the giant frog, whose body is seven inches long and whose hind legs are another nine inches, as "one of the most remarkable creatures in the world."

There is a worldwide folklore about Brazil's giant serpents, the anaconda and boa constrictor. Particularly has the length of the former or *sucurijú* become the subject of tall tales at home and abroad. Specimens over 20 feet long are occasionally reported, and probably the largest *skin* vouched for by Brazilian scientists had a length of 45 feet. A fantastic yarn of a *sucurijú* killed in an epic battle near Tabatinga on the Solimões and measuring over 130 feet is typical of the exaggerations for which the animal is responsible. The repute of the relatively inoffensive and lethargic boa is built around the myth that it is given to squeezing men—or man-and-horse—to death in its fire-hose coils.

While the stranger instinctively associates poisonous snakes with the tropical forest, the chances of encountering one in the jungle are really small. During almost a year in which I traveled nearly 25,000 miles in the Amazonia I saw exactly two, and those at the same time, or fewer than I have seen in a Virginia county in an equal period of time. One rarely finds a snake in the upland forest, and of 20 or 25 that he encounters in the Amazon Valley, probably not more than one would be venomous. Most accidents from snakes are likely to occur in the *cerrado* or badlands of Mato Grosso or in the *caatinga* country of northeastern Brazil where snakes are found in larger numbers than in the Amazonia. They are especially liable to attack the *caboclo* who is working with his machete in tall grass or light undergrowth. Most feared of the poisonous varieties are the black jararaca, the rattler or *cascavel,* and the ugly and aggressive bushmaster, which is the largest and most dangerous venomous serpent in Brazil.

To deal with the medical problems raised by the frequency of snakebites in the interior of the country, the famous Butantán Institute was founded many years ago in the outskirts of São Paulo. It has been the world's outstanding center of research in the field, and from the thousands of poisonous snakes that are sent to it each year, it prepares the series of anti-ophidian serums that are now indispensable equipment for anyone who ventures into the snake-infested areas of Brazil.

To the casual visitor to Brazil who is not a seasoned "bird watcher" the most obvious bird is the *urubú* or buzzard. When not gliding about in the sky or engaged in devouring a piece of carrion, this lugubrious specter is liable to be seen sitting on the housetops or otherwise prominently displayed in the cities and towns of the more backward parts of the country. There he gives the impression of one waiting for the very city to die. As an unpaid member of the local bureaucracy, this employee of the municipal sanitary department has a special status in the community, a position which he also holds in certain other parts of Latin America. However, he has long since outlived his time, and his public presence would not be tolerated in such progressive centers as São Paulo, Porto Alegre, or Belo Horizonte, and he cannot expect to be admitted to Brasilia. As a scavenger, he saves "the taxpayer's money," but he is "bad public relations" for a nation that is increasingly sensitive to world opinion.

The first bird to be identified with Brazil was the parrot. As José Carioca, the friend of Donald Duck, he has since had an important role in Brazilian-American relations. The *papagaio* was an important item of export in the sixteenth century. He accepted foreign residence and changes of language with grace and good temper. He gave a light touch to the grim realities of an age that took itself too seriously, and he must have helped many a bored noblewoman in the chateaux of the Loire to pass the time in Touraine. He comes of a large and vocal family of parrots, parakeets, and macaws, whose colorful members are both ornamental and entertaining, so that his place in the future of Brazil is well and deservingly assured.

A Brazilian in a sentimental or nostalgic mood is still likely to associate his country with the *sabiá* that, appropriately, sings at dusk and even in the rain. Popular sentiment about this bird was crystallized by the poet, Gonçalves Dias, in his "Song of Exile," which was written in Portugal in 1843. The poem begins with the lines:

> My country has palm-trees (*Minha terra tem palmeiras*)
> Where the *sabiá* sings. (*Onde canta a sabiá.*)

And the second line is the refrain that ends each verse. Henry Bates, who arrived in Belém two years after the poem was first published in Brazil, was charmed by "the sweet and plaintive" song of the *sabiá.* "In the course of time," he wrote, "the song of this humble thrush stirred up pleasing associations in my mind. . . . The Brazilians are not insensible to the charms of this, their best songster, for I have often heard some pretty verses in praise of the Sabiá sung by young people to the accompaniment of the guitar."

The Indians named the birds of Brazil, as they named the rest of its wildlife. So the *jacurutú* is an owl, and the *jurutý* is a sort of turtledove, and the *arapacú* hunts bugs in the bark of the trees. Sometimes, the *caboclo* or the Portuguese renamed the birds, so that the nomenclature of ornithology is very confusing and unscientific. Thus the pretty yellow bird with the orange head that one often sees in cages is a *canario,* and the *picapau* is really a woodpecker. But the *rouxinol* is not a nightingale nor is the *cardeal* our crested cardinal. Sometimes the name is expressive of the bird's habits, as is that of the hummingbird, which is a *beijaflor* or "flower-kisser," or that of the friendly *joão de barro* or "John the potter," who builds his nest of mud in the trees near the habitations of the natives. Many birds have onomatopoetic names that are reminiscent of their call, like the *hudú* and the *urú,* the *teu-teu* and the *cri-cri-ó.* One bird is called a *mariá-ja-é-dia* or "Mary, it's already day." One of the most popular birds is the *bem-te-vi,* which means "I got a good look at you." These very properly belong to the family of the Tyrannidae and literally "rule the roost" wherever they are. Like the jay, they are noisy and aggressive, and more timid birds generally keep out of their way.

The Indians and other dwellers in the Amazonia are very sensitive to the bird sounds in their dark and lonely world, and the Indian considers some of them as of ill omen. One of the most depressing is the deep croak of the grand *potoo* or *mae da lua* ("mother of the moon"), which utters its chilling cry from the treetops at nightfall, and "the long-drawn melancholy and almost human call" of its smaller and more common species. There is also a large hawklike bird of prey whose call resembles a wild burst of laughter.

The largest bird in Brazil and, except for the emu or *nhandú* of the River Plate lands, in all South America is the *jaburú-moleque* or *tuyuyú*. It is a stork and belongs to the same general family of wading birds as the African marabou and its cousin, the adjutant bird of India. Theodore Roosevelt shot one in Mato Grosso which he said was "as tall as a man." Probably the most repugnant of Brazilian birds is the archaic *cigana* or *hoatzin,* which lives on the low-hanging branches of trees along the rivers. An evolutionary freak, it has only incipient wings and cannot fly, hopping awkwardly from branch to branch. Its cry and its odor are as disagreeable as the rest of its forbidding ensemble.

Brazil is rich in game birds, some of which are domesticated by its inhabitants. Besides varieties of pigeons and pheasants, there are several larger varieties in the Amazon country such as the *mutúm,* the *inhambú,* and the *jacú,* some of which might advantageously be imported into other countries.

Most noteworthy of Brazilian animals are the insects. Naturalist Henry Bates identified 7,000 species of them in the vicinity of Ega alone. They live in the air and in the bark and foliage of the trees, on the ground and beneath its surface, and in the water. They live in houses and the very stuff of their walls. They live in the hair and on the bodies of the larger animals. Some, like the *bicho de pé,* may burrow into the human body. They breed all the year, and there is no harsh winter to slow down the astronomical process of their multiplication. Nearly all of them are enemies of man—of his comfort, his health, or his economics. Their extinction or control is a major problem in the future development of Brazil. They should prove to be even more of a boon to the insecticide industry than they have been to the entomologists. As for the locale of their operations, the tropical forest is the seat of their empire, though many prefer to live in the open country. In the cities of the south they are under control and no more a plague than in Europe or the United States.

In the *lingua geral* of the Tupís a *carapaná* is a mosquito. On one of the upper rivers of the Amazon system there is a village named Carapanátuba or "many mosquitoes." A Brazilian once proposed that the Amazonia be renamed as Carapanálandia. Although there are stretches of the rivers and areas of the high forest that are relatively free from mosquitoes, the traveler is seldom far from them. Probably the most widespread and pestiferous is the ordinary culex variety, which the Brazilians share with the United States and many other countries. The anopheles and other disease-carrying species are also common and associated with particular health problems.

Since mass extermination of the mosquitoes is obviously impracticable by any means short of atomic weapons, any protective measures are necessarily very localized or exclusively personal in their scope. Even the Indian suffers much from their bites. He may try to sleep at night in the choking fumes of a fire on the floor of his hut, or he may anoint his naked body with ill-smelling unguents of his own concoction. If he wears clothes, it is for protection against mosquitoes rather than for modesty's sake. People in the towns generally sleep under mosquito nets that are hung over their hammocks by means of a clever contrivance of local origin. The principal source of rotenone, a basic ingredient of DDT, is in the Amazon Valley, and people are becoming increasingly accustomed to the use of insect repellents.

In addition to mosquitoes, an assortment of other insects torment the inhabitants of the Amazonia. Among the more nefarious of them are the *piúm,* a tiny fly that is a terrible scourge on the upper rivers, the *motuca,* a bloodthirsty gadfly larger than the mosquito, and the miniscule *mocuím,* a reddish tick whose bite causes a disagreeable itching.

According to Adolph Ducke, the Swiss scientist who lived at Belém for many years, "the basin of the Amazon is richer in wasps than any other region on earth." People walking in the jungle are liable to make a detour when they sight the hanging nest of a colony of these belligerent monsters, some of which are almost two inches long. These big *maribondos* attack the face with a dive-bombing motion, as I once learned when one stung me between the eyes. My eyes were swollen shut immediately and it was nearly an hour before I could open them.

Sometimes to a traveler in northern Brazil the country seems like one vast formicary, so ubiquitous and pestilential are the ants. The very land is theirs, and man can never coexist with them except in a perpetual "cold war" in which the advantages are on the side of the ants. Their organization and methods are more efficient than those of men. The anteaters and the birds cannot even "make a dent" in the infinitude of their numbers.

Some are large, like the savage *tucandeira,* biggest of all ants. They are over an inch long and are equipped with strong pincers. Their bite is extremely painful and may cause a fever for several hours. Among certain Indian tribes part of the ceremony of initiating a young man into the class of warriors is to force him to hold his arm in a hollow section of bamboo that is full of these terrible ants.

Some ants are very small, like the lesser variety of fire ants or *formigas de fogo* which are scarcely visible. They live in the vegetation of the *varzea* along the rivers, and anyone who brushes against the undergrowth or the branch of a tree is liable to be attacked by what feels to him like a myriad of tiny burning coals. I once leaned inadvertently against a cecropia tree, and in an instant my body seemed covered with a fiery plague of ants, from which my only relief was to jump into the river as I was.

Some ants are only annoying and uncomfortable. Others are highly destructive. The outstanding example of the latter is the *sauba* or leaf-cutter. It is a common saying that either Brazil must destroy the *saubas* or the *saubas* will destroy Brazil. Its habitat is by no means limited to the Amazon Valley, but it operates far and wide over the country. Its depredations are a major threat to agriculture, and some areas have been abandoned because it had made farming impossible. I once saw a countryman on the banks of the distant Abuná who had laboriously constructed a "hanging garden" where he could cultivate some vegetables beyond the reach of the *saubas*. He had built a large "bed" about 12 feet long and filled it with earth in which he planted his crops. His aerial farm was suspended on piles about eight feet high that were set in large cans filled with water. He tilled and harvested his vegetables with the aid of a ladder, which he took down when it was not in use, so that the ants could not use it. Incidentally, I have seen a stream of *saubas* descending a *castanha* or Brazil-nut tree that was at least 150 feet high with their endless load of leaf particles. On the floor of the forest one may find their well-marked roads over which the workers carry the raw material of their food supply into their veritable underground cities. These subterranean labyrinths may reach down into the earth from 15 to 25 feet and may occupy an area of ground 60 feet or more in extent. Within the elaborate chain of passages there may be hundreds of small compartments in which the leaf particles are stored and processed as a fungous food for the colony.

A special variety of the leaf-cutters is known as the *carregadeira*. It lives at a lower level than the *sauba,* which avoids the floodlands, but its habits are equally destructive and even more omnivorous. Once when I was sleeping in my hammock, which was tied to two trees, the hammock suddenly crashed to the ground as the *carregadeiras* had eaten through the ropes at both ends.

Equally devastating are the termites or "white ants," known to the natives as *cupim*. These voracious wood-eating insects are one of the curses of the light forest country in particular, and houses that have been undermined by them sometimes collapse in a heap of ruins.

On the other hand, the termites' own "house" is a large stony lump on the landscape that is impregnable except to a pickax or the powerful claws of the *tamanduá bandeira*. In this elaborately tunneled structure the termites live their extraordinarily busy and well-ordered lives, often in company with other "guest" creatures whose company they accept. Inside the walled city the reigning queen may reproduce her kind at the rate of over 10,000,000 a year. Sometimes at night one may observe lights on the termitaries that are made by the phosphorescent larva of certain beetles which reside there.

Most earth-shaking of the nearly 500 varieties of ants in Brazil is the formidable Eciton or "forager," known to the natives as *taoca*. There are several varieties known to science by such significant names as *rapax, legionis,* and *praedator*. The warriors of this ferocious order are equipped with steel-like prongs or tweezers that are larger than their heads. For some reason known only to themselves, a community of millions of these terrifying creatures begins a concerted move in a wide area of forest. They move as a relentless army in serried ranks while the entire animal life of the jungle becomes aware of their approach. They destroy every living thing in their path—other insects, reptiles, and small animals—and at the sign of their coming, frightened natives even remove their young children to safety as an added precaution. Writing of the natives' fear of the drepanophera, a species of ant, Bates writes: "There is no course left but to run for it," and he adds: "Wherever they move, the whole animal world is set in commotion, and every creature tries to get out of their way."

Brazil is as rich in butterflies as it is in noxious or disagreeable insects. "Flying flowers," Konrad Guenther called them. Bates found over 700 species of them within an hour's walk of Belém, and at Ega or Teffé on the Solimões, where he lived for several years, he collected 550 varieties. Most striking of them all is the famous Morpho of the metallic blue wings. Sometimes it has a wingspread of eight inches. Large numbers of them are caught for the decoration of trays and other objects sold to tourists in Rio and São Paulo. In their native haunts in the tropical forest there is no more beautiful sight than one of them flying lazily in a sunlit glade.

There are also fireflies of an uncanny brightness. Sometimes the countrywomen decorate their hair with them at night. There are Titanus bettles six inches long, such as Paul A. Zahl describes in the May, 1959, number of the *National Geographic Magazine*. And there is a phosphorescent beetle whose eyes project a red light while it has a green light in its tail.

CHAPTER 9

The Gods

THERE IS A SAYING IN BRAZIL THAT "GOD IS A BRAZILIAN." But, as in pre-Diocletianist Rome, deity has assumed many forms in Brazil, and new faces and images continue to appear in the overcrowded national pantheon. The religious unity that prevailed for so long has disappeared in a confusion of faiths and sectarian interpretations of Christian doctrine. In the eager competition for his soul the Brazilian is only bewildered as he seeks to recover something of the comforting assurance of a less complicated age. Floating on the current of a real River of Doubt, he is too willing to grasp any passing log that might seem to offer him the sense of spiritual safety which he craves.

The Brazilian is by nature tolerant in matters of religion. He lacks the Castilian's or the Arab's capacity for fanaticism, and the messianic mysticism of the *sertão* is a purely local phenomenon. The gentle gospel of St. John is more congenial to his nature than is the more intellectual and exigent dogma of St. Paul. He has no relish for theological controversy nor is he given to philosophic meditation. There is too much of the pagan in him to accept the ascetic denials of Puritanism as a condition of salvation. He does not consider the body as the seat of original sin, and to him austerity and denial can only have their roots in economics and not in religion. His concepts of the godhead have mental associations of beauty and of a certain genial magnificence. At times there is a certain irreverence in him, as exemplified by the popular precept "Pray to the Virgin Mary and run." When a world championship football team returned from triumphs in Europe, a cartoonist in Rio pictured the "Christ of the Corcovado" in a familiar Brazilian, but unbiblical, gesture of welcome. The huge white statue of the Savior stands with arms outstretched, as though blessing the city and its inhabitants; in the cartoon, He joins His hands above His head.

In point of time the first divinities in Brazil were Indian. When the Portuguese arrived, the aborigines had developed a cosmogony which primarily satisfied the basic needs of their Stone-Age minds. They had peopled the dark forest with spirits, baneful and beneficent, usually in the transfigured likeness of familiar beasts. The hold of these animistic bogies on the imagination of the Indian was so deep-seated that it has survived to the present, even among the *caboclos* of the Amazon Valley. Probably the best known and most feared of these superstitious fancies is the legend of the *curupira,* the misshapen monster who is the bearer of bad luck to the fisherman and the hunter.

When the Portuguese came to Brazil they had already been exposed to many creeds, both at home and abroad. While they accepted none of them in toto, they inevitably borrowed certain forms and observances that suited their own temperament. The Christianity they brought with them to the New World was an earthy and plebeian faith whose expression, in its fresh environment, became as homey as an old-fashioned county fair. Yet it was as orthodox in the essentials of its doctrine as the most rigid cleric could demand, for the settlers were simple men who had no taste for dogmatic ratiocination. Even if they had been inclined to religious speculation, they did not wish to expose themselves to the punitive consequences of heresy.

The Catholic Church followed two different lines of development in Brazil. One was a transplant of the popular faith of Portugal, as altered in its details by the special social and economic conditions prevailing in the "sugar civilization" of the north. It was, therefore, a local and even familial Church, with only remote ties with the supreme episcopacy in Lisbon. There was a bishop in Bahia, but the hierarchical structure and controls of this segment of the colonial Church were always weak. Its true center of authority and inspiration was the individual plantation, whose owner was practically omnipotent in all matters that concerned the welfare of his numerous dependents.

Under the circumstances the priest was to all intents and purposes only a chaplain of "the Big House." He was actually a retainer of the lord of the plantation, and was dependent on his largesse for a living. He officiated at the regular religious services in the chapel, conducted the prescribed rites on the numerous occasions of marriages, christenings, and burials, catechized the Indian or Negro slaves, served as schoolmaster at a primary level to the young sons of the planter, and organized and supervised the many religious festivals. Beyond the recounting of stories of the saints, he would seldom have been capable of any intellectual stimulus to his captive congregation. Generally affable and kindly, he was not an overwhelming force for a rigorous morality, though an easygoing and indulgent guardian of the accepted rules of behavior. Not even complete celibacy was expected of him, though his free and easy ways in this respect were ultimately to raise a major issue in church affairs in the time of the Empire.

In the large families that were the rule, one of the sons was generally expected to enter the service of the Church, either as a parish priest or as a member of one of the regular orders which had establishments in Olinda and Bahia. Daughters of the planters also frequently entered the nunneries in the cities. However, there was apparently little of the ascetic in the conventual life of either sex. The young ladies became experts in the making of sweets and indulged their tastes for music as they never could have done in the confused existence of the Big House. However, in view of the customary shortage of marriageable females, this choice of a celibate life, in preference to the responsibilities of a *dona da casa* in a man's world, created a social problem of proportions and tended to promote the sexual irregularities that were chronic in colonial society. This seems to have been the reverse of the situation prevailing in Goa, the capital of Portuguese India, which Linschoten, the Dutch navigator, visited in 1583. "The Towne," he wrote, "hath in it all sorts of cloysters and churches, as Lisbon hath, onely it wanteth nunnes, for the men cannot get the women to travell so far, where they should be shut up, and forsake Venus."

In the jurisdiction of this localized Church there was much emphasis on garish ceremonials and pageantry, of which pyrotechnic displays, feasts, and elaborate processions were the principal features. Frequent occasions were provided for these affairs by the plethora of religious holidays, the crowning celebration of the year being the festivities in honor of the patron saint of the locality. In the daily observance of the faith, considerable emphasis was also laid on the wearing of such insignia as amulets and charms and on the preservation and display of holy relics and evidences of miraculous cures. In the processions the order of march was organized in terms of social status, the Negro slaves heading the line, with the other elements of the population following in order of category, down to the members of the patriarchal families, resplendent in the finery that was a mark of their superior position. To the other familiar aspects of these religious fetes the Negro added a special colorfulness and exuberance. He treated the images of the saints or of the *Bom Jesús* with warm familiarity, and in spite of the social lines drawn, entered into the spirit of the occasion with a mixture of unrestrained delight and reverence.

The other Church in colonial Brazil was that of the Jesuits. In contrast to the homespun, grass-roots religion of the sugar plantations, Christianity as exemplified by the Jesuits was formal, centralized, and international in its organization. It was concerned with the spiritual welfare of the Indian population rather than with that of the Portuguese and their dependents. And since the Indians were the object of enslavement by the Portuguese planters, a deep-seated incompatibility early developed between the two elements.

Jesuit priests arrived in Brazil in 1549 in the company of Tomé de Souza, first governor of the colony. The leader of the group was Manoel de Nóbrega, one of four extraordinary members of the Society who were to gain fame in Brazil. The others were Antonio Vieira, one of the world's great preachers, José de Anchieta, and Fernão Cardím. As a fifth there might be added Father Samuel Fritz, a Bohemian, the scene of whose labors was the upper Amazon country.

Though the Jesuits had considerable influence for a time in the higher circles of power in Bahia, their impact on the religious and social development of Brazil was largely in connection with the proselyting of the Indians. In this work they adopted the same general plan of action as that followed in other missionary areas, like the famous Guaraní "reductions" in Paraguay. After winning the confidence of the tribe, their objective was to erect on the tribe's foundations an isolated theocratic community dominated by two or three priests. Against the opposition of the local Shaman or "medicine-man," they carried on their missionary and civilizing program, catechizing the Indians, with special emphasis on the young, organizing musical bands, and teaching the rudiments of certain industrial skills. Though the Society of Jesus was expelled from Brazil after a little more than two centuries and the Indians were abandoned to the chance ministrations of an inferior lay clergy, some of the Society's influence in the former areas of its activities has persisted to the present day. And, few as they were, the Jesuits had represented during their stay most of the culture that was spread so thinly over the sprawling world of Brazil.

Agents of the Inquisition were stationed in Brazilian ports, but the institution, true to its Portuguese antecedents, never had the direful aspects of its Spanish counterpart. Since heresy was a threat to the state, the agents had the status of security police or immigration inspectors, bent on assuring the orthodoxy of newcomers to the colony, or lecturing stray—and often inebriate—Dutch or English sailors on the errors of their Protestant ways. One of their particular concerns was to investigate the sincerity of the conversion of the numerous "New Christians" or Sephardic Jews, whose faith was always suspect. When religious freedom was proclaimed in 1806, heterodoxy was virtually nonexistent in Brazil.

If there has since been a lack of true religious peace, the problem has largely been an internal one. The specific issues of controversy have been concerned with the priesthood and with the organization of the Church, as well as with raising the general level of the popular faith and its observances.

There have never been enough priests to provide the needed religious services for a widely distributed population. In an article on "Brazilian Catholicism" which appeared in a Rio newspaper in 1959, Antonio Carlos Villaga wrote of "the monstrous lack of priests in Brazil." He pointed out that the country has only a little more than 10,000 priests when it should have at least 60,000. Half, he said, are foreigners "without roots in the country." The customary source of recruits for the parish clergy was gradually cut off by changed conditions in the dominant planter aristocracy of the Northeast, and there was no adequate supply of novices for the priesthood to fill the personnel gap. Young Brazilians have not been inclined to choose the Church as a career, and until recently there was a lack of training seminaries of the superior intellectual standards that might have attracted them. In many village communities in Brazil the position of the priest may be assumed by some old man or woman who has memorized the prayers of the liturgy or by a lay reader who is supported by a local brotherhood of the priestless parishioners of the locality.

Most of the "foreign" priests are Europeans who lack a familiarity with local customs and the mental habits and attitudes of their congregations. Many are really descendants of Italian immigrants. During the Empire, devoted Italian Capuchins took over much of the work of providing religious and charitable ministration to the poorer classes of the population. German Franciscans moved into some of the old monasteries of the cities, where they acted as parish priests for their Brazilian neighbors on the outside. The bishop of the Tapajóz country in the Amazon Valley is an American Franciscan from Chicago, and the convent at Santarém is occupied by other Americans of the same order. There have long been Italian mission stations on the upper Amazon, and American friars operate up-river from their base in Belém.

The moral and intellectual standards of the domestic clergy have long been the subject of comment by foreign visitors and native Brazilians. The issue came to a head during the Empire, which was then headed by Dom Pedro II, a man of exemplary personal life and considerable intellectual attainments. As might have been expected, Protestant missionaries were inclined to be critical of the conduct of their Catholic counterparts. For example, the Reverend Daniel Kidder wrote: "There is no class of men in the whole empire whose lives and practices are so corrupt as those of the priesthood. It is notorious." However, some laymen were equally open in their criticism of priestly ways that were a carry-over from the laxity of colonial times. According to the Agassizs, who visited Brazil over a century ago, "as a general thing, the ignorance of the clergy is universal, their immorality patent, their influence very extensive and deep-rooted." Yet they were patriotic, tolerant, and liberal. Henry Bates, the English naturalist who was in the Amazon Valley a little earlier, was generally very critical of the clergy, though he notes a few exceptions to the general rule. Of the parish priest at Obidos he remarked that "the vicar Padre Raimundo do Sanchez Brito was an excellent old man, and I fancy the friendly manners of the people and the general purity of morals, were owing in great part to the good example he set to his parishioners." On the other hand, the priest at Santarém, a little farther down the river, "showed remarkably little zeal for religion," and the curate at Altar do Chão on the Tapajóz was "a most profligate character." "I seldom saw him sober," Bates observes, and he continues: "I may as well mention here, that a moral and zealous priest is a great rarity in this province [Pará]." He found the vicar at Ega, where he lived for several years, "a thoroughly upright, sincere, and virtuous man." And he adds that "It is a pleasure to be able to speak in these terms of a Brazilian priest, for the opportunity occurs rarely enough."

One of the issues most widely debated under the Empire was the ancient question of sacerdotal celibacy. Since a large part of the Brazilian clergy had never made a pretense of observing the rule of clerical chastity, but lived quite openly with their wives or concubines, the scope of the controversy was indeed very broad. The circumstance that the general public was prone to accept such arrangements as in accord with human nature, the climate, and long-established custom further complicated the problem and precluded any objective solution. A group of persons, both lay and clerical, high in imperial circles, openly declared themselves in favor of legitimizing the practice, even at the cost of setting up a separate Brazilian Church divorced from the authority of the Vatican.

Other phases of the over-all controversy regarding the mores of the cloth in Brazil involved the widespread presence of Freemasonry among the clergy and the active participation of the priesthood, even of some members of the hierarchy, in political affairs. A number of the higher clergy were senators of the Empire, and a few occupied cabinet positions whose jurisdiction was unrelated to matters of religion or public morality. Richard Burton, the British orientalist—and Africanist—who was consul at Santos in 1865, made some pertinent and provocative observations on the general subject after a long journey through the highlands of Minas:

> The Mineiro, like the Paulista, is a religious man but a lax Catholic. Catholicism is here far removed from its legitimate centre, and has undergone some notable changes. At the same time, he has, like the Paulista, a certain horror of any non-Catholic. He is rather superstitious than fanatic. . . . Many of the highly educated, if not the vulgar, advocate the marriage of the clergy. . . . The parishioners have little objections to a vigario who takes a wife and makes an honest man of himself. The climate is not favorable to chastity; the race, especially where the blood is mixed, is of inflammable material. . . . The superior dignity of virginity or sterility, either enforced or voluntary, is an idea revolting to reason and common sense, especially in a young country, where polygamy is morally justifiable, the evils being more than counterbalanced by the benefits.

Commenting on the historical role of unrestrained procreation in the original settlement of Brazil, Gilberto Freyre has observed that "An ascetic, orthodox Catholicism, by hampering the freedom of the senses and the instincts of generation, would have prevented Portugal from straddling the world."

Under the later republic the leaders of the Church have maintained a course at once conservative and constructive. Relations with Rome have been close and friendly, and the Brazilian Church was rewarded for its decorous and prudent orthodoxy by the award of the first cardinalate in Latin America.

For many years a group of influential laymen, now associated with the wider organization of Catholic Action, has carried on a program designed to raise the general level of religious observance in the nation. Among those prominent in its work have been José Carlos Rodrigues, former editor of the *Jornal do Com-*

mercio of Rio, and Alceu Amoroso Lima, the distinguished writer. Meanwhile, the disciplinary controls of the National Primacy over the priesthood have been strengthened, with a corresponding improvement in clerical standards. The Church, as represented by clergymen of the type of Dom Helder Cámara in Rio, is also taking an increasingly active part in problems of social welfare.

Among the things that still remain to be done in order to bring Brazilian Catholicism up to the standards which its heads have set as their goals is the inculcation of a sense of community or group participation in the urban congregations. The Brazilian Church has been torn between the traditional claims of family loyalty and the individualism of the upper and middle classes which often makes co-operative effort so difficult. The rural Church, some of whose practices are still colonial, nevertheless has a much stronger bent for united action than do the otherwise more correct worshippers of the cities.

A peculiar manifestation of religious fervor has long been endemic in the drought-ridden *sertão* country of northeastern Brazil. The inhabitants of this vast area, that covers parts of 12 states, are a mixture of Portuguese with Indian and Negro. Isolated from the main currents of national life, they have developed from long residence in their trying habitat a special character that is compounded of asceticism, physical hardihood, intensity of purpose, rebelliousness, and mysticism, as an expression of deep religious feelings. Their Christianity is a grim and tragic cult. They have a capacity for an apocalyptic messianism that is lacking in the typical Brazilian, and which they share with desert peoples from ancient Sinai to modern Arabia. Roused by some leader with a messiah complex, they have from time to time indulged in violent outbreaks against the established order.

Most famous of these affairs was "the war of Canudos" in the 1890's. This revolt of epic proportions has been described in R. B. Cunninghame-Graham's biography of *A Brazilian Mystic,* and is the theme of Euclydes da Cunha's classic work, *Os Sertões,* which was translated by Samuel Putnam under the title *Rebellion in the Backlands.* This prolonged series of disorders, that ended in mass annihilation, was provoked by an old *sertanejo* named Antonio Vicente Mendes Maciel, later to be better known by the name of Antonio Conselheiro, conferred on him by his followers. Embittered by the persecution of local government agents in Ceará, he began an aimless pilgrimage through the back country in 1876. Begging alms from farm to farm, he preached repentance to all who would listen and gradually gained a far-flung reputation as a holy man. Growing crowds joined him as he moved through the country, until the predacious host of thousands became a menace to all authority.

The multitude finally holed up on the abandoned fazenda of Canudos in the interior of Bahia. Here they built and fortified a town, while they lived off the surrounding country. Government troops sent against them were ignominiously defeated. By this time the situation was long since out of hand and reflected seriously on the prestige of the national administration in Rio. A supreme effort was eventually made by the harassed government and an army sent against the stronghold. When, after a long siege, the town was taken by storm in early October, 1897, the last of its defenders were slaughtered. It was 21 years since Antonio Conselheiro had begun his fateful pilgrimage of penance.

For many years, beginning contemporaneously with the career of Antonio Conselheiro in the 1870's and ending with his death in 1936, another extraordinary figure appeared in the same region. This was the famous Padre Cicero, who assumed the role of apostle of the *sertão.* From his seat in the village of Joazeiro his reputation as healer of the sick and comforter of the unfortunate spread throughout the Northeast. Though the Church tried to expel him from its ranks and sent another priest to replace him, his thousands of devoted followers remained loyal to him. In time he became the dominant political power in the area, and when American and British engineering firms undertook the construction of irrigation dams in the field of his influence in the 1920's, they had first to assure themselves of his approval. A few years ago a similar phenomenon occurred on a lesser scale in another part of the country in the person of Padre Antonio Pinto, hailed as a "miracle priest."

For a time Positivism, the formalized religion which Auguste Comte, the French philosopher, developed from the base of his ethical cult of humanity, had considerable influence in higher circles in Brazil. One of the founders of the Brazilian branch of the Positivist church was Benjamin Constant, who was one of the leaders in the establishment of the republic. The national motto of *Ordem e Progresso,* or "Order and Progress," which appears on the Brazilian flag, reflects the strong position of Positivist ideas at that time. Most of the small body of Comtean proselytes were members of the intelligentsia, the officer corps of the armed forces, and the political leadership of the country, but particularly in the state of Rio Grande do Sul. Positivism largely represented an organized protest against the failure of the familial or patriarchal system of society and of the traditional Church to solve the more pressing social problems of the nation. A Temple of Humanity survives in Rio as a reminder of its former influence, but its select membership has steadily diminished in numbers and it is no longer a factor of importance in the religious scene.

The first Protestants in Brazil were the French Calvinists who settled briefly on islands in Rio Bay over 400 years ago and the Dutch who later occupied for a time much of the northeast coast. But their stay was short and their influence in the religious history of the country ephemeral. The first group of Protestants who came to Brazil to stay were German immigrants who arrived during the Empire. Some were of conventional Lutheran faith, but a minority were Anabaptists who did not harmonize with their compatriots, either Catholic or Protestant, and much less with their Brazilian neighbors.

Meanwhile Protestant clergymen from the United States and

England had begun to explore the possibilities of the missionary field in Brazil. There were no longer any legal obstacles to the entry of once heretical faiths, and the majority of the public was at least indifferent to their introduction. Protestant sects were to establish themselves in Brazil long before the end of the last century. The Methodists came in 1836 and the Congregationalists in 1855. In 1859 the Reverend Ashbel Green Simonton arrived in Rio to initiate a Brazilian branch of the Presbyterian church. A hundred years later the World Presbyterian Alliance held a conclave in Brazil, during the course of which President Kubitschek, a Catholic, sang a Protestant hymn in the company of five Calvinist pastors, in the interest of religious harmony and coexistence. In 1960 the Baptists staged a world convention in Rio. The first Episcopal clergymen probably came to Brazil to minister to the religious needs of the large English business community, and by the 1890's the Anglican Church was well established in the country. One of the pioneers in Brazilian Episcopalianism was Bishop Lucien Lee Kinsolving, whose Brazil-born son is Episcopal bishop of Arizona.

The various Protestant churches in Brazil have made important contributions to education and social welfare. They have founded superior schools, like the Presbyterians' Mackenzie College in São Paulo, one of the best institutions of higher technical instruction in the country. Other schools include the Methodists' Bennett College for girls in Rio, the Colegio Americano in Porto Alegre, the Colegio Isabel Hendrix in Belo Horizonte, the Granberry School at Juiz de Fora, and a large Baptist institution in Recife. The Presbyterians also operate an agricultural training school and experiment station at Lavras in Minas Gerais.

Some churches have set up medical facilities in remote parts of the back country, as the Adventists have done in the Amazon Valley. The Adventists maintain a mobile medical service on the rivers by means of a fleet of nine well-equipped launches. They treat from 25,000 to 50,000 persons a year, and in 1958 their itinerant doctor-dentists pulled a total of 13,663 teeth. The

Reverend Leo B. Halliwell and his wife, a trained nurse, recently retired after 37 years as Adventist medical missionaries in Brazil, most of that period spent on a launch on the Amazon. The Adventists operate a total of eight hospitals and clinics in Brazilian cities and towns.

Confronted by the difficulty of obtaining entry visas as missionaries only, an organization known as Co-Laborers, Inc., was formed a few years ago for the purpose of settling 150 families on farms, from which they would spread their particular gospel to their neighbors.

In order to dispel any suspicion that they might be instruments of foreign cultural penetration or imperialism, the older—and more respectable—Protestant churches have taken pains to identify themselves as closely as possible with the national life. As a rule, the pastorate is Brazilian, and organizational ties with the mother church tend to grow weaker as the Brazilian branches become more capable of maintaining their independence.

Since Brazil has been widely publicized as a promising mission field, other denominations have continued to enter the country. As an example of this propaganda, a Presbyterian minister recently called it a "great frontier of the Protestant movement," adding the observation that "Roman Catholicism never really took possession of the Brazilian sub-continent." Some of the new sects are ill prepared for the delicate task of adjusting to the demands of an alien culture. This missionary proliferation, with its attendant fragmentation of basic Christianity, only adds to the religious confusion of the Brazilian, who may begin to "shop around" for the church that will best suit his spiritual fancies of the moment.

In the meantime, the Protestant missionary movement, which was of very modest proportions at the beginning of the century, has since had a phenomenal success. In 1900 there were less than 50,000 acknowledged Protestants in Brazil; at the end of 1956 there were about 1,700,000.

An abnormal number of Brazilians—nearly 600,000 of them in

1956—seek in spiritism solace for their concern about man's relation with the unseen. Part of the widespread phenomenon doubtless represents the individual's search for a solution or easing of his own mental anxieties. For a time there was a tendency for the communicants to retain their connection with the more traditional and earth-bound sects, but there is a growing inclination to accept spiritualism as a religion in its own right, equipped with a complete apparatus of doctrine and ritual.

It is by no means a unified movement. There are, in fact, several different gradations of creed and worship that are social and intellectual in their bases. These may vary from a definite metaphysical context at the upper level to a clearly animistic association, verging on primitive Indian or Negro beliefs, at the bottom. The only thing which they have in common is the presumption of communication with the dead. There is a considerable literature in the field, which one may sometimes find for sale in small cubbyholes along the streets of cities in the interior. Predominant among treatises and guides for the illumination of believers are the enunciations and commentaries of Alan Kardec, the Parisian, who is a sort of thaumaturge or high priest of the largest of the spiritualist bodies.

The faiths brought into Brazil by the Negro slaves were a jumble of Islamic and pagan cults. Most of the Negroes like the superior Haussas, who came from the region to the west of the Niger, were Mohammedans. As a rule, they did not prove to be as culturally malleable as those of Bantu stock, and for a long time there were nuclei of Moslem slaves and freedmen that continued the worship of Mohammed. The variations among the groups of pagan slaves largely depended on the part of Africa where they originated, and were classified as Nago, Angola, Congo, Gégé, and so on. Their gods were sometimes interchangeable, and rites from different sources might be merged. One element which the pagan cults had in common was their habit of direct communion with their deities, somewhat after the manner of the ancient Greeks. The ceremonials involved a complex mixture of dancing and music, feasting and drinking, the wearing of special garb, the giving of gifts to the particular deity of the occasion, and the recital of ritualistic invocations and petitions.

Both pagan and Moslem Negroes generally accepted the elemental concepts of Christian theology and its more spectacular observances with readiness, though the Mina peoples were originally more disposed to conserve the basic elements of Islam. However, much of the African religions survived, either to color the forms of Christian worship and other phases of life in northern Brazil, or as an integrated and distinct system of relationships with the supernatural within the domain of the official Church.

The celebration of the rites known as *candomblé* has continued to the present in the region of Bahia. It is primarily a woman's religion and it is colored "mothers" who officiate at its elaborate rites. A related form, called *macumba,* persists in the vicinity of Rio, where it is sometimes made a public spectacle for the entertainment of tourists. As practiced in Bahia, *candomblé* evidently represents a serious display of atavistic religious feelings that has found no satisfactory substitute even in the warm and demonstrative Christianity of the country. To avoid the embarrassment of a spiritual dualism, the simple followers of the African faiths have endeavored to identify some of their deities with Christian saints. For example, Xango is the alter ego of St. Jerome, who serves as a special patron of the Negro in Brazil. Oxalá is generally regarded as the counterpart of the infant Jesus. Olorum is a sort of black Jupiter or supreme god, and Exú is the equivalent of Satan. Yemanjá, as goddess of the sea and, incidentally, of fertility, is the object of special rites in early February, when sailors and fishermen cast into the waters offerings of flowers and perfumed soap and cheap perfumes and gaudy baubles for her adornment. Other colored folk who dwell by the sea may observe the same rites, as I once found by chance on a secluded island in Rio Bay. And fine ladies have been known to alight from their chauffeured cars at night along the beach at Copacabana and toss a cluster of orchids into the surf in obeisance to the female Neptune.

Of other religions in Brazil there is no end. The Mormon Church has a growing membership. There are Christian Science reading rooms and meeting centers. The Salvation Army has won a very special place in the charitable hearts of Brazilians by its good works. Some of the cults of Asia have found a congenial atmosphere in Brazil. For the contemplative there is a branch of the Theosophical Society, and for those who yearn for human brotherhood in a contentious world there is a Bahai congregation in Rio. Of nearly 200,000 Buddhists, not all are immigrants from the Orient. In the official religious census of 1950 nearly 300,000 Brazilians registered as avowed atheists.

PART III
THE ACTION

CHAPTER 10

The School

LIKE POLITICAL DEMOCRACY AND THE INDUSTRIAL REVOLUTION, public education came late in Brazil. In fact, the polls and mills preceded the schools and provided much of the impetus for them, on the principle that an illiterate people can be neither good citizens nor good workers. But the nation is now obsessed with the urge to fill the educational gap that was so wide and so deep. The Brazilians are a people in a hurry to catch up with lost time—to make up the classes they missed because there were no classes. Their specific goals are the elimination of illiteracy and the creation of a school system that will adequately serve their intellectual, economic, and social needs in the new tempo and scope of national life. The task they have set themselves is enormous and, in spite of all they have accomplished in the past 30 years, they still have far to go. After all, the republic started educationally, as well as politically, almost from scratch, for in 1890 only about 250,000 of its 13,000,000 people were in elementary school.

The Jesuits had left Brazil 130 years before, and with them

went most of whatever interest and competence in education there was in the colony. Other religious orders carried on some schooling of sorts in the cities, and occasionally a wealthy planter or miner sent a promising son to the old Portuguese university at Coimbra. The routine of learning varied little in two and a half centuries.

When the royal family moved to Rio in 1808 to get away from the French, the king undertook what amounted to a real revolution in education. Among the cultural institutions that were set up during João VI's stay in Brazil were two medical schools, a military academy, a school of fine arts, two schools of applied arts, a museum of natural history, the botanical gardens in Rio, a national library, and the first printing press in the history of Brazil. All of these innovations were related to the field of higher education. Elementary education was left to shift for itself.

During the Empire, which began in 1822, little progress was made in educating the mass of Brazilians. A large part of the labor force still consisted of slaves, and anyway, the idea then prevailed that education was bad for the lower classes. In other words, it was believed that learning and sophistication would spoil the *caboclo*. The aristocratic concept of education as a monopoly of the elite remained the rule. As a mark of caste, like a gold-headed cane, the privileged scion of the Brazilian gentry was expected to accumulate an impressive volume of unrelated knowledge. Beyond its ornamental aspects, this educational philosophy served no functional purpose, either as it affected the professional career of the individual or the national welfare of Brazil. Moreover, it resulted in little creative literary or scholastic effort of consequence, and its respect for authority ignored the value of experiment and observation as educational techniques.

Another impediment to educational progress during the past century was the Brazilian's awe of French culture, which for a long time prevented a realistic approach to the intellectual needs of his own country. Adulation of the encyclopedic element in the culture of France set the tone for the Brazilian approach to higher education, but French emphasis on scientific inquiry met with little response in Brazil until the present century. The prestige of French letters and thought was based on the appeal of their clarity and universality to the mental temper of Brazil at the moment of her emergence from an era of provincial tradition into independence. It also represented the reaction to a passing inferiority complex or mood of depreciation of the cultural attainments and potentiality of Brazil. There was later to appear a certain snobbery in the Gallophilia, as when Brazilians fell into French in conversation with one another or used the French language in preference to Portuguese when making an address in Brazil.

Yet during the imperial regime some very creditable additions were made to the educational structure of Brazil, and behind the fashionable façade of pseudo-Europeanism, much mind-searching must have gone on, to the eventual advantage of Brazil. Law schools were established at São Paulo and Olinda-Recife, the Escola Polytecnica, an engineering school, at Rio, and a school of mines at Ouro Preto in Minas Gerais. In 1838 the Imperial High School was founded in the national capital. Better known as the Colegio Pedro II, it was to become a Brazilian Eton and has maintained a position unique in secondary education to the present. Also, though elementary education had been turned over to the provinces, several normal schools were created for the training of teachers, the first in 1835 at Niteroi across the bay from Rio. There must have been others, like the modest school that was described by "Helena Morley" in her delightful diary of a young girl's life in Diamantina in the first years of the republic.

One of the most important educational institutions to be founded in the time of the Empire was the school in São Paulo that is now Mackenzie University. It began in 1871, on the initiative of a Presbyterian missionary's wife named Mary Annesley Chamberlain, as the Escola Americana or American School. Starting as a one-grade primary school, it was to become one of the cultural landmarks of Brazil. It provides a cross-section of all educational levels, from the original elementary school through a multiple-offering university. When one of the early buildings bore the inscription of a New York lawyer who had made a bequest to the school, the students called it "The Mackenzie," by which name the institution has ever since been known.

Of the many foreigners who commented on the state of the Brazilian mind in the nineteenth century, Spix and Martius, the German scientists who came to Brazil in 1817 just after the king had put his educational program into effect, remarked that "the capital disposes of various good institutions of learning." However, they noted the lack of a university and the absence of any interest in experimental science. As an index to mental activity in Brazil, Martha Graham, the Englishwoman who visited the country a few years later, reported that there was no bookstore in Recife and, while there were two shops in Bahia, books were only an expensive luxury for the rich. Of the country at large she wrote that "The state of general education is so low that more than common talent and desire of knowledge is requisite to attain any." In mid-century Henry Bates found in isolated Santarém in the Amazon Valley three schools: one for boys, another for girls, and a third that taught Latin and French in preparation for admission to the institutions of higher education in Belém. Of the citizenry of Santarém, Bates remarked that "The people seem to be thoroughly alive to the advantages of education for their children." As for the pupils, "It is remarkable," he says, "how quickly and well the little lads, both coloured and white, learn reading, writing, and arithmetic." Bates' observations on what then passed for higher education in Belém would probably have been generally applicable to conditions in most Brazilian cities of that period:

> The course of study must be very deficient, for it is rare to meet with an educated Paraense who has the slightest knowledge of the physical sciences, or even of geography. . . . The

> young men all become smart rhetoricians and lawyers; any one of them is ready to plead in a law case at an hour's notice; they are also great at statistics, for the gratification of which taste there is ample field in Brazil, where every public officer has to furnish volumes of dry reports annually to the government, but they are woefully ignorant on most other subjects.

Louis Agassiz and his wife, both of whom were educators, conducted a scientific expedition to Brazil in 1865. While they found the intellectual development of the nation to be generally retarded, they had discriminating comments to make on particular facets of the educational system. They considered the "universities," i.e., law or medical schools (*faculdades*) in São Paulo, Bahia, and Recife good, though the area of instruction was perhaps too limited. Scientific education was "one rather of books than of facts." They declared field studies "foreign to Brazilian habits," including "personal indolence," and reported that "their naturalists are theoretical rather than practical. They know more of the bibliography of foreign science than of the wonderful fauna and flora with which they are surrounded." Of the Colegio Pedro II, they wrote: "It may be compared to our New England high schools and fully deserves the reputation it enjoys." Also, they praised the work of the Polytechnic School in Rio and the practical instruction that was provided by trade schools in the cities, where blacks and whites mingled "without any discrimination."

Difficult as it is by any standards, Brazil's educational dilemma, which the republic inherited, full-grown, from the Empire, is further complicated by interrelated demographic and financial factors. The magnitude of the problem is not a fixed quantity, for the population of Brazil is, meanwhile, increasing at the phenomenal rate of 1,500,000 persons a year. As a result, some responsible Brazilians fear that, in spite of everything that has been done, the national illiteracy rate may actually be increasing.

Moreover, due to the peculiar age grouping of the population, of which more than 52 per cent are under 19 years of age, the financial burden of educating so many children, even at a low level of schooling, falls on a proportionately small group of income earners and taxpayers.

Responsibility for the financial support of education is divided between the federal, state, and municipal governments. Public expenditures for education in 1957 of approximately 20,743,000,000 cruzeiros were shared on a ratio of respectively 37, 52, and 11 per cent. There is considerable assistance from private sources, including schools supported by churches, student fees for enrollment in secondary schools, and the contributions of private business, especially in the field of industrial education. In every sector of the school system the long-continued inflation seriously affects all calculations of cost, as in every other phase of Brazilian life. Even if it were constitutionally feasible, the government of the union is unable at the present juncture of its affairs to finance another "crash" program in the interests of education, like that by which it has moved the federal capital to Brasilia.

Though the Constitution of 1946 specifies that the federal government must devote at least 10 per cent of its budget to the support of education, only in 1950 have federal expenditures for education reached that proportion of the total. In 1956 the percentage was only 3.82 and in 1957, 5.33. In the latter two years the armed forces accounted for respectively 19.19 and 21.82 per cent of the outlay of the federal government, or five and four times the appropriations for education.

Furthermore, the existence of a dual society in Brazil, one modern, as represented by São Paulo and the other southern states, and the other archaic, as exemplified by the more backward states of the north, places a disproportionate financial burden on the former. As an example of the economic disparity, the average daily income of a Paulista is about eight times that of a wage earner in Piauí.

The direction of the national school system is vested in a Ministry of Education and Culture, which in its present form dates from 1953. Previous to 1930 no single branch of the federal government was entrusted with over-all responsibility in educational matters, but authority was scattered among several administrative departments. Besides its supervision of secondary and higher education, the ministry is specifically authorized to oversee and support a number of institutions and organizations, such as the Colegio Pedro II, the National Theater Commission, and the Oswaldo Cruz Institute for research in biology and pathology. It is aided by the National Institute of Educational Research and the National Council of Education, which is the supreme advisory body in the field.

The weakest part of the Brazilian school system is elementary education. Thus its strongest phase, that of higher education, is paradoxically built on an inferior foundation. Since the basic criterion of its quality is the ability to read, national and regional rates of illiteracy are the essential index of its effectiveness. The federal Constitution declares that "Education is the right of everyone" and adds that "Primary schooling is obligatory." Meanwhile, estimates of the illiteracy rate for persons over nine years of age vary from the official figure of 51.65 per cent for 1950 to recent private guesses as high as 70 per cent. The general consensus of responsible opinion in Brazil would probably place the illiteracy rate at about 60 per cent. Whatever the actual rate, it is obviously too high, and is so recognized and lamented by Brazilians.

On the basis of government census reports, of about 36,500,000 over nine years old in 1950 there were nearly 19,000,000 illiterates. The illiteracy rate varied from 80 per cent in Alagoas to around 35 per cent in Rio Grande do Sul, São Paulo, and Santa Catarina. It is heaviest in the rural regions of the *sertão,* where there are isolated villages in which it is almost total. Much of the illiteracy in otherwise advanced localities of southern Brazil is due to the inroads of ignorant northerners in the past few decades. For example, the swollen *favellas* or slums of Rio are immense nuclei of imported illiteracy.

In 1956 there were a little over 5,000,000 children in elementary schools in all Brazil. Of these, approximately 56 per cent were enrolled in state-supported schools, 32 per cent in municipal schools, and 12 per cent in private schools. In that year there were nearly 83,000 elementary schools of all kinds and about 183,000 teachers, which would appear to show a preponderance of one-room schools. However, the actual ratio of teachers to schools is affected by the frequent resort to two—and even three—sessions in the same classroom. School plants run the whole gamut from super-modern buildings designed by the great Oscar Niemeyer to decrepit shacks in forlorn villages of the back country, that are devoid of elemental pedagogic and sanitary facilities. Meanwhile, as a phase of the massive movement for educational reform, hundreds of new schoolhouses are being built.

The great majority of elementary schoolteachers are women, and in the municipally supported schools men have left the teaching profession almost entirely to women. Except in the more progressive states and cities, teachers are shamefully underpaid, even by current income standards in Brazil, and in order to meet the rising cost of living thousands of teachers are forced to work at two jobs.

In spite of the growing number of normal schools, there is still a serious shortage of well-equipped teachers. Only about 40 per cent of those enrolled in the normal schools intend to teach, and many who graduate refuse to live in the backward communities where teachers are most needed. Much of the hope for improved education in Brazil lies with its women. Devoted and intelligent, if they were properly trained and rewarded they could revolutionize elementary education in this generation. As an example of their possibilities for initiative in the field of education, a woman teacher who was a school inspector in Minas Gerais aroused the community of Sete Lagoas to build and equip a school by their own efforts and to assure local interest and support for its maintenance.

One of the several co-operative projects carried on by the Education Division of the United States Operations Mission or

Point 4 in Brazil is the comprehensive program which it has set up for training those who train the teachers of Brazil. A pilot elementary education center, staffed by Americans and Brazilians trained in the United States, has been established in the Institute of Education in Belo Horizonte. To participate in its intensive training courses, normal school instructors and school supervisors and inspectors are brought in from all over Brazil. Eventually, as with all the Point 4 projects, responsibility for the operation of this national training center will be turned over to the Brazilians. Much is also being accomplished in certain areas of the same general field by excellent model schools which are conducted by the Ministry of Education in Salvador, Recife, and Rio.

Supplementary to the purposes of the regular elementary school system is an extensive national program for providing some primary instruction to illiterate adults. The response to this campaign, as also occurred previously in Mexico with a similar program, has been very heartening. For the benefit of those who are employed, classes are generally held in the evening in the local school premises.

In its basic structure, elementary education in Brazil differs greatly from the American system. Instead of eight years, the elementary course is of only four years, though a supplementary year may sometimes be added for special pupils, and we may find retarded 14-year-olds in this prolonged course. A striking predicament of the elementary schools is the extraordinary drop-out rate, known to the Brazilians as "evasion." Only about one child in 10 who enrolls at the beginning "graduates" from the four-year course of study, and about 60 per cent fail to complete even the first year. Many do not "pass" the required tests, others lose interest, and the early demands often made on children to help in the home and the fields remove many from school before they have learned to decipher a simple sentence. Of the many problems which beset elementary education in Brazil, this is one of the most serious.

There are two levels of secondary or high school education in Brazil. Only to that extent does it parallel the American pattern of junior and regular high school. The lower-level school is called a *ginasio* and the continuation school is a *colegio*. There is no exact equivalent for these terms in American practice, though adaptations of them are common in Europe. The first stage of the seven-year cycle of secondary education lasts four years and it requires another three years to complete the advanced curriculum of the *colegio*. Students in the *colegio* may register in either a classical or scientific course of study.

In 1956 there were 2,066 schools of the *ginasio* or lower-level type and 746 *colegios*. Of the former, about three-fourths were privately owned and of the latter, about two-thirds. Thus the public high school as it exists in the United States is the exception in Brazil.

In the same year, approximately 900,000 students were enrolled at both levels. Private secondary schools which meet the standards prescribed by the Ministry of Education are certified as eligible for the enrollment of tuition-paying students and may receive government aid in the form of financial subsidies. There has been considerable criticism of the predominance of private interests in secondary schooling, and a prominent Brazilian writer has called the private high schools in Rio "one of the most profitable of small businesses."

The original concept of the secondary school in Brazil was as an avenue to the university, and its course of study was planned accordingly. However, a change of emphasis as a result of legislation and directives of the Ministry of Education has broadened somewhat the basic purpose of secondary education by identifying it more closely with the interests of national development. Thus the completion of a high school course may become an end in itself, unrelated to the university.

The Colegio Pedro II in Rio, the classical institution of secondary education, still remains the paragon of schools in its field and has continued to maintain its high standards of instruction.

Another important influence in secondary education is the Colegio Novo Friburgo, which is located in the pleasant town of that name in the state of Rio de Janeiro. It was founded as an experimental school in 1950 on the initiative of the Getulio Vargas Foundation. It is a residential school and receives students from all parts of the country.

As a rule, high school teachers at either level know the subject matter of their courses better than do the majority of elementary teachers. However, too much stress is generally laid on lecturing as a teaching device and not enough on student discussion, so that well-filled notebooks tend to have a value beyond their deserts. There are too many required courses and there is an overemphasis on passing examinations and on such external insignia of learning as diplomas. Associated with these propensities is the *doutorado* complex or undiscriminating use of the title of "doctor" as a symbol of the "status" appeal of higher education. The tradition of secondary education in Brazil is so high and its social standing is so high that it still remains a powerful conservative force in national life, and in the content and methodology of its teaching, change is liable to come somewhat slowly and grudgingly.

Whereas Mexico and Peru have had a university since 1551, there was none in Brazil until 1920, although there had long been separate institutions—"faculties" or colleges—in the field of higher learning. Under the Empire, they were usually law or medical schools. Then in 1920 the separate schools of law, medicine, and engineering in the Federal District were united administratively as the University of Rio de Janeiro, now the University of Brazil. At present, Brazil has 21 universities and many other specialized institutions of higher education. Five of the universities are Roman Catholic and Mackenzie is Protestant in origin. Three are classed as "rural" universities. The total university enrollment is over 75,000. The largest university is that of São Paulo, followed by the University of Brazil in Rio. Five other universities have over 3,000 students. By faculties or departments, the heaviest enrollment is in law and medical studies. In the Brazilian equivalent of the American liberal arts college, the majority of the students are women.

Except for certain controls exercised by the Ministry of Education, the Brazilian universities generally follow the "autonomous" pattern common in other Latin American countries. They are, in effect, largely self-governing, with authority vested in a council of the faculty which, among other powers, elects the rector. As elsewhere in Latin America, the students exert a great deal of influence in university affairs. While rules for their conduct are specifically laid down by law, they have sometimes resorted to public demonstrations, so that more staid and responsible members of the community frequently complain of their indiscipline and wayward habits.

Though the lack of a full-time professoriate may detract from the internal cohesion of the university, the custom of supplementing the regular instructional staff with lectures from outside has the effect of strengthening the university's ties with the community. It also enables the university to draw on the best minds of the country—writers, diplomats, research scholars, leaders of the press and the arts, and outstanding figures in the professions and the national economy. In addition to local talent, permanent or occasional, visiting American or European professors are frequently found on the faculties. The average quality of instruction is high, though classroom techniques may differ considerably from American practice.

These are the more conventional forms of Brazilian education. The actual structure is much more complex, as new programs and instrumentalities of training are added to the traditional framework. These include, among many others, the Escola Superior de Guerra, which is like the United States Army's War College and is one of the best institutions of higher learning in Brazil; the Escola Livre, or Free School of Economics and Politics, in São Paulo; a new school of advanced social studies in Recife, that is designed to provide a background of sociological knowledge for public administrators; a school of music in the University of Bahia; and a new school of the drama, headed by the able Martím Gonçalves, that is attached to the same university.

One of the most important and effective sectors in Brazilian education is economic in its purpose. It represents a variety of special training programs which are urgently needed to meet the growing demands of agriculture, transportation, industry, and trade for competent personnel. The scope of the programs ranges from the shop worker and the farm hand to the managerial level. In manufacturing industry, the principal needs are for skilled machine operators and repairmen and, above all, for foremen. The tremendous increase in air transportation in Brazil requires not only the preparation of pilots, navigators, and radio operators, but of ground crews, and even of meteorologists. Similarly, the expansion of the national highway system has made the occupation of truck or bus driver a coveted calling for young Brazilians, and has created a special training problem of magnitude for the operation and maintenance of commercial motor vehicles. In mercantile business, the demand is especially for accountants to deal with the complex and monumental intricacies of Brazilian taxation, for persons familiar with import and banking regulations and procedures, and for qualified sales employees.

Plans for agricultural education have run afoul of the special difficulties inherent in the backward practices that perennially bedevil farming in Brazil and in the outmoded social structure of her vast rural population. The crux of the problem is to reach the millions who perform the actual work of cultivation or stock raising. On this uncertain ground, the dilemma of agricultural education coincides with that of the retarded system of elementary education. The rural worker is demeaned in the national esteem, and the influence of this barrier of caste is reflected in the *caboclo*'s indifference to efforts for improving his efficiency by changing the routine of his backwardness. So the educational program of the Ministry of Agriculture on his behalf has met with little response that would be reflected in figures of farm production. The more advanced segments of the official program are designed for the training of agronomists, who tend to seek a career of ill-paid respectability in the government service, and for the managers of fazendas owned by absentee landlords. In this limited field, they have done much good work, though the repercussions of their superior training on the ultimate tillers of the soil are limited. Only a long-term campaign of agricultural extension, on the lines of the county agent system in the United States, would appear to offer a promise of breaking the present obsolete pattern of farming.

There are 12 agricultural colleges in Brazil, in addition to eight veterinary schools. They are generally well staffed and equipped, and in spite of the basic handicaps under which they operate, they have contributed much to the improvement of agriculture. The oldest of them, in the state of Bahia, dates from 1870 and has profited from long and close ties with Texas Agricultural and Mechanical College. Another, at Pelotas in Rio Grande do Sul, was also founded during the Empire. Probably the best known of the colleges is that at Piracicaba in São Paulo, which has also had the advantages of co-operation with similar American institutions. There are two excellent agricultural schools in Minas Gerais, one at Viçosa and the Presbyterian College at Lavras.

The organized training of personnel for commercial aviation began in the early 1940's with an in-service program in the United States conducted by the Civil Aeronautics Administration. Training is now concentrated in the Technological Institute of Aeronautics, which is located at São José dos Campos on the road between São Paulo and Rio. This superior school trains flyers and other technical personnel for both civilian airlines and the national air force. It has American advisors, provided by the United States Operations Mission in Brazil, and altogether is one of the best educational institutions in the country.

To take care of the requirements of Brazil's expanding industrial development, there is a large network of schools at different levels. They are supported by federal, state, and municipal government, sometimes with the active co-operation of private business, which is vitally concerned with the success of the program. Those who received training in them, whether as machinists or supervisors, are a purposeful lot who have an immediate personal stake in their education.

The importance of commercial instruction in the Brazilian economy was attested by the more than 1,300 teachers and administrators who attended the third Brazilian Congress of Commercial Education held in Porto Alegre in August, 1959. At a somewhat higher level than the training provided by the conventional commercial or business school are several new institutions and programs of recent origin. The most ambitious project in the field is the College of Business Administration that was established in São Paulo in 1954. It has a four-year course, and during the initial stages of its development has been largely staffed by professors from Michigan State University. Other examples of educational offerings in the same general field were courses on "the administration of business enterprises" and "sales promotion," offered in São Paulo in 1959 by the Brazilian Institute of Cultural Extension, and a series of lectures on industrial sociology announced by the Roberto Simonsen Forum in the same city.

At another level is the extensive program for teaching English to adults that is conducted by the 58 co-operative Brazilian-American cultural centers. Though sponsored by the United States Information Service, most of their operating income is derived from student fees. Nearly 50,000 students are enrolled in their language classes, of which about 7,700 are in Rio. Comparable information is provided by similar British organizations and, in French, by the Alliance Française. There are also large American community schools in Rio and São Paulo whose classes, largely conducted in Portuguese in accordance with Brazilian law, are open to Brazilian children. Because of abuses in the German schools at the time of World War I, the government adopted rigorous policies for the control of foreign schools within the country, particularly as regards the language of instruction.

American programs of student interchange, supported both by the United States government and private foundations, have been a valuable auxiliary factor in Brazilian education. In 1959, 560 Brazilian students were enrolled in American institutions of higher learning, of whom 70 per cent were men. Of the total, 163 paid their own way and an equal number had financial support from foundations or other private sources; 134 were engineering students. Of 137 whose major interest was in the humanities, 40 were attending theological schools, 47 were enrolled in medical schools, 59 were specializing in the physical and natural sciences, and about an equal number in the social sciences. In the opposite direction, relatively few American students are enrolled in Brazilian universities, though New York University has made a beginning in a real student-exchange program with the University of Bahia.

CHAPTER 11

The Clinic

TO PERO DE MAGALHAES GANDARO, WHO WROTE OF BRAZIL nearly 400 years ago, as to all laymen of his time, health was largely a matter of climate, that is, the air was either salubrious or pestilential. He had much to say about the air of Brazil. "The Province," he wrote, "is the most suitable of all the provinces of America for mankind, because usually the air is good." If the country was so "healthful and free from sickness," it was because of the winds that blew off the sea for most of the time. "The air is so pure and well-tempered," he continued, that it "restores and prolongs human life." However, he reported that "the land breeze is very dangerous and unwholesome, and if it happens to continue for many days many people die." Of the enervating influences of the tropical environment on the newcomer from Europe, he commented as follows: "The land itself is slack and lazy; there men find themselves a little weak and their strength less than they had in the Kingdom [Portugal], on account of the heat, and the food that is used there." But after they are acclimated—and accustomed to the native diet—"they are as lusty and strong as if this land were their native country."

So much for health conditions in Brazil in the early 1570's, when most of the settlers still lived in the zone of the trade winds along the coast of Pernambuco and Bahia. If Peter Magellan should return today, he might have a less sanguine story to tell. The same winds still blow, but 65,000,000 people live in the country—and too many of them are ill. A few years ago, Hernane Tavares de Sá wrote a book about his fellow-Brazilians, and in a chapter entitled "Thirty Million Economic Zeros" he quoted Dr. Miguel Pereira, a distinguished physician of the early 1900's, as saying that Brazil was then "a vast hospital."

If modern Brazil has serious problems of public health, it is not natural conditions of climate and physiography that are to blame. Louisiana is hotter and a larger proportion of its area is swampland. *With reasonable precautions,* men can live as long in the tropics as elsewhere, but the penalties for heedlessness are greater. Two of the best-known figures of the Amazon Valley in this century, J. G. Araujo of Manaus and Nicolas Suarez of the Bolivian Beni, lived to over 90 years of age.

The roots of the problem are in economics and custom rather than in heat and humidity, though both may be contributory factors. The "precautions" are restricted by ignorance and poverty. And most of the rural population are ignorant and poor. When they are ill, they "let nature take its course," which may only lead to another grave with a wooden cross for marker. Or perhaps they call on the nearest *curandeiro* for his ministrations, that are liable to be a mixture of folklore medication and magic. For, until the "health posts" of the Saude Pública began to come to their rescue, there were no professional physicians in their part of Brazil. Moreover, the mobility of the roving *caboclos* provides the germs with long-distance transportation for spreading infection over the country. Few of them have any knowledge of sepsis or of the part that insects play as vectors of disease. The governor of a Brazilian state once contended to me that mosquitoes had nothing to do with malaria, but that it was caused by the night air. The *caboclo* lives in a tropical world without refrigeration or other facilities for preserving food or for filtration of the water he drinks from open streams or pools. He dwells in a wattled hut that admits and harbors every kind of noxious bug. He walks barefoot in the polluted soil about his house.

When the *caboclo*'s child is weaned there is no more milk for it. It is then put on the traditional diet of Brazilian country folk, which is a combination of *farinha de mandioca,* or manioc meal, black beans, and *xarque* or jerked beef. Not only is this diet monotonous and, for lack of any other flavoring than salt, unpalatable, but it is deficient in proteins, minerals, and vitamins. The *farinha* is produced from the poisonous manioc tubers by extracting the cyanide and roasting the residue. It looks like browned sawdust and is about as tasty. Its advantages are that it keeps well in a warm climate and is handy to carry on long trips. There is also a non-venomous variety of manioc, which is boiled like potatoes. The non-nutritious tripartite menu of meal, beans, and "jerky" is a major curse of Brazil, and is primarily accountable for the inability of the *caboclo* to resist the ills which assail his body. As their teeth bear witness, the country people eat large quantities of raw sugar that comes in hard brown chunks. Any local variation in the rural diet, whether from fruit, an egg, or a meal of fresh meat or fish, is a welcome windfall for the individual's health and vitality.

The Brazilian government has long been aware of the country's health problems and has made steadily increasing efforts to deal with them. Major responsibility is vested in the federal Ministry of Health, popularly known as the Saude Pública. Since the ability of the states to take care of their own sanitary needs is unequal and often inadequate, more and more of the burden has fallen on the federal agency and its specialized bureaus.

Among the multiple activities of the federal government is a large-scale project of physical education, which is designed to acquaint the public with the basic facts of living. Much of the program is centered in the schools, where the children are encouraged to take part in outdoor games and sports. Also, audio-visual media are used to familiarize adults with such matters as the danger of infection from mosquitoes, flies, and other insects, and with elementary rules for first-aid.

Above all, Brazil desperately needs more doctors. The medical profession has great prestige and is a lucrative career. Some Brazilian doctors, like Oswaldo Cruz and Carlos Chagas, have had an international reputation. But in 1956 there were only 29,232 registered physicians in all Brazil for a population of about 60,000,000. At that time the ratio of physicians to population was less than one-third that of the United States. Of the total, about 37 per cent were in the state capitals and in Rio de Janeiro, and over one of every five doctors was in Rio or São Paulo. There were only 131 doctors in the huge state of Amazonas, of whom nearly half practiced in Manaus. Another large northern state, Maranhão, had only 172 physicians, and its neighbor, Piauí, had only 120. But the state of São Paulo had 7,522 doctors, or more than a quarter of those in the entire country.

Since the graduates of the medical schools have no desire to locate in Pigui or Peixe, the gap of medical services in the back country has to be filled by the federal *postos de saude,* or "health posts." These are government clinics, established and maintained by the Special Public Health Service, better known by its initials as S.E.S.P. This beneficent service was initiated in 1942 by a co-operative agreement between the Saude Pública and the Office of the Co-ordinator of Inter-American Affairs, the wartime agency headed by Nelson Rockefeller. Later known as the Office of Inter-American Affairs and since merged into the International Co-operation Administration, it still maintains its association with the Brazilians in an advisory capacity. The only professional medical care available to millions of people is provided by the technicians, both men and women, of S.E.S.P. In certain remote areas, particularly in the Amazon Valley, their work is supplemented by the activities of missionary doctors, both Catholic and Protestant.

There are 23 medical schools in Brazil, of which 12 are private institutions. The largest schools are under government auspices and include, among others, those of the University of Brazil in Rio, and of São Paulo, Bahia, Recife, and Belo Horizonte. In 1955 over 10,000 students were enrolled at the beginning of the year, but only a few more than 1,500 completed the course in that year. As a rule, the professors in the medical schools are practicing physicians who lecture on a part-time basis. However, the medical school in Belo Horizonte has made an approach to a full-time faculty whereby the doctor is primarily a teacher but is permitted to carry on a private practice on the side as a secondary career. It has long been customary for many Brazilian medical students to go to Europe or the United States for postgraduate study. Some are dependent on their own resources, but others are aided by grants from the Rockefeller Foundation, from the Medical Division of the I.C.A., or from the State Department. In July, 1959, 12 such students returned to Belo Horizonte from a period of advanced study in the United States, the majority of them with American wives.

In 1956 only 1,749 graduate dentists were registered in Brazil. However, since 1,278 completed the course in the previous year, it would appear that a large proportion of those who graduate from the 24 dental schools of the country do not utilize their professional training. Meanwhile, at the beginning of the school year in 1958, a total of 2,378 students were enrolled in the dental departments of 12 universities and even more in as many private institutions.

Brazil's hospital tradition goes back to the sixteenth century when the Jesuits established the first sanatorium in the colony. For a long time the large Santa Casa de Misericordia has been a haven for the needy ailing in Rio. Another important element in the development of the nation's hospital system has been the

Portuguese Beneficent Society's chain of hospitals, the most modern of which is located in São Paulo. Other communities of foreign origin maintain hospitals of their own, as the Americans and British do in Rio de Janeiro. The large Samaritano Hospital in São Paulo was founded by Dr. Job Lane, a descendant of one of the post-Civil War immigrants from our southern states.

In 1953 there were 1,374 hospitals in Brazil, with a total of 171,000 beds. This represented a ratio of approximately three beds per 1,000 persons or about 325 inhabitants per bed. This compared with corresponding ratios in the United States of nearly 10 beds per 1,000 of the population or 101 persons for each hospital bed. Only about one-sixth of the Brazilian hospitals were public or governmental, though they had one-third of all the beds. Of the remainder, probably the majority consisted of independent clinics maintained by private physicians and surgeons. Fifty-five per cent of the total were general hospitals as against 74 per cent of all American hospitals. Of specialized institutions, the largest number were devoted to the treatment of nervous and mental diseases. In the category of miscellaneous hospitals were 31 state leprosaria with a total of nearly 23,000 beds. Three years later, in 1956, the official statistical service of the Brazilian government reported a total of 2,505 hospitals or an apparent increase of 82 per cent in the interim! Since there was no hospital building program of corresponding magnitude in the meantime and the increase in the number of beds was only 25 per cent, the figure for 1956 would seem to result largely from the inclusion of smaller clinics hitherto omitted from the census of public health facilities.

The quality of professional medical and surgical services provided by many of the Brazilian hospitals is very high, and, among them, the vast Hospital das Clinicas in São Paulo ranks with the best hospitals in any part of the world. The principal hospital problems are difficulties of internal administration and the shortage of nurses. Until quite recently the hospitals were very largely dependent on nuns as nurses, but as the expansion of the hospital system outgrew this dwindling source of supply, it became necessary to attract ever larger numbers of women from the laity into the nursing profession. The program encountered serious obstacles in the conservative mores of middle-class Brazilian families, from which most of the candidates for nursing positions might be expected to come. A great impetus was given to the program in the 1920's by the Rockefeller Foundation's establishment of a nursing school in Rio.

In spite of the advances made by official and private initiative, in 1956 there were only 9,346 registered nurses in Brazil, or at a ratio of less than four for each hospital in the country. About 40 per cent of these were in capital cities, including Rio. In the period from 1917 to 1955 only 4,052 nurses were graduated from training schools, so that many of the registered nurses must have obtained their credentials on the basis of experience. Practical nurses are being employed in increasing numbers to meet the deficit in hospital staffs. In 1956 nearly 20,000 women were licensed by government health agencies to provide nursing service wherever needed. Similarly, there is still a dearth of laboratory technicians and X-ray operators. In 1956 only 1,123 of the former and 856 of the latter were registered by government authorities as professionally qualified.

The pharmacy fills an unusual place in the Brazilian health picture, particularly in provincial towns and villages where there is a shortage, often complete, of professional medical services. It is usually well stocked with basic medicinals and is frequently the best-appearing place of business in the community. It is not a Bagdad bazaar, but an "ethical" institution that restricts its field to the service of the curative arts.

In default of a graduate doctor, the pharmacist probably fills the role in the village and its rural environs. Garbed in a white robe and addressed as *"doutor,"* he mixes and dispenses remedies, prescribes treatments, gives injections, performs minor operations in first-aid cases, and on the side may serve as dentist and optician. Though most of his therapeutic knowledge may be pragmatic, he serves for the time being a useful purpose in the changing structure of public health. To dilute his own deficiencies and the whims and vagaries of his customers, he usually has a deep fund of common sense and human understanding. If his clientele have a passion for panaceas or a naïve faith in "injections" for their own sake, he adjusts his techniques of treatment accordingly. From living long among them, he can generally distinguish the hypochondriacs and psychosomatics from those whose ailments are corporeal. It is to his credit that he would rather have his "patients" survive than otherwise, and he is certainly preferable to the rank and file of *curandeiros,* who may offer the only competition to his ministrations pending the arrival of the government "health post."

Twenty-one institutions offer pharmaceutical courses in Brazil. In 1954, 547 students completed the course of study and were awarded diplomas. In 1955, 1,653 students enrolled in the pharmacy schools, but in the following year only 527 graduate pharmacists were registered with the federal Ministry of Health.

There is a large domestic production of proprietary medicines and of the standard antibiotics. The Oswaldo Cruz Institute of Manguinhos near Rio is a dependency of the Ministry of Health, devoted to medical and biological research and to the preparation of certain serums for national distribution, as the Butantán Institute at São Paulo is a center of anti-ophidian research and serum production. In the matter of pharmacopoeia, the flora of Brazil would appear to have further possibilities. The Tupí-Guaraní peoples developed by trial-and-error an extensive system of therapy, which greatly impressed the Jesuits. Among several medicinal plants from Brazil which have been accepted by modern pharmacology is ipecac. The *curandeiros* or "curers," who are modern heirs of the Tupí "medicine men," draw on other native plants for their own *materia médica.* This marginal —and scientifically disreputable—area of medicine may eventually provide additional contributions for the war against disease.

Between the two periods, 1939–41 and 1949–51, life-expectancy in the larger Brazilian cities increased by eight to 10 years. In the latter period the rates ranged from 36.2 years for Natal and 37.7 years for Recife to 51.5 years for Porto Alegre, 52.8 years for Rio, and 57.6 years for São Paulo. The corresponding rate for the same period in the United States was a little over 68 years. Continued improvement in health conditions in the cities would presumably indicate a further rise in life-expectancy since 1951, though probably not at the same rate as in the previous decade. However, these gratifying figures are by no means an index to conditions in the country at large. Particularly in the rural areas, the infant mortality rate continues to be abnormally high and is reflected in a diminished life-expectancy for the population in general.

For the first four years, the principal cause of death is gastro-enteritis, and for the large age group of 10–40 years it is respiratory tuberculosis. Grippe and pneumonia are also important causes of death among young children. In the 20–29 years age group, accidents rank second as a cause of death in Recife and Rio and the neighboring city of Niteroi. Suicide holds third place in Porto Alegre and ranks fourth among causes of death in Belo Horizonte for persons of the same age level. For the middle-aged segment of the population, from 40 to 49 years, syphilis ranks third in Recife, fourth in Belo Horizonte, and fifth in Porto Alegre. Cancer and heart disease also take a considerable toll of lives in this age group, and after 60 they are the main causes of death. In the past half century, yellow fever and bubonic plague, or *peste,* have practically ceased to be a health problem in Brazil, and deaths from smallpox are very rare. Though still widely prevalent in certain areas of the country, the mortality from malaria has been reduced to insignificant proportions. Contaminated food and water are still major health problems. For example, of 2,421 municipal districts in 1956, only 1,148 or less than half had a central water supply. Drinking water is still a hazard in much of Brazil. Lack of effective inspection of food supplies in public markets or in low-class eating places, as well as ignorance of personal hygiene among the poor and more backward part of the population all contribute to the high incidence of dysentery, typhoid, and other gastro-intestinal diseases.

The radical changes in the incidence of disease in the larger cities in this century is exemplified by a comparison of the causes of death in Rio between the five-year period 1900–1904, when its population was about 700,000, and the year 1957, when it had nearly 3,000,000 inhabitants:

	Bubonic Plague	Yellow Fever	Smallpox	Malaria	Diphtheria	Typhoid	Dysentery	Tuberculosis
1900–1904	1,344	2,305	7,785	4,875	193	619	383	14,609
1940–1949	—	—	19	941	736	599	1,536	30,062
1957	—	—	4	6	77	134	107	2,742

On the general basis of conditions prevailing in 1950, a comparison of causes of death in Rio and São Paulo with those in the United States shows the following diseases were responsible for a higher mortality rate in the United States than in the two Brazilian cities: polio, diabetes, arteriosclerosis, degenerative heart disease, and cardiac disorders resulting from hypertension. In deaths from accidents, poisonings, and violence, the record of the United States was slightly higher than for Rio and about 17 per cent more than that of São Paulo.

The excessive rate of infant mortality is largely the result of gastro-enteritis, which results from improper feeding and a general disregard of the rules of hygiene. It is associated with the poverty and ignorance of much of the rural population and of those who live in urban slums, as in the *mucambos* at Recife and the *favellas* at Rio. More specifically, it is related to the lack of a pure milk supply within reach of the population affected. For the period around 1950, the yearly rate of deaths of children under one year of age per 100,000 ranged from 3,274 at Rio to 4,755 at Belém and 8,542 at Recife. At that time, over half the babies born in the Afogados district at Recife died in their first year. The corresponding rate in the United States was then about 105 deaths per 100,000 persons, or only about 2 per cent of the average of six large Brazilian cities.

For a long time malaria was Brazil's principal sanitary problem. Natural conditions in much of the country were highly favorable to the propagation of the anopheles mosquito, and measures of defense were limited to the use of quinine and the drainage of foci of infection—pools of stagnant water and swamps like the extensive Baixada Fluminense or tidal flats near Rio, in itself a Herculean undertaking. The normal incidence of morbidity from malaria was between 6,000,000 and 10,000,000 cases. Of these a large proportion reached a state of malignancy and the mortality rate was high. The economic loss which resulted from the chronic devitalizing of so much of the population was a severe burden on the country.

By 1959 the Ministry of Health announced that there were only about 200,000 cases of malaria in Brazil and that the extermination of the disease was only a matter of a relatively short time. This phenomenal record has largely been the work of the National Malaria Service of the Ministry of Health, aided by the Rockefeller Foundation and the Medical Division of the Point 4 mission in Brazil. Among the measures taken in the war against malaria has been the spraying of millions of homes with DDT. The latest device to be used has been a chloride-quinine salt which, mixed with the food, serves as a deterrent against infection by the mosquito. Large quantities have been distributed to the inhabitants of the Amazon Valley, where ordinary procedures are ineffectual.

The most dramatic incident in the history of malaria in Brazil was the appearance of the Aedes Gambiae mosquito in the north. This mosquito was introduced into Natal, the capital of Rio Grande do Norte, in 1930 by a French destroyer which carried the "airmail" between Dakar in Africa and Natal. The Gambiae produces a particularly lethal variety of malaria, and within a few months the epidemic caused the death of thousands of persons. It was only by a relentless campaign of extermination, carried on by the Rockefeller Foundation in co-operation with the Brazilian health authorities, that this dangerous mosquito was wiped out. If it had reached the forest zone of Brazil, no measures could have extinguished it. The Aedes Gambiae reappeared in 1938 and was not completely suppressed until two years later.

Epidemics of yellow fever broke out in the ports of Brazil over 100 years ago and continued their periodic ravages until the identification of the Aedes Egypti or Stegomya mosquito as the carrier of the disease in 1900. When Henry Bates was in Belém in 1850 an outbreak killed 4 per cent of the population. The authorities and public were helpless against its attack, but the city government had cannon fired at the street corners to purify the air! Sometimes the crews of ships in the harbors of Rio and Santos were stricken to a man. The visitations of the pestilence did not cease until the war against the Stegomya mosquito began in this century. The leader of the campaign was Dr. Oswaldo Cruz, who ranks with Gorgas in Panama among the great sanitary engineers. With the support of the government he cleaned up every breeding place of mosquitoes in Rio. His *matamosquitos* or mosquito-killers, armed with a ladder and kerosene can and dressed in a distinctive uniform, were authorized to enter any home or other building in the city in their search for receptacles that might hold standing water where the larvae or mosquitoes could breed. The fact that the Stegomya is a house mosquito made it easier to control, once its relation to yellow fever was demonstrated. However, in later years, another mosquito, of outdoor habits, has appeared as a vector of yellow fever. It is a forest insect, frequently breeding in the small pools of water in the tops of palm trees and therefore difficult to combat. Certain species of monkeys are chronically infected with yellow fever and provide endemic foci of the disease in some jungle areas. There have been occasional isolated outbreaks of this sylvan form of the disease from the Amazon rain forest north by the Colombian Llanos into Central America. The principal reliance in combatting the vestiges of yellow fever in Brazil is now vaccination. Since 1937 over 21,000,000 persons have been immunized by this method.

Leprosy is still a subject of concern to health authorities in Brazil, though the head of the National Leprosy Service declared in 1959 that it is no longer a serious problem. The government estimates the total number of lepers in the country at around 70,000. The majority of these are in the Amazon Valley, very few are in the Northeast, and a sizable contingent of them are in the southern states. They are isolated in a number of farm colonies, where they are given treatment and prepared for possible rehabilitation and reintegration into society. Although the method of treatment is slow and still of doubtful effectiveness, a certain number of reclaimed lepers are released each year as no longer capable of transmitting the contagion to others.

Three debilitating diseases constitute grave health problems in Brazil. The most serious of these are cistosomiasis and Chagas' disease. The other is ankylostomiasis or hookworm disease. While these three ailments are not directly a major source of fatalities, by weakening the organism they are important contributory factors in the incidence of other secondary maladies. Above all, they are devitalizing elements that rob millions of their energies and therefore comprise a prime economic liability for a country that needs all its human potential.

Cistosomiasis is a liver fluke disease, caused by a flat parasitical worm that enters the body through the skin and then settles in the liver. The parasite was evidently introduced into northeastern Brazil by African slaves in colonial times. In the meantime, it lay dormant in that part of the country until it found a suitable host in which it could breed. The intermediate host was a certain variety of snail which is common in the muddy bottoms of Brazilian rivers. Utilizing that medium of development, it has spread in the past few decades from the Northeast into Minas Gerais and, more recently, into the streams of São Paulo, due to the migration of infected persons into those areas. The Ministry of Health has recently estimated at over 4,000,000 the number of persons now afflicted. The disease is easily contracted by contact in water with the worms that issue from the snails. Women who wash their clothes in infected streams or persons who wade or swim or even drag a hand in the water, are liable to contamination.

The custom of drinking water from open streams is another factor in the widespread transmission of the disease. The Brazilian government has instituted a special campaign to deal with the problem, but is handicapped by a lack of therapeutic knowledge and the difficulties inherent in the habits of the population affected. Medical measures for the treatment of those already infected by the parasite are still of doubtful efficacy, so that for the present the principal reliance is being placed on the extermination of the snails by means of chemicals that include lime, copper sulphate, and pentachlorophenate of sodium. Entomologists have recently expressed confidence in a plan for destroying the snails by means of the larvae of marsh flies. Meanwhile, as part of its program, the Brazilian government has increased its plans for providing a safe public water supply for localities where the disease is particularly rampant or threatening.

Chagas' disease derives its name from Dr. Carlos Chagas, the distinguished Brazilian scientist who first analyzed the malady and traced its causative cycle. It is popularly known in Brazil as "*barbeiro*" from the blood-sucking louse-like bug that is the carrier of the disease and whose bite irritates the face and throat like a barber's dull razor. The disease is prevalent in several South American countries and has been found in other parts of the world, so that its control is an international problem. Children are particularly susceptible to its attack, and after an incubating period of several days, they suffer from prolonged high fever. Unless checked in its initial period, it ultimately causes anemia and hypertrophy of the liver and spleen, and a predisposition to chronic heart trouble. The disease is caused by a parasite of the trypanosome family, which uses the armadillo as incubating host or reservoir, and enters the human body by means of the "*barbeiro*" bug.

The favorite habitat of this insect is the cracks in the mud-and-wattle walls of the Brazilian countryman's hut, from which it emerges at night to bite the occupants. Its living habits prevent the effective use of DDT and other insecticide sprays, and it is only by sealing the chinks in the homemade walls which provide a hiding place for the bug that its ravages can be stopped. A homemade answer to the dilemma was found by filling the cracks in the huts with a crude plaster that has a dried cow-dung base. This concoction is reported to have been applied with complete success in a pilot project involving several thousand homes that were previously infested with the nefarious insect.

The hookworm has been a factor in the backwardness of depressed areas in Brazil. This parasite, which flourishes in polluted ground, burrows into the body through the skin of the feet and lodges in the small intestines. This process is facilitated by the popular habit of going barefoot and by the lack of the most elementary sanitary facilities about rural homes. The symptoms of the disease are anemia and general weakness and fever, with abdominal pain. The individual becomes apathetic and listless, and where the infection is widespread a community has a general appearance of lethargy and spiritlessness. In the 1920's a joint campaign by the Rockefeller Foundation and Brazilian health authorities was directed at the eradication of hookworm disease in large areas of the interior. Beyond medication for those already afflicted, the measures employed were preventive and involved a crusade for the wearing of shoes and the large-scale construction of outhouses. The campaign resulted in the eventual rehabilitation of many communities and the reactivation of sluggish multitudes.

CHAPTER 12

The Farm

IN SPITE OF THE GREAT ADVANCES MADE BY MANUFACTURING industry, about two-thirds of all Brazilians still live in the country and make a living from the land. It is seldom a good living, but it has improved in recent years. At least the production of foodstuffs has kept well ahead of population growth, and while population increased by over 26 per cent between 1948 and 1958, agricultural output was more than half again as large. Not only must 2.5 per cent more people be fed each year, but the income from agricultural exports has to pay for most of Brazil's imports and take care of the service on the foreign debt. Exports of agricultural products normally account for about 85 per cent of the total, and in 1957 coffee alone comprised over 60 per cent of all Brazilian exports. Other agricultural exports of importance are cacao, cotton, and sugar, though their value and volume vary considerably from year to year. Brazil is the largest source of United States agricultural imports, and in 1957 and 1958 this trade amounted to respectively $615,100,000 and $496,300,000. In both years coffee represented about 84 per cent of these totals, followed at a distance by cacao, castor beans, Brazil nuts, hides and skins, and sisal fiber. In the opposite direction, Brazilian purchases of agricultural products from the United States amounted to only $40,100,000 in 1958, of which three-fourths consisted of wheat and flour. Only a little more than 2 per cent of Brazil's 2,100,000,000 acres is under cultivation.

According to a study by the United States Department of Commerce, the production of the principal crops in Brazil in 1959 was as follows:

Crop	Units	Amount	Rank in World Production
Bananas	1,000,000 stems	240.1	1
Beans	1,000 100-lb. bags	26,147	1
Cacao	1,000,000 lbs.	410	2
Castor beans	1,000 short tons	165.0	1
Coffee	1,000,000 bags	36	1
Corn	1,000 bushels	275,000	3
Cotton	1,000 bales	1,650	4
Jute	1,000,000 lbs.	77.0	
Manioc	1,000 metric tons	16,000	1
Oranges	1,000,000 boxes	22.5	
Peanuts	1,000 short tons	420.0	
Pineapples	1,000 70-lb. boxes	6,214	
Potatoes: sweet	1,000 short tons	1,205	
Potatoes: white	1,000 short tons	1,100	
Rice	1,000,000 lbs.	9,080	1 outside Asia
Sisal	1,000,000 lbs.	330.0	
Soybeans	1,000 bushels	5,512	
Sugar	1,000 short tons	3,562	4
Tobacco	1,000,000 lbs.	273.5	5
Wheat	1,000 bushels	24,000	

In the same year the approximate numbers of livestock were as follows:

	THOUSAND HEAD	RANK IN WORLD
Cattle	72,000	5
Hogs	46,000	3
Horses	7,600	2
Mules	3,500	1
Sheep	22,000	

The natural conditions of climate, soil, and topography present many problems to agriculture in Brazil. There is a definite dry season of between four and six months in most parts of the country, during which crops cease to grow, and if the rains do not return at the normal time there may be heavy losses from drought. This condition is particularly prevalent in the vast region of the *seccas* in the Northeast, where a whole year—or even more—may pass without rain, with devastating effects on agriculture and on all life in the *sertão*. Occasionally, the same area may suffer from an excess of rain, with destructive floods, as occurred in 1959. Freezing is only a crop hazard in the highland country to the south of the Tropic of Capricorn, which crosses the state of São Paulo. However, the frost line has invaded the part of the state above the tropic at least once, with serious consequences to the coffee industry. Farmers seldom have to reckon with the chance of windstorms, and tropical hurricanes of the type found in the Caribbean are unknown.

When the Portuguese arrived in Brazil in the 1500's and took to farming for lack of any other way to make a living or fortune, they were lucky in finding some of the best soils in the country. It was only later that there began the myth of unlimited reserves of deep black soil in the backlands which has persisted to the present. As a matter of fact, there does not exist in all the expanse of Brazil a concentrated pool of fertility comparable to the

Argentine pampas or the American Midwest. No extensive surveys of the soil resources of the nation have been made. The total of good land is clearly considerable, but it consists of many pieces, some large and others small, narrow strips of river bottom, or isolated pockets among the hills, scattered over the broad face of Brazil. There is much less than there used to be. For Brazilians have despoiled their country of its greatest source of wealth by farming methods that mined the soil or exposed it to wholesale erosion by the rains. It has been overcropped for too long or the rain has leached the organic matter out of it. Or the topsoil is gone altogether and the land is dead beyond revival. Over the large area of the misnamed *campo cerrado,* or "closed lands" that are, in reality, *open* lands, extending across much of Mato Grosso into Goiás and cropping out in other parts of the union, the soil is hardpan. Even if it had any fertility in it, it could only be worked with dynamite and bulldozer. For beneath a thin layer of sand or clay there lies an impenetrable mass of *canga* or concrete-like crystalline rock. Nothing grows here but a coarse grass that contains little nourishment for the rachitic cattle that wander over it, and other scrub vegetation of no economic value whatever. The treeless *campos gerães* of the province of Rio Branco and other parts of the Amazonia are of the same general composition. For in the rain tropics the natural ground cover is forest.

Another basic obstacle to agricultural development in Brazil is the lay of the land. There are very few sizable tracts of even relatively level ground except in southern Mato Grosso and Rio Grande do Sul. São Paulo and Minas Gerais, the "key states" of the republic, are all "up-and-down-hill." And the enormous Amazonian plain is broken everywhere by humps and knolls and ridges. The Brazilians have always farmed the slopes of the land, often up to angles of 40 degrees or higher. The inevitable result is that, barring an unlikely resort to terracing or contour tillage, most of the topsoil disappears down the hillsides, eventually to find a permanent lodging in the bottom of the Atlantic Ocean.

The tilt of the terrain not only promotes erosion but in regions where irrigation may be desirable and otherwise practicable, it is not feasible because of a lack of uniformity in the ground level. This is an important consideration in the use of irrigation, both in the valley of the São Francisco and in the interior of states like Ceará and Rio Grande do Norte.

A rural pattern that was fixed in the early period of the colony long dominated the agricultural development of Brazil, and many of its elements have persisted into the present age. Whatever useful purpose this system may have served in its beginnings, when immense areas of virgin land were to be had for the taking, it is now an anachronism and a deterrent to the sound economic growth of the nation. The bases of a pattern that became traditionally identified with Brazilian agriculture were *latifundia* or large land holdings, monoculture or a one-crop economy, high speculative profits, and a servile labor force, at first Indian and later Negro.

Land-owning, as in Spanish America, was—and still is—a mark of gentility. *Latifundia* was associated with social prestige and political power, and provided a fit setting for the patriarchal family system that was to remain the model for Brazilian society until the present. The estates of some of the early landowners were veritable empires, within which their will was the only law, and the proprietors of the sugar mill and the "big house" were the great lords of the land, as their successors, the "colonels" of the north country and the coffee *fazendeiros* of São Paulo were to be after them.

When the Portuguese found the coastal lands of Pernambuco and Bahia well suited to the cultivation of sugar cane, they concentrated all their efforts on its production, save for an occasional minor venture in cotton. In a Europe where sugar was just ceasing to be a "drug" for the sick and becoming a staple food of the rich, there was suddenly opened a vast and lucrative market for the commodity. So until the competition of the West Indian plantations broke their monopoly and prices declined, the Brazilians felt security in their dependence on sugar. The only serious interruption to the sugar cycle was due to the Dutch occupation in the seventeenth century. Meanwhile, the profits had to be high to compensate for the risk of loss at sea from shipwreck or piracy, or from disorders in Europe attendant on the wars, or to meet the usurious interest rates of the Jews in Recife and Salvador who were their only source of credit.

As the favorable conditions of the industry declined and gold was discovered in the highlands of Minas, many of the sugar planters migrated with their slaves to the goldfields. However, except for the change of locale and product, the basic economic pattern remained much as it had functioned in the sugar lands of the Northeast. It was always an exploitative and "get rich quick" formula that was dependent on an unlimited supply of cheap and compliant labor.

For all his initial cost, the Negro slave met these requirements. He remained the mainstay of the rural labor force, though of ever-decreasing importance, until the emancipation of the remaining slaves at the end of the Empire. Then, as many of his kind drifted into the cities, the *caboclo* supplanted the former slave as the farm laborer in the republican era. A mixture of Portuguese with Indian or Negro, or a compound of all three, he had long been a familiar figure in the backlands, particularly on the big cattle *estancias* along the Rio São Francisco. Without pride of race or status, he was willing to accept the inferior position that was the traditional lot of the rural worker in a society which considered manual labor as associated with a subject people. No bondman or chattel slave, but with a certain independence of spirit of his own, he nevertheless bore the social stigma of servitude. Yet, though depreciated under the republic for his ignorance and shiftlessness, he was to become a sort of grass-roots symbol, and sometimes politicians would remark, "I am a *caboclo*," as American office-seekers once put an aura of glory about the log cabin. If he was ignorant, it was because there were no schools in his world. And if there had been, and his sons had learned to read and write and make numbers on a slate, he was afraid that they would leave him and go off to the cities to live. If he seemed shiftless, it was because he saw no reason to be otherwise. Beyond a natural urge for survival, he was practically wantless. He was trapped in a closed society that was the only one he knew. He was interested only in producing enough for his most elemental needs.

Somewhere his Indian ancestors had left a certain legacy of beliefs and habits in his being. One is his addiction to *farinha de mandioca,* the tasteless manioc meal that is the eternal *pièce de résistance* of his diet. Another is his nomadism. He is by nature a restless wanderer and, except for the *sertanejo* of the drought-stricken region of the Northeast, who generally has an urge to return to his inhospitable homeland, he feels little attachment to place. Ever since colonial times, government has been trying to stop his endless journeying and to locate him on the land. For his benefit there is even a "squatter's rights" clause in the Brazilian Constitution. Often with his family, he travels endless distances on foot, sleeping at night by the roadside and carrying his few belongings on his back, or perhaps in a pushcart or on a burro. Occasionally he may stop to put in a few days of work at some ranch along the way. The thousands of his sturdy breed who worked on the building of Brasilia did not travel to their destination by airplane. When I asked one of them from where he had come, he answered: "I am from Sergipe." And to my question of *how* he had come, he said, "On foot, like most of us." But nowadays, since the big north-and-south road has been opened, he may ride, standing in an open truck with a couple of dozen of his fellows, for 1,000 miles or more to Rio or São Paulo in search of a job.

It is the *caboclo* who is responsible for a system of agriculture that is a major evil of modern Brazil. On the move, somewhere in the back country he finds a piece of forest in which he decides that he would like to settle for a while. The land may be of the public domain or part of a large private property. If the latter, he makes the necessary arrangements with the owner, perhaps a certain number of days of work during the year. He then clears an acre or two of the woodland, and when the debris has dried he sets fire to it and burns it. Then he plants some corn and beans and manioc among the charred stumps. Meanwhile, he has built a hut with a frame of poles, a thatched roof, and mud-and-wattle walls. Since his house contains no glass or hardware or plumbing, it costs him nothing in terms of money. In time his crops ripen and he gathers them. As the land is new, the soil is very productive and his harvest is good. The next year the yield is much less, and if he plants the same patch of ground a third year the crop does not repay him for his labor or provide enough food for him and his family for another season. So he either clears an adjoining tract for another two years' stay or moves to another locality, where he starts all over again. The land that he has farmed so briefly is now fit for nothing but inferior pasturage. As the devastating process is repeated interminably by many thousands of *caboclos* over the face of Brazil, the land is impoverished. Responsible Brazilian leaders are the first to condemn this itinerant and predatory system of cut-and-burn agriculture. Typical of their views is the remark of a prominent economist who declared before the National Economic Council in 1959 that Brazilian farming methods are those used by the Tapuya and Tupí aborigines before the coming of the Portuguese. Writing of "the pattern of traditional agricultural practices," a publication of the Brazilian Embassy in Washington said that

> man is largely responsible for the erosion observed in many agricultural tracts in Brazil; the indiscriminate removal of forests and other wooded areas, along with poor agricultural techniques, specially the yearly burning of the land preparatory to cultivation, has led to removal of the top soil and consequent exhaustion of the arable land.

Immigrants—Italians, Germans, and others—have done much to improve agricultural practices in Brazil. They have made their influence felt by the results of the superior methods used on their own farms and by their work as farm laborers alongside native Brazilians on large fazendas in the southern states or in the new agricultural colonies where the two elements are deliberately interspersed. Since the foreigners avoid the northern part of the country with its lower living standards, the direct influence of their example is largely limited to São Paulo and other states in the south, where they have settled in large numbers. In the early period of European immigration many peasant farmers without capital were forced to descend for a time to the level of the *caboclo,* but the great majority of them have materially improved their status.

In the structure of the present-day agricultural system, the large property remains the characteristic unit of land tenure, though inroads have been made in its solidarity. Its roots are deep in Brazilian history, and though the number of small farms has increased greatly, new economic forces which have appeared in this century have not seriously affected its dominant position. The best accessible land had already been pre-empted, and a combination of circumstances has operated to maintain the status quo. One is the reluctance of the *fazendeiro* to dispose of his land, however extensive, unless forced by economic considerations. However, for lack of a law or custom of primogeniture, large properties have frequently been parceled by inheritance among the sons of the owner. When slavery was abolished, a good many of the large landowners in the north, who measured their estates in terms of the original *sesmarias* or "six Marys" of colonial times, found it unprofitable to continue the operation of their properties under the new conditions.

Another impediment to the breakup of the traditional system of landholding is the amount of ready cash required for the purchase of a fazenda, since real-estate sales "on time" are not the rule in rural Brazil. Also, because of the many ties, sentimental and familial, including the loyalties of dependents and retainers, and various long-term commitments associated with its posses-

Resources of
BRAZIL
EGEND
Cotton
Sugar
Bananas
Rice
Rye
Rope Fibers
Vegetable Oils
Cattle Hides
Sheep Wool
Coffee
Cocoa
Titanium
Tannin
Industrial Diamonds
Quartz Crystal
Zinc
Rubber
Gold
Coal
Mica
Beryllium
Iron
Chrome
KEY TO LAND AREAS
Intensive Agriculture
Grazing Lands
Lands Largely Forested
Agriculturally Unproductive

sion, the transfer of a large fazenda not only represents a complex economic and legal transaction, but is likely to involve the acquisition of a long-established social institution. Also, in some parts of the country titles of ownership may be a problem, and in default of fencing or other adequate marking, the boundaries of properties may not be clearly delimited.

The large coffee plantation or fazenda in the state of São Paulo is the prototype of its kind. It has generally been managed with more intelligence than its counterpart in the north, and has been less dependent on a *caboclo* labor force. Until the coffee zone moved on to new lands, the fazenda had a stronger economic base, and its owner has been more receptive to new ideas than, for example, the land-poor "colonel" in Maranhão or Piauí. The traditional Paulista *fazendeiro* is the member of a genuine aristocracy, whose only rivals for political power in the state have been the new industrialists and urban property owners of São Paulo. While the old fazendas, like Guatapará and São Martinho, had large and comfortable homes, the *fazendeiro* usually owned a town house on the Avenida Paulista in the city, where he and his family spent much of their time. In addition to much absentee landlordism, another deficiency of the system was a tendency to keep too much of the land fallow.

In 1950 there were 2,064,000 farms in Brazil. Of these, 85 per cent were less than 100 hectares or 247 acres in size, but the other 15 per cent accounted for 83 per cent of all the land in farms. Some 711,000 small farms had less than 10 hectares each. There were 1,611 properties of over 10,000 hectares or 24,700 acres, and 60 of at least 100,000 hectares or 247,000 acres. Over half of these extreme examples of latifundia were in Mato Grosso and the Acre Territory. The number of small independent farms has continued to grow, though the rate of acceleration is moderate. Government policies favor in principle the increase of small landowners, mainly as a device for fixing the nomadic population on the land, and also to slow down the movement of the landless into the cities. On the other hand, an influential element in the state of São Paulo defends the institution of the fazenda as the only unit capable of the large-scale mechanization of farming.

The answer to the question, and to many other agricultural problems in Brazil, depends on the availability of credit. Money is needed, not only for the purchase of land, but to buy tools and implements, seed and breeding stock, fertilizer and insecticides, to build houses and sheds and fences, and to install private water systems. The total requirements are beyond the capacity of government to provide. At present, most agricultural credit is supplied by the Bank of Brazil, but loans are generally limited to large landowners. The ordinary commercial banks keep out of the field and restrict their transactions to commercial business, industry, and the sounder type of building operation. A branch of the American International Association, a Rockefeller organization, has eased the situation somewhat. But there are no instrumentalities for financing the small farmer, who has no credit rating and seldom any assets to offer as security beyond his character and industry and whatever growing crops he may have in the field at the time. For lack of any regular banking facilities at his disposal, he is accustomed to receive cash advances on his crop from a middleman at rates of interest which probably leave him little net return from his harvest. Rates of bank interest are very high and loans for any purpose are for short terms. For example, 10- or 20-year mortgage loans are unheard of. Meanwhile, government and business leaders are greatly concerned over this basic problem, but have been daunted so far by the magnitude of the financial operation involved in any practicable solution short of a long-term self-liquidating program.

The "agrarian reform" that is a perennial source of discussion in Brazil concerns far more than questions of land tenure, methods of cultivation, and availability of credit. The problem reaches into all the complex ramifications of distribution and marketing, to the point where the product is loaded onto a steamer for export or is served on the table of "the ultimate consumer." In the first place, more rigid standards of quality grading are needed.

Such a system of grading has long been established in the coffee industry, but it is lacking in nearly all other branches of food production and distribution, so that there is little or no relation between quality and price. Also, from the farm of origin to the public market in the city, there is a dearth of facilities for preserving foodstuffs from the agents of spoilage, whether in the form of flies, unclean hands, the weather, or other causes. For example, meat is displayed in open stalls where it is exposed to swarms of flies and handled by prospective buyers. The itinerary of milk from the cow to the child's stomach is liable to be a sequence of progressive dilution and corruption. The official inspection of food for public distribution is generally inadequate and appears to ignore such precautions as refrigeration, screening, and proper storage facilities. The high rate of spoilage for all such perishable foodstuffs as vegetables, fruit, meat, and dairy products is a major item of loss in the accounts of Brazilian agriculture.

The local distribution of farm products involves not only the mechanics of transportation and sanitation, but at the middleman level, a predatory and unscrupulous group of wholesalers exacts a heavy tribute from both suppliers and consumers. The efficient provisioning of a large city like Rio, which is distant from its sources of supply, is difficult at the best, but is particularly susceptible to the sharp practices of those on whom the retailer is dependent for his supplies. Government price-fixing policies, designed to protect the interests of the consumer, are liable to be directed against the food processer rather than the middleman, as happened in 1959 with the seizure of stocks in meat-packing plants.

The primary objective of Brazilian agricultural policies is increased production. This can be attained either by improving methods of cultivation or by opening new areas to development or reclaiming areas ruined by the traditional techniques of farming. Since the nature and intensity of the basic problem differ from one part of the country to another, programs must vary accordingly. Plans that may serve the needs of backward Piauí have no place in progressive São Paulo or in Rio Grande do Sul. Government, federal and state, has created a maze of alphabetical agencies to deal with problems on a national or regional scale. Some of these are bureaus or dependencies of the Ministry of Agriculture and others are departments of state governments. The United States Operations Mission (Point 4) has the usual cooperative arrangements for providing technical assistance to the corresponding Brazilian entities. In the drought-ridden zone of the Northeast, a small mission from the World Agricultural Organization of the U.N., headed by an Arizona agronomist, is training young Brazilians under the aegis of the Bank of the Northeast to take over the task of reconstructing the agricultural economy of that region. An international commission of the UNESCO has recently completed a comprehensive survey of the Amazon Valley with the object of appraising its possibilities for agricultural and other lines of development. The geographical scope of its work corresponded with the jurisdictional field of one of the regional agencies of the Brazilian government. The series of long-established commodity "institutes" include specialized bodies for the promotion of the interests of the coffee, cacao, sugar and alcohol, and rice industries, among others. High-level statements of policy and recommendations for the improvement of agriculture include the *"metas"* or "targets" of President Kubitschek, the report of the Joint Brazil–United States Economic Development Commission, prepared in 1953, and the "plan of action" of Governor Carvalho Pinto of São Paulo.

Suggestions for improving methods of cultivation consider measures for raising productivity per man and per hectare while reducing production costs per unit in order to strengthen the country's competitive position in export markets and to reduce the cost to the domestic consumer. As a device for achieving these ends, much stress is laid on the prospects for mechanization. Subsistence farmers in Brazil still depend on the heavy hoe and a machete as standard equipment. In 1948 there were less than

100,000 plows and 6,000 tractors on the more than 2,000,000 Brazilian farms. Ten years later the number of tractors had risen to nearly 50,000, but by no means all of them were employed in farm work. Tractors are particularly useful in rice and wheat cultivation in the southern states, but their possibilities are definitely limited elsewhere by terrain, size of properties, and mechanical knowledge of potential operators. The greatest need is for more animal-drawn plows, cultivators, and harrows. The increasing manufacture of farm implements within the country should provide a marked impetus to their use by native farmers.

In the matter of soil conservation—and restoration—dependence must largely be on the increased use of chemical fertilizers, which would doubtless require a considerable extension of the existing fertilizer industry. Also, the price range would have to be kept within reach of the small farmer. However, the generality of coffee planters have ignored the use of fertilizers almost as completely as have the *caboclos,* as demonstrated by the impoverishment of the soil in the older coffee-producing areas of São Paulo. Other factors in reducing soil exhaustion and erosion are a greater use of crop rotation and contour plowing, filling eroded gullies, reforestation of the steeper slopes, and controlling the practice of burning over harvested fields.

The widespread destruction of forests for fuel and to provide clearings for cultivation has affected not only agriculture and the fuel supply, but such other phases of the economy as underground water resources and the flow of rivers, which influence navigation, irrigation, flood control, and the production of hydroelectric power. Because of deficiencies in coal and petroleum supplies, Brazil has been dependent to an inordinate degree on wood as a source of energy. Locomotives, river steamers, and stationary engines are stoked with firewood, and enormous quantities of wood are used for making charcoal, which is the staple cooking fuel in rural and village homes. Much charcoal has also been consumed by small furnaces in the production of pig iron. The progressive cutting off of forests in the interior has created serious fuel problems for the inhabitants of towns in those areas. Many years ago the Paulista Railway carried out a vast reforestation program in the state of São Paulo within the area served by its lines. Millions of eucalyptus trees were planted, but in the meantime no comparable efforts have been made by either government or private interests.

Other means of improving the position of agriculture in Brazil are the use of better seed and the increased diversification of products. Much has been done in the former connection through the introduction of hybrid corn on the initiative of the Rockefeller brothers' International Basic Economy Corporation. Superior varieties of wheat have also been introduced. Of new crops in this century, the most important have probably been the industrial fibers, jute and sisal. The large demand for jute for bagging is now met from domestic production, and sisal is a major raw material for cordage and other purposes. Among other crops introduced in recent years is pepper, grown in the Amazon Valley by Japanese farmers. Also, certain new varieties of fruits and vegetables have lately entered the domestic market.

Of areas increasingly opened to settlement and cultivation in the past decade, the best known are western Paraná and southern Mato Grosso, including the zone bordering on Paraguay. New highways that lead from Curitiba down the valley of the Iguaçú to the Paraná River and from Campo Grande in Mato Grosso to the Paraguayan frontier have facilitated this movement by providing outlets for the products of farms in those areas. It is also likely that the building of Brasilia as the federal capital and the opening of roads from São Paulo and Rio will result in a sizable migration into the rural areas of southern Goiás. As an inducement for settlement, the provisioning of Brasilia should offer a growing market for farm produce.

Coffee: To Americans, Brazil is, above all, the land of coffee. And those Americans who refer to coffee as "Java" are speaking a dead language. For all the islands of Indonesia now produce less than 4 per cent of Brazil's total coffee crop, and American imports of Indonesian coffee would supply our needs for about five hours out of the year. In 1959 nearly half the coffee we drank came from Brazil.

On its long travels from Mocha on the Arabian Gulf to Maringá on the outer edge of the new zone of production in Brazil, the coffee tree has made many stops. The coffee that enlivened the cities of Europe from the middle 1600's came from Arabia. The Dutch planted coffee in the East Indies before the end of the century, and in the early 1700's there were young plants in the botanical gardens at Paris. It was from here that coffee trees were transplanted to Cayenne, which was the origin of the first trees to be grown in Brazil. In 1727 Sergeant-Major Francisco de Melo Palheta, a young officer in the colonial service of Portugal, was sent on an official errand to Cayenne by the governor of Maranhão. Though the occasion of his mission was a border dispute between Brazil and French Guiana, Palheta carried secret instructions from his superior to bring back coffee cuttings and seeds for planting. These were not planted in São Paulo, but in the locality of Belém at the mouth of the Amazon, and it was only later that the tree spread into the southern part of the country. The first plants were set out in Rio about 1760, and in the next few decades there were large plantings in the neighborhood of Rio and in the near-by province of the same name. The lower valley of the Paraiba, which flows north through the hills behind Rio, early became the center of the coffee industry. From this nucleus, cultivation extended up into the highlands of Minas and southward up the valley into São Paulo, leaving behind it the barren hillsides that one still sees on a ride between Rio and São Paulo. The industry did not attain its full stature until it reached the vicinity of Campinas, deep in the red-earth country of São Paulo. In time the soil was exhausted around Campinas and the area turned to cotton and manufacturing as the coffee zone moved out into new lands. By 1910 what was to be the classical pattern of the industry was well fixed. By then it was the very cornerstone of the Brazilian economy and the source of the extraordinary position which São Paulo held among the states of the union.

The problems of the industry were an adequate labor supply, insect pests and frost, and overproduction. After the freeing of the slaves in 1888 there was a serious shortage of hands, which was ultimately met by the systematic immigration of large numbers of Italians, Slavs and Japanese, fostered by the government of São Paulo. Most serious of the natural plagues which attack the coffee plant is the so-called *broca do café,* which first appeared in the Campinas area in 1924. Heavy freezes have occurred several times in this century, notably in 1918 and in 1953, when the crop was cut by over 60 per cent. The new coffee zone in northwestern Paraná is particularly liable to the hazards of frost, and, in fact, the likelihood of freezing sets definite limits to the further expansion of coffee production in that direction.

Coffee is a capricious crop. The factors on which production depends are weather, the number of new trees that come into bearing in the year, and the stimulus or deterrent of prices. If prices are high, growers will strip every tree of its berries; if they are low, harvesting old stands of trees may not repay the cost. The industry formerly counted on the cycle of alternate large and small crops, on the theory that every other year the trees were "tired" and needed to rest up for a boom crop the next year. Thus the carryover from the large crop would take care of the deficit for the following year. However, this proved to be a fallible guide, as a three-year succession of large crops glutted the market. Moreover, there still remained an inexplicable margin of error that added to the normal speculative element in the industry, so that any formula for prediction was virtually valueless.

In the crop year 1870–71, Brazil produced 3,764,000 bags of 132 pounds each, or a little over half of world production. By the end of the century Brazilian output had risen to 11,373,000 bags, which represented more than three-fourths of the world total. In 1939–40, Brazil's ratio of the world product was about 64 per cent, but five years later it fell to less than 38 per cent. In 1956–57, when Brazil had a crop of only 18,000,000 bags, following the frosts of the previous winter, her share of world production was still about 40 per cent of the total of all producing countries. In 1958–59 a bumper crop of 31,000,000 bags only restored her temporarily to her position of 60 years earlier as supplier of half the world market.

The ups and downs of production had long since created a serious problem, not only for the growers and business in general, but for the federal and state governments, which had become dependent on the revenues from coffee for a large part of their expenditures. The effects of periodic shortages and surpluses are illustrated by the wide range in New York prices for Santos 4s, the standard of the trade, over a period of 50 years. The year's average for 1910 was 10 cents a pound. For the five years beginning in 1924, it was 22 cents. During the Depression, prices fell to disastrous lows, reaching a bottom of 7 cents as late as 1940. In 1950 the average spot price for Santos 4s had risen to 51 cents, and for 1953 it was 88 cents, reaching an all-time high of one dollar a pound in the first months of the following year. By 1958 the average had declined to about 48 cents, and at this writing the New York price is 36 cents a pound.

To relieve the desperate situation of all interests affected by overproduction, with its accompaniment of large unsellable surpluses and consequent low prices, the government has resorted to a series of radical expedients to control coffee prices. The best known of these is the device known as "valorization," whereby the government purchases and withdraws from the market a large part of the crop in order to create an artificial scarcity that would raise prices to a remunerative level. This program represented a major financial operation that strained the credit of the government and, moreover, aroused a good deal of controversy and consumer resistance in foreign markets. The coffee that was withdrawn from the open market was stored in state warehouses from which lots were sold on the rise of prices to figures that might appear to reimburse the government for its outlay. The balance was either destroyed by burning or by dumping it in the ocean, or it was utilized in the manufacture of plastics or fertilizers. Another measure adopted by government was a ban on further plantings, though the success of this device was qualified by difficulties of enforcement and also by the effects of the time lag of 10 or 12 years between planting and full production of the tree. In the meantime, the opening of a new coffee zone in southwestern São Paulo and particularly in the adjoining areas of Paraná has given a considerable impulse to increased production, with the result that Paraná has supplanted São Paulo as the first coffee state in Brazil. Other states, in order of production, are Minas Gerais, Espirito Santo, Goiás, and Bahia. There is also sizable production in the states of Rio de Janeiro and Pernambuco.

The major factors in overproduction are now the possibilities of the new Paraná zone and the competition of African coffee in world markets. The output of 11 districts in Africa has doubled in 10 years and now represents almost 20 per cent of world production or enough to upset all the calculations of Brazil and the other Latin American producers. This is mostly what is known to the coffee trade as *robusta,* an inferior grade, and excludes some 50,000 tons of superior coffee from Ethiopia, the original home of the plant.

One of the effects of Brazil's price-support policies has been to encourage more planting in the other Latin American countries, with the eventual result that increased production in those areas has only aggravated the general world depression in the industry. In 1957 an agreement was signed between Brazil and 14 other producing nations of Latin America in an effort to control prices by withholding a certain percentage of the crop from the market. Under this pact, Brazilian producers were to turn over 40 per cent of their next crop to the government. In Colombia, the second producer, the government received 15 per cent of the crop, and in other countries the government's share was less.

Since the pact encompassed only a part of the coffee world, this application of the principle of "valorization" to the hemispheric problem was bound to have only limited results on the price range in import markets. In 1959 the scope of the pact was extended to countries outside Latin America by means of the so-called International Coffee Agreement. However, its failure to include all important producing nations clearly limits its effectiveness for the purpose it was created, and even its promoters recognize it as little more than a makeshift solution of the basic problem of overproduction.

There is much responsible opinion in Brazil to the effect that little headway can be made in finding a long-term solution for the problem without an overhauling of the industry to reduce production costs, coupled with intensified efforts to increase consumption abroad. Except for a relatively few progressive *fazendeiros,* a cultivation routine has long been established that varies little from one area to another or from one generation to another. The emphasis has been on *extensive* methods of cultivation and maximum quantity, often with little relation to unit costs, and the good years have paid off so well on this rule that the bad ones are likely to be written off to the caprices of nature or the perversities of fate.

On the other hand, to solve its perennial problem Brazil would have the world drink more coffee, or stronger coffee. The per capita consumption of coffee varies widely among the peoples of Western Europe, and this inequality would appear to offer a promising field for Brazilian propaganda. However, it is difficult to change national beverage habits by outside persuasion, as the Pan-American Coffee Bureau has learned in the United States, where coffee drinking is already a deeply rooted habit. To Brazilians, the notion that coffee keeps people awake when they should be sleeping is an international affront, and the use of chicory is a form of gastronomic depravity. The popularity of the "coffee break" has been a welcome bonus for Brazil, partly counteracted by the end of the free refill at American lunch counters. Meanwhile, Brazilians consider American coffee brew too weak to be drinkable and devoutly hope that the American housewife will come to put an extra spoonful in the pot.

The United States has long been the mainstay of the Brazilian coffee industry and thus of Brazilian export trade. As early as 1818 coffee was shipped from Rio to New York and Boston. In 1957, when Brazil exported 8,640,000 bags to the United States, her second largest market, Western Germany, took only 717,000 bags. Exports to other countries in that year in order of their size were Sweden, Argentina, France, Britain, Finland, Denmark, Norway, and Italy. Each of these countries, half of which were Scandinavian, bought over 300,000 bags. In 1959, when the United States bought 46 per cent of its coffee needs from Brazil, the Soviet Union, scarcely a coffee-drinking nation, bought 69,000 bags or 58 per cent of all its coffee purchases for the year.

In that same year the United States acquired 13 per cent of all its coffee imports from Africa and Asia, and another 41 per cent of the total came from the "mild" coffee countries of Latin America, chiefly from Colombia. The amount of green coffee used for the processing of soluble coffee was 3,728,000 bags, a growing phase of the coffee business that concerns the Brazilians. The usual branded blend sold in the United States is a mixture of Brazilian coffee and Caribbean "milds" in varying proportions. In 1958 United States purchases from major sources of supply came, in order, from the following countries: Brazil, Colombia, Mexico, Guatemala, British East Africa, El Salvador, Angola, Congo, Peru, and Ethiopia.

Cacao: Cacao—cocoa, to the trade—which came from Aztec Mexico, is Brazil's third largest export. After African Ghana, it ranks second in world production, though its share of total world output is normally only about one-sixth. Its competitive position in the face of the possibilities of West Africa is, therefore, precarious, and its present rank can only be maintained by changes in cultivation methods which would improve the quality of the product and reduce costs. The industry, which is more than two centuries old, is concentrated in the southern part of the state of Bahia. In the humid belt that centers in the port of Ilheus, over 800,000 trees produced over 170,000 tons of cacao beans in 1958, most of it for the United States. There is much slipshod management of plantations, with special problems arising from itinerant and seasonal labor, insect pests, and antiquated processing methods. However, the Cacao Institute of Bahia, a government entity, is conducting field research whose findings, if applied by the conservative growers, might materially improve the prospects of the industry.

Sugar: Sugar cane, the classic crop of Brazil, was introduced into Bahia from Madeira in the early 1500's. Until the decline of the industry because of Antillean competition and the advent of the gold era in Minas, sugar was the basis of the colonial economy. After a long slump, the industry has regained much of its old momentum, and in the 20 years between 1938 and 1958 production almost trebled. With an output of well over 3,500,000 tons a year, Brazil is now in fourth place among sugar-producing nations, after Cuba, the Soviet Union, and the United States.

Nearly all of this large production is consumed within the country, and exports are relatively unimportant—only 4,000 metric tons in 1956 and 27,000 tons in 1957. In the latter year, the principal markets were a strange medley of countries: Spain, Czechoslovakia, and Pakistan. In the time of the colony, Pernambuco was the center of the industry, but most of the sugar is now produced in the south, chiefly in the state of São Paulo. Through the medium of the powerful Institute of Sugar and Alcohol, the government gives preferential treatment to the northern segment of the industry, much of which is antiquated. In fact, there are areas of sugar production in the hill country of Pernambuco that could have changed very little since the seventeenth century. Without government protection, most of this outmoded business would be recognized as uneconomical and the land diverted to other uses. The basic structure of the industry is probably the most bizarre outside India. There are over 66,000 "mills"! Of these, only 375 are classed as *usinas,* large mechanized operations which produce centrifugal sugar for the national market. The others are mostly little *engenhos* where the cane is crushed between wooden rollers and the juice boiled and crystallized over a bagasse fire. Motive power for the grinding is supplied either by a water wheel, by oxen walking round and round in a circle, or, in the more modern establishments, by a small stationary engine stoked with firewood. About half of these Lilliputian outfits are located in Minas Gerais, but examples of them may be seen along the highway that leads west out of Recife to Garanhúns in the uplands of Pernambuco. These primitive apparatuses turn out raw brown sugar known as *rapadura* for the local market. It is an important item in the subsistence diet of the rural population and is sold in chunks, from which pieces are broken off to sweeten coffee or to chew in the field or on the road. The total production of this class of sugar is immense and in some years may reach nearly 1,000,000 tons. Some of it is produced in every state and territory in the union.

By-products of the sugar industry provide valuable additions to the national income. They include molasses, rum, large quantities of alcohol, and bagasse for the manufacture of paper and cellulose products.

Tobacco: In the 1550's, Jean Nicot, French ambassador to Portugal, is said to have visited Bahia, then a new settlement, where he found the tobacco that he later presented to Catherine de Medici with a dissertation on the weed. Brazil is now one of the major tobacco-producing nations of the world. Only four other countries, headed by the United States and including the U.S.S.R. and two Asiatic countries, surpass it in the output of leaf tobacco. The annual yield runs at an average of a little over 140,000 tons, of which about 20 per cent is normally exported, largely to Germany, the Netherlands, and Spain. The domestic production of cigarettes is very large, and cigars of excellent quality are produced in Bahia. The largest producers among the states are Rio Grande do Sul, Bahia, Minas Gerais, and Santa

Catarina. Several different types of leaf are grown, including some of the world's strongest tobacco in Pará.

Corn: Among Brazilian cereals, corn is predominant. Only the United States and China exceed Brazil in its production. For several years the crop has been estimated at slightly under 300,-000,000 bushels a year, and total acreage at around 13,500,000. The type of cultivation is not the large-scale operation found in Illinois and Iowa, but corn is grown in myriads of small lots or patches that defy normal statistical procedures. Heaviest production is in Minas, São Paulo, Rio Grande do Sul, and Santa Catarina. Little sweet corn is raised, and the field corn is mostly used as stock feed, but especially for fattening hogs. Large quantities are also utilized as food for humans, and the eating of roasted ears of corn is one of the symbols of St. John's Eve. By-products of corn farming include starch, oil, glucose, and special processed foods.

Wheat: Urban Brazilians are a white-bread people, but Brazil has no pampas or Great Plains. The best wheat lands are also the best grazing lands; the cattle were there first. So, to satisfy the mounting bread hunger of her city dwellers Brazil has had to resort to a massive program of state intervention in wheat production. However, in spite of the success of the government's program so far, the spread between population growth and increased wheat supply is almost certain to widen.

The traditional locale of wheat farming in Brazil is the hill country of Paraná, Santa Catarina, and the northern part of Rio Grande do Sul. The farmers here were mostly of immigrant stock and their methods were biblical. The land was too rough for the use of machinery and the only harvesting tools were scythe and sickle and pitchfork. Man and wife worked the field, and any extension of acreage was dependent on the number of children able to heave a hoe or swing a sickle.

In those days most of the bread was made with flour imported from the United States or milled from Argentine wheat. American exports of flour to Brazil began early in the last century. In

1802 the U.S. ship *Belem,* out of Philadelphia, arrived at Bahia with a cargo of, among other goods, wheat flour and well-seasoned butter. Seven years later, at least six American ships called at Olinda and Recife with flour, codfish, cheese, hams, and more butter. In 1811 Joseph Bryan of New York set up an importing business at Recife that lasted until 1824. Along with soap, paper, sailcloth, and other commodities, he sold large quantities of flour. Travelers in the Amazon Valley in the first half of the century often wrote of finding American flour in remote towns. The flour trade, which reached as far south as Rio and São Paulo, later began to recede as mills were established in the south to grind wheat from Argentina and Uruguay. Then, after the First World War a special chain of circumstances made it imperative for Brazil to increase her wheat production. The urge for industrialization, which received its greatest impetus after World War II, required the importation of ever larger quantities of machinery, with a corresponding demand for foreign exchange. Also, when there was a deficit of raw materials for the new factories—including even rubber—these had to be imported. Since imported wheat was the largest consumer of foreign exchange until petroleum displaced it, the government decided to make the country as nearly self-sufficient as possible in the matter of wheat.

Another factor in the situation was the dietary revolution that was going on in Brazilian cities. With industrialization, incomes were rising and people were spending more money for food. Much of these increased earnings went into the purchase of more bread and other baked goods, including the pastries for which Brazilians have a special weakness. Also, during this period many thousands of rural workers moved into the cities to take jobs in factories or construction work. As they adjusted themselves to urban life, they tended to shift from a manioc meal diet to one that was based on bread. The net result of these developments, together with the normal 2.5 per cent annual growth in population, was an enormous increase in the demand for wheat flour.

It was this dilemma which the government faced when it undertook to draw up an elaborate plan to foment the greater production of wheat. The main features of the plan were a policy of price-fixing at levels designed to encourage prospective growers; liberal credits through the Bank of Brazil for the acquisition of machinery, seed, and other materials; the government purchase of foreign, chiefly Argentine, wheat, and its distribution to millers, but only after they had bought their specified quota of domestic wheat; and a special large-scale research program in the problems of wheat production.

Since the only area appropriate for the purposes of the campaign was the open rolling land of southern Rio Grande do Sul, emphasis was centered on that region. However, that part of the country had long been devoted to the raising of cattle and sheep, and acceptance of the new order of things required a major reversal of customary land use. Though the larger landowners were reluctant to embark on an agricultural program for which they were unprepared by past experience, many of them were willing to lease part of their holdings to others for the purpose. As a result, most of those who have actually produced the bulk of the wheat under the program were so-called "suitcase farmers," attracted by the high scale of prices offered by the government. The results have been statistically gratifying, but the renters have only been concerned with quick profits and have no interest in preserving the fertility of land which they expect ultimately to turn back to its owners. However, production increased 45 per cent in the three years between 1951 and 1953, and average production in recent years has about quadrupled since the decade of the 1940's. Due to weather conditions and other factors, the yield has not been steady, varying between 28,700,000 bushels for 1957, 20,000,000 bushels in 1958, and 24,000,000 bushels in 1959. While the "crash program" appears to have met its basic objectives for the time being, it has not succeeded in keeping up with increased demand, and as time goes on, the country will doubtless have to accept the inevitable and resign herself to continuing the importation of a large part of its wheat.

Rice: Brazil is the largest rice producer outside of Asia. In recent years the country has grown an average of about 4,500,000 tons a year, or more than half the rice of the entire western hemisphere. Yet until 1917 it imported rice.

Rice is eaten by all classes of the population and in steadily increasing quantity. In a Brazilian restaurant an order of meat is liable to be topped with a large heap of rice. With growing domestic consumption, there is little likelihood of it becoming an important export crop. However, contrary to the situation in the wheat industry, there is virtually no limit to the rice-producing capacity of the country, since both upland and paddy varieties can be grown. As usual, São Paulo ranks first in total yield, with Minas in second place and Rio Grande do Sul in third. The most modern methods of cultivation, including large-scale use of irrigation and machinery, are found in the latter state.

Cotton: Cotton has been grown in Brazil since very early times. In fact, as in other parts of the New World, an arboreal species of cotton existed prior to the coming of Europeans. Brazil is now the world's fourth largest producer, after the United States, India, and China. However, in spite of the magnitude of the industry, it has had an unsteady growth. For example, production was about the same in 1938 as in 1955, but in the three years 1957–59 it increased from 1,350,000 to 1,650,000 bales. The rising home market absorbs most of the crop, so that the margin remaining for export tends to decline.

While, in the long run, cotton is Brazil's number-two export, foreign sales are liable to be very irregular. Thus, exports during the five-year period 1954–58 varied by over 85 per cent. These fluctuations were partly due to increased needs of the national textile industry, which has pre-emption rights in the distribution of the domestic crop, to shifts in cotton acreage to other crops, and partly to the normal hazards of weather and insects.

The most dependable foreign markets for Brazilian cotton have been Japan, Germany, Great Britain, Italy, and the Netherlands, but in the highly competitive and unsettled situation prevailing in the world cotton market, the future of these markets is problematical.

Cotton is raised all over Brazil except in Rio Grande do Sul, and possibilities for expansion are limited only by market prospects. Again, the largest producer is São Paulo. There are two distinct cotton belts in the country, with different planting and harvesting seasons and quality of product. One, in the northeastern states, produces about one-third of the total output. Its cotton is characterized by cream-colored fiber and medium to long gauges, whereas Paulista cotton is generally of the short-staple variety.

Vegetables: The most important Brazilian vegetables are, in order of their production, manioc or mandioca, beans, and sweet potatoes. The official figure on the yield of manioc root in 1957 was over 15,000,000 tons, but the cultivation of manioc is so widely disseminated that any statistics as to its production can be little better than a distant guess. However, the output is obviously enormous, both of the poisonous (cyanide) variety used for the preparation of *farinha* or meal and the non-poisonous tubers, which are eaten boiled or used in the preparation of tapioca or for manioc flour which is mixed with wheat flour for bread-making.

Brazil is the center of the bean world. The 1,600,000-odd tons of *feijão preto* or black beans allows each Brazilian an annual ration of about 50 pounds. Yet, in 1959, Brazil ran out of beans, and, to her humiliation, was forced to import some from the United States. Beans are so much a *sine qua non* for Brazilian living that, when a Brazilian football team went on a triumphant tour of Europe, it took along with it a large stock of *feijão* as necessary for its training regime and general morale.

At least 27 countries, including Peru, the original home of the "Irish" potato, exceed Brazil's 1,000,000-ton output of white potatoes, which Brazilians call "English potatoes." However, Brazil raises still more sweet potatoes than white, both for human consumption and stock feed. As in Spanish America, there is a large production of onions, and in recent years the tomato crop has reached a high of 300,000 tons. Much of the new interest in the growing of garden vegetables is due to the initiative of Japanese and other immigrant farmers.

Fruits: The three most important fruits grown on a commercial scale in Brazil are bananas, oranges, and pineapples. No other nation on earth produces or eats so many bananas. With production at a level of around 240,000,000 stems or bunches a year, there are nearly four bunches for every Brazilian. The state of São Paulo alone is now producing at a rate of over 50,000,000 a year. The banana plant is as much a mark of the Brazilian landscape as is the coco palm of the long coastal zone, and outside nearly every home in rural Brazil there is the familiar patch of long green leaves. There are several varieties, including a small banana of excellent flavor. In comparison to the total product, exports are relatively small, only some 13,000,000 bunches in 1958, of which the bulk go to Argentina and the balance to Great Britain and Uruguay. In spite of the large market potential in Europe, the Brazilian industry is not organized at present to take the fullest advantage of this export potential. Cultivation methods are often haphazard, and handling and transportation practices and facilities are liable to be defective.

The growing of oranges, another old Brazilian crop, has shown marked progress in recent years, with present production at around 23,000,000 boxes and exports at about 3,000,000 boxes, mostly to England and the Benelux countries. However, much of this growth has been speculative, with large plantings hastily made and sometimes as hastily abandoned for another crop that appeared more promising at the moment. The citrus industry has great possibilities of expansion, both at home and abroad, but it needs to be stabilized and more efficiently organized. It is not enough for Brazil to be content with her present place as the world's second producer of citrus fruits, for no other country on earth holds such potentialities for expansion. Brazil could well be the orangery of the world.

There is a vast output of pineapples or *abacaxis,* but the fruit, which is of excellent quality, is mostly eaten fresh within the country. Present production runs at a level of around 220,000 tons a year. Prospects for export and for canning should be good.

Except for watermelons, wine grapes in Rio Grande do Sul, and strawberries in São Paulo, temperate-zone fruits are of little importance in Brazil. Most of the apples and pears sold are from Argentina, chiefly Delicious-variety apples sold from open boxes on city streets at prices that make them a luxury item for the average Brazilian.

However, there is a large array of tropical and semi-tropical fruits, many of which, like the proliferous mamão, better known in the United States as the papaya, are native to the country. Some fruits, like the mango, a poor man's fruit in Brazil but which often sells in the United States for 50 cents apiece, were introduced from Asia or Africa. Several others, like the avocado and the guava, are common to Latin American countries with a similar climate. The guava is widely used for the making of marmalade, which is served with cheese as a favorite Brazilian dessert. Sometimes the juice is served as a soft drink or fermented to make a country wine, as with the yellow *cajú* or cashew.

The Indian names of many of these native fruits are evidence of their indigenous origin. The Tupí, like the Greek, always had a name for them, as he did for every other manifestation of nature. So, among them are the *acaí,* the *bacurí,* the *biribí,* the *cambucá,* the *cupúaçú* of the Amazon country, the *guaximama,* the *jaboticaba* that is like a big blue grape, the *maracujá,* and the *pitanga.* They are not produced commercially and they do not enter into international trade, but they are part of the infinite variety of Brazil. Whether eaten out of hand or served as a dessert in simple homes, made into marmalade or jelly, or as the basis of a refreshing drink, they add something to the delights of living of millions of Brazilians and a much-needed variety to their diet.

Livestock: Almost as soon as they settled in Brazil the Portuguese began the breeding of cattle. Large ranches, or *estancias* that were little more than vast areas of open range in the lower valley of the São Francisco and the *sertão* to the north, provided a beef supply for the population along the coast. The half-Indian *caboclos,* who were the *vaqueiros* or cowboys of the region, came to dress themselves in leather clothing to protect themselves from the thorny growth of the *caatinga.* Thus there developed a "civilization of leather" in the backlands that was so distinct from the "civilization of sugar" in the coastal lands of Pernambuco and Bahia. The *sertão* is still cattle country, though its economy is much more diversified than it was in the 1600's.

Today there are well over 70,000,000 head of cattle in Brazil, more than in any other country except India and the United States. Moreover, no other nation has such possibilities for the raising of cattle, for the area that can be devoted to grazing is almost unlimited. This phenomenal growth has come about in spite of a multitude of problems that bedevil the industry: insect pests and resultant cattle disease, jaguars, rustling, lack of transportation facilities, often ill-conceived government regulation of the meat supply, scarcity of veterinarians, inferior breeding stock, a shortage of good forage crops and processed stock feeds, and antiquated methods in general. It is testimony to the potential of Brazil that, for all these handicaps, the cattle, like their owners, continue to increase at so fantastic a rate.

The cattle industry is no longer concentrated in the *sertão* of the Northeast but has spread into every state and territory of the union. Its present center is in the state of Minas, particularly in the so-called "Triángulo Mineiro" or triangle that centers on Barretos. Not only do many cattle originate in this area, but the *invernadas* of the Triángulo are one vast fattening station for cattle that are driven in from Mato Grosso and Goiás for later distribution to the packing houses and *matadouros* or slaughterhouses in the heavily populated zone between the Triángulo and the coast. Millions of head come out of Mato Grosso to the west, driven in the long *boiadas* that are as much a feature of the Brazilian frontier as were once the famous drives over the Chisholm Trail to the railheads in Kansas. The Noroeste railroad, which was built largely to serve the needs of this traffic, has deteriorated through bad management until it is completely inadequate for the task of moving the vast supplies of cattle to market. Many of the Mato Grosso herds are in the swampy area of the *Pantanaes* or flood plain of the upper Paraguay. There, close to the Bolivian border, was located the famous Descalvados ranch that was managed for many years by Murdo Mackenzie, an American from Ohio. Also, millions of cattle graze over the open *campos de vaccaría* or "cattle lands" that lie between the long wall of the *chapadão* or "rim" and the frontier of Paraguay.

It was only natural that Rio Grande do Sul, which is adjacent to the River Plate lands of Uruguay and Argentina, should become a major cattle area. The best cattle in Brazil now graze on its rolling plains, where they compete for the best lands with sheep, rice, and the new spread of the wheat industry. Its picturesque gauchos have long been noted for their skill in handling cattle and for their pride in their trade. However, São Paulo, which offers the largest market for meat in the country, has surpassed the border state to the south in the number of its cattle.

At the opposite extreme of Brazil, two areas in the Amazon Valley are the site of unique segments of the cattle industry. One is the large island of Marajó at the mouth of the river, which was described in Desmond Holdridge's book, *Feudal Island.* Here, in the periodically flooded plains, there lives a race of half-amphibious cattle which supply the large city of Belém with beef. Many of the cattle mire in the mud or are killed by jaguars or snakes, but the industry is so well established that it has managed to survive all of the natural obstacles of one of the most forbidding locales on earth. The other cattle zone is situated near the Venezuelan border in the *campos geraes* or "open lands" of the Territory of Rio Branco, where enough cattle are raised on inferior pasturage to provide meat for Manaus, several hundred miles to the south on the Rio Negro.

It was not until well along in this century that serious efforts were first made to improve the stock of cattle in Brazil. When packing houses were established by American and British firms in São Paulo and Rio Grande do Sul, they promoted the introduction of better breeds of beef cattle with good results. The traditional *caracú* variety, which ran to horns and legs, may have served well enough for the making of *xarque* or jerked beef, or even for canning, but it was clearly unsuited for the requirements of the packers and for the increasing demand for better beef from the growing market of the cities. Experiments with Herefords and Shorthorns generally proved unsuccessful, as the odds of adjustment in tropical areas were against these too-civilized animals, however well they might adapt themselves to living conditions in Rio Grande do Sul. Reliance early came to be placed on the *zebu* as more resistant to ticks and other forms of infestation, as generally more hardy, and as offering a much larger carcass than the native breeds. Therefore, the *zebu,* mixed with other varieties, tended to become the standard of the industry. Santa Gertrudis stock have since been imported from Texas, and a branch of the famous King Ranch has been established in Brazil with the special purpose of breeding this breed. Over the country there is still a wide range in the quality of cattle, but the general trend is toward a definite improvement of the herds in the principal commercial areas. Among assorted bovine species, I once saw a large and flourishing herd of carabao or water buffalo wallowing in the mud at Aramanduba on the lower Amazon, from where they supplied down-river markets with meat, milk, butter, and cheese.

The dairying branch of the industry has not kept pace with the raising of beef cattle. As a result of the malpractices of dairymen and distributors, milk has a bad name in Brazil. For children, once weaned, it is no longer considered important, and adults generally shun it as infantile and insidious. There is a considerable dairy industry in the vicinity of large cities like Rio, São Paulo, and Porto Alegre, and good milk is obtainable, though at a price beyond the reach of the average Brazilian. A long-established industry in southern Minas Gerais produces large quantities of cheese of a very good quality.

Hogs have long lived in Brazil and pork is the favorite meat of Brazilians. Hog-raising has had a boom in recent decades, and the number of animals has doubled since 1935 to a total of over 46,000,000. The country now ranks third in swine, after China and the United States, though the U.S.S.R. may have put it in fourth place by now. Hogs of colonial lineage are raised by *caboclos* in the back country. Resourceful, resolute, and robust, they usually forage for a living, but may have access to their owner's house. They stand high off the ground, and their mobility simplifies the problem of transport to market. In the area of commercial hog-raising there has been a marked improvement in breeds. Berkshires and Poland Chinas have been introduced in quantity and either mixed with the native varieties or bred separately on their own merits. Since lard has been increasingly replaced by vegetable cooking oils, the emphasis is strongly on meat production, and the packing houses now turn out large quantities of excellent hams and bacon. The business would appear to have good prospects provided improvement continues at the present rate, and exports of pork products should increase materially.

Brazil is not a major sheep country, being exceeded by at least 10 other nations, including the United Kingdom and Turkey. Most of the country is too warm for woolly animals and the bulk of Brazil's flocks of some 22,000,000 are therefore in Rio Grande do Sul. Only the Soviet Union has as many horses as Brazil and no country has so many mules. Only China and Mexico have more donkeys or burros. The small but sturdy Brazilian mule has performed invaluable service to farming and transport. It would be difficult to conceive of the backlands of Brazil without the mule trains. Anyone who knew the interior of the country before the era of motorized highways remembers the muffled sound of the pack trains, led by the bellwether mule, passing through the towns at night, to stop for rest in some woods by the road in the heat of the day.

CHAPTER 13

The Countinghouse

THE INDUSTRIAL REVOLUTION CAME LATE TO BRAZIL. BUT when it did, it came with a rush. The government of Portugal, in accordance with the mercantilist philosophy of the age, tolerated no manufacturing in the colony beyond the simplest household processing of cotton, leather, and wood for local needs. Industry fared little better during the imperial era between 1822 and 1889. The barons of the Empire, who set the tone and tempo of national life, were great landowners, and with few exceptions, like the farsighted Viscount Mauá, thought only in terms of agriculture. The economics of Brazil remained as colonial as ever; her traditional place in the world was as a supplier of raw materials to the industrialized nations of Europe and North America. The lords of the land were suspicious of factories as foreign contraptions that were incompatible with the life of Brazil. And when the change finally came under the republic, the pioneers of industry were to have such un-Lusitanian names as Matarazzo, Renner, Farquhar, Lundgren, Klabin, Marvin, and Wollman.

There were a few cracks in the wall, represented by some struggling cotton textile mills, a few small charcoal furnaces for making pig iron, *xarqueadas* or jerked-beef plants, their location marked by *urubús* wheeling overhead or perched in the trees. It was not an impressive industrial park.

With the coming of the republic there was much searching of hearts and taking of stock. The uncompensated liberation of the slaves had dealt a hard blow to the old landed aristocracy which had managed the country for so long, and the immediate future of agriculture was problematical. Many of the political leaders were new men without associations with the old regime, and immigrants from Europe were bringing in fresh ideas unrelated to the historic currents of Brazilian life and thought. Government had no economic policies that might guide the nation in the crucial period of change, and economists had not yet invented the "five-year-plan." Economics was then a matter of hit-or-miss pragmatism, and there was little foreign experience for a young nation to go by, so that the new forces which were on the loose in Brazil had to find their proper place by a process of trial-and-error. The first 20 years of the republic were, therefore, a time of much muddling and confusion. The prospects of the normal outlets for coffee and other products were already threatened by the growth of new colonial empires with their ties of reciprocal trade and closed markets, so that calculations of future income from that traditional source had to be discounted in advance. The international springs and channels of investment capital were still uncharted and the flow of money and credit between countries was as yet irregular. There was no World Bank or Export-Import Bank or International Development Fund to finance new projects and no International Monetary Fund to relieve stringencies of currency and exchange. Private bankers were accustomed to driving hard bargains with governments, and the movement of risk capital across borders, where the potential debtor lacked an established credit rating, was liable to have definite speculative and promotional undertones.

It would have been strange if the course of events in Brazil at this time were orthodox or regular. In a quantitative sense the investment climate appeared promising—an "underdeveloped" country with primary assets of vast natural resources and a fast-growing population. But if the climate seemed good for the long run, the weather was uncertain for the time being. The clouds on the horizon were as so many unanswered questions. The X-quantities in the formula included the adequacy of certain essential tangibles like the supply of energy, the capacity of the transportation system to move matériel and product, the competence and soundness of public administration, the readiness of the nation to accept and co-operate with what would virtually amount to the creation of a new economy, the availability of a labor force fitted for the massive task of industrialization, and the existence of the necessary pool of managerial and technical skills.

The weather has not entirely cleared to this day and some of the questions are still unanswered, but the nation has at least been long aware of them and has striven to solve them. It was not until this century was well under way that the economy got its bearings again and could move ahead at forced draft. For a while there was an orgy of speculation that defied all rules of good business sense and morality. Brazilians may have a natural flair and urge for speculation and quick returns, but this has seldom been so unrestrainedly orgiastic as it was during the last decade of the nineteenth century. Spectacular and hollow stock companies were organized for the covert purpose of profiting from the maneuvered rise of shares. The chance of dividends was only an incidental consideration in those wildcat schemes, most of which wound up in bankruptcy or prolonged stagnation and liquidation. Meanwhile, there was also much well-intentioned bungling and ill-concealed quackery, but by 1910 the country had recovered from its initial spree and was definitely well on its way to a sounder order of things.

Three events had a great deal to do with setting the patterns of economic progress in this century. One was the First World War, which had the effect of isolating Brazil for four years from its customary markets and sources of supply. If anything were needed to convince the nation of the urgency of industrialization, the huge vacuums in its international flow of goods created by the war would have provided the decisive argument. The country managed to assemble and install enough equipment so that her industrial output more than doubled during the four war years. Though some of this expansion was improvised and makeshift, it nevertheless served the purposes of the country by relieving shortages in many lines. Moreover, its beneficial effects continued after the war to become part of a larger and more definitive program.

The progress which was subsequently made was interrupted by the Depression of 1930, during which coffee exports and prices fell to a catastrophic level and imports of industrial machinery were even lower.

The beginnings of the Depression coincided with serious political disturbances that accompanied the armed revolt of the state of São Paulo against the federal government in 1932, and which continued in other forms during the long Vargas regime. Getulio Vargas took over the presidency in November of the same year and ruled for 15 years. By 1937 his role as dictator was firmly established, and with it a widespread distrust of his economic policies among businessmen, native and foreign, that hindered the course of national development. The momentum of previous years and the further impetus given to industrialization by the circumstances of World War II carried the economy through the years of uncertainty without major setbacks. The rate of economic growth would certainly have been much greater under a more moderate and constitutional government in which political passions and the individual caprices of an opportunistic ruler were absent. The return of Vargas to power in 1951 only renewed the anxieties and tensions of business until his regime was liquidated three years later by his suicide. However, his ghost continued to haunt the nation for a time, and, added to the radical administrative and constitutional changes that were his work, the economic picture was further clouded by the growth of Communism in the country and the rise of an aggressive and xenophobic nationalism that was a heritage of the Vargas era.

Brazil's industrial progress has been particularly rapid since 1955. In the 10 years, 1948–57, the rate of increase was nearly 200 per cent and was later accelerated. The government estimated that by 1957 manufacturing had come to account for about 23 per cent of the total national income of something over a trillion cruzeiros (Cr. 1,049,700,000,000). In this connection, while the reckoning of industrial output is feasible within limits of a reasonable margin of error, in view of the massive imponderables and incalculables in the Brazilian economy, any estimate of "gross national product" must be qualified to the point where it would have little value for economic evaluation.

A growth that was once haphazard and helter-skelter had become more orderly and systematic, so that there was less waste and lost motion and better co-ordination of the parts. An over-all program was presented in 1953 by the Joint Brazil–United States Development Commission, in which recommendations were made for improvements in nearly every part of the economy. Five years later another comprehensive working plan was provided by President Kubitschek's "program of *metas*" or goals, which was designed to spur high-speed development in the principal fields of power, petroleum, steel, chemicals, automobiles, and other branches of heavy or capital goods industry. Remarkable progress has been made in several of these lines, even at the risk of overstraining the financial solvency of the state. As examples of accomplishment, the production of steel and cement almost trebled in the decade 1948–57. On the other hand, consumer goods industries, like food processing and cotton textiles, were well established by 1950, and it was now largely a matter of modernizing plants and methods and extending the general scope of the business.

Of the principal elements in industrial development—raw materials, investment capital, labor supply, sources of energy, transportation, markets, and government administration—Brazil's position, actual and foreseeable, in the first category shows some important deficiencies. Some of these are problematical and dependent on the chance of further discoveries, as in the case of petroleum. A group of foreign scientists, most of whom were Americans, laid the foundations of geological research in Brazil, and while their work has been ably continued by men like Avelino Ignacio de Oliveira, the survey of the nation's mineral resources is still far from complete. Of the ferro-alloys and other industrial metals, there is a deficit of copper, lead, tin, and zinc. About 1,400 tons of tin is produced annually in the state of Rio and about 3,500 tons of lead in Paraná, but copper imports run at a rate of about 30,000 tons a year and domestic production is very small. There are ample supplies of manganese, and there may be enough chrome and nickel in the Tocantíns basin in northern Goiás, but transportation difficulties have prevented the working of the deposits. The electric lamp industry is using domestic tungsten for filaments. There is probably enough bauxite for any expansion of the aluminum industry, which is already well established. The paradoxical shortage of rubber can be overcome if the country is willing to employ on a larger scale the same methods that have given southeast Asia a dominant position in the field, but meanwhile there are plans for the production of synthetic rubber. There exists a plentiful supply of fibers, soft and hard, for a wide variety of textile and cordage manufacturing. The hard fibers include not only a large output of cultivated jute and sisal, but several native plants, such as *caroá, piaçava, guaxima* or *malva,* and *tucúm,* the fibers from which the best and strongest hammocks in the world are made. A similar situation prevails in the vegetable-oil industry, for which there is a large supply of ingredients, both for use in cooking and for lubricants. Cooking oils include babacú and other oils derived from palm nuts and peanuts, as well as cottonseed oil.

Brazil is the world's largest producer of castor beans or *ma-*

mona—over 200,000 tons a year. The plant is cultivated commercially and grows wild over much of the country. Trains developing a "hot box" may stop while the crew searches the countryside for beans to stuff about the axle. Large quantities of the castor beans are shipped to the United States and Germany, and in 1957, 48,000 tons of the oil were exported, mostly to the United States. Except possibly for wheat, where it is doubtful whether Brazil can economically produce enough for her needs, any present deficit in basic foodstuffs can be met by increased domestic production.

There are plenty of hides and skins, including goatskins, of which she is a major exporter, for any requirements of the Brazilian leather industry. Though she has the largest forested area of any country, Brazil has failed to utilize adequately her immense resources of wood, except for fuel! The varieties of trees vary in density from the light balsa to the hardest of timber woods. She has some of the finest cabinetwoods on earth and woods that, for construction beams and piling, possess the best qualities of reinforced concrete or steel. Yet the only tree which is systematically exploited on a commercial scale is the Paraná pine, or Araucaria, a medium-weight wood used for interior finishing and a variety of other purposes, even paper manufacturing. It is the country's third largest export, and in 1957 over 800,000 tons of the lumber were exported, mostly to Argentina.

Brazil has had a veritable revolution in sources of energy. The rapid changes in the use of fuels are illustrated by the following percentages for the years 1949 and 1956:

	1949	*1956*
Firewood	83.2	11
Coal	8.7	9
Petroleum	5.9	49
Hydroelectric	1.3	21
Others: Charcoal, Alcohol, Bagasse	0.9	10

The government estimates that in 1949 over 3,000,000,000 cubic feet of firewood were used for stoking the engines of locomotives, river steamers, thermal power plants and factories, and for other purposes. Other fuels used have included babacú nuts, sugar cane bagasse, and even surplus coffee. Large quantities of charcoal have long been consumed for household cooking, and during wartime gasoline shortages, smoky *gasogenios* or charcoal engines were installed in automobiles. In parts of northern Brazil, motorists were long required to mix a certain proportion of alcohol with gasoline for automobile fuel, and occasionally, after adjusting the carburetor, tanks were filled at roadside saloons in the back country for a spin across the *sertão*.

To meet the growing needs of industry the government has given high priority to hydroelectric power in its development plan. The goal fixed was 5,000,000 kilowatts by 1960 and 8,000,000 kilowatts by 1965. In 1958 total capacity was 3,924,000 kilowatts, of which 744,000 kilowatts were in thermal plants. This was double the installed capacity in 1952. The hydroelectric potential is estimated at about 25,000,000 kilowatts. Much of this is in remote and thinly settled parts of the country, like the Amazon Valley. This estimate also includes the vast reserves of the Iguacú falls and the Sete Quedas or Guayrá in the Paraná River, both of which, like Niagara, are international sites.

The first large electrical power enterprise was the Brazilian Traction, Light & Power Company, Ltd., a Canadian concern, which supplies Rio and São Paulo with electricity, and operates local transport utilities, like the famous street railway or "bonde" system of Rio. The company was organized in 1912. The total capacity of its plants is about 1,500,000 kilowatts. Its dual plant at Cubatão, at the bottom of the Serra da Mar between São Paulo and Santos, which was conceived by the genius of Asa Billings, an American engineer, is one of the most remarkable electrical installations in the world. Its source of power is derived from large reservoirs to the east of São Paulo, which were made by damming a number of streams that flow out of the high rain belt of the Serra and whose normal outlet was toward the west. The head of water accumulated in this way was then diverted backward through the hills and into the powerhouse 2,000 feet below. The second largest private concern in the country is the Companhía Auxiliar de Empresas Elétricas Brasileiras, which is a subsidiary of the American & Foreign Power Company. It operates a network of plants in nine states of the country, including the large Peixoto plant in Minas Gerais. Its installations in Rio Grande do Sul were expropriated by the state government in 1959. It has a $250,000,000 expansion program that is designed to double the total capacity of its plants by 1963.

Though most of the present hydroelectric development is located in Minas Gerais, the federal government has erected a large plant, with an ultimate capacity of 1,000,000 kilowatts, at the Paulo Affonso falls on the lower Rio São Francisco. The site of the plant is about 250 miles from the important coastal cities of Recife and Salvador, which it will serve, with other smaller cities in the Northeast.

At Tres Marias, on the upper reaches of the same river, another major hydroelectric project is under way. This multiple-purpose operation is designed, not only to furnish power at an ultimate rate of 520,000 kilowatts, but by means of its earthen dam to regulate the flow of water in the São Francisco and make possible large-scale irrigation of the lands along its course.

The largest of the new power complexes is represented by the gigantic Furnas plant under construction on the Rio Grande in Minas, which will have a capacity of over 1,000,000 kilowatts. This plant will serve the economic heart of Brazil, an area of nearly 400,000 square miles containing 25,000,000 people and about three-fourths of the nation's industrial production.

Petroleum is one of Brazil's several major problems. With new roads a-building and more planes flying, there is not enough oil to go around. The nation's biggest foreign bill is for petroleum products—over $250,000,000 in 1958. That same year her own wells produced about 19,000,000 barrels; the next year, 23,000,000.

It is a very new industry. In 1939 oil was found in the state of Bahia, which is still the center of the industry. The National Petroleum Council, responsible only to the president, was created the same year. As exploration proceeded and production slowly climbed, the issue of foreign participation in the industry was raised and debated for several years. The question did not come to a head until the second reign of Getulio Vargas, who adopted an ultra-nationalistic policy, expressed in his famous slogan, "*O petroleo é nosso!*"—"The oil is ours!" Government was to have full charge of exploration and production, and to serve these ends a special body known as Petrobras was created in 1953 and placed under the control of the National Petroleum Council. Though its stock is held jointly by government and private investors, the state is assured by the basic law of full authority over its policies and activities. Foreign geologists and other technicians have been employed on a contractual basis to serve until sufficient nationals have been trained to fill their places. The product of the Petrobras fields is sold to private companies, mostly American, who distribute it through their own outlets to consumers. Petrobras has three refineries and a fleet of tankers, and there are a couple of private refineries. A useful base has been provided by these refineries for petrochemical industries. To make up the deficit in the national supply, Petrobras imports crude oil from the Middle East and Venezuela. Imports of diesel oil, gasoline, and any other petroleum products come from Venezuela and Trinidad. Since the potential of the field in the Bahian Reconcavo is limited, an exploratory campaign is being conducted from the Amazon Valley to Rio Grande do Sul, but no new strikes have been made. Meanwhile, with output running at a level of over 70,000 barrels a day or 10 times that of 1955, the industry is satisfying about 30 per cent of domestic needs.

In respect to coal, Brazil is no Ruhr or Wales or Pennsylvania. Its highest output was about 2,300,000 tons, in 1955; the official goal for 1960 was only about 800,000 tons more, which represents about its normal rate of imports from the United States. However, Brazilian coal has too high an ash content and has to be pulverized, washed, and otherwise processed before it is suitable for use in the steel industry or in locomotives. The country will probably always have to import coal, and may have resigned itself to this fact. After all, imports of codfish and olive oil are a heavier drain on foreign exchange.

The largest coal field is located in Santa Catarina, where mining began on a commercial scale in 1916. The reserves in the principal seam are estimated at between 200,000,000 and 300,000,000 tons and for the entire country at around 1,700,000,000 tons. The second producing field is in Rio Grande do Sul and there is a small field in Paraná. The government hopes to give a further impetus to coal mining by encouraging the establishment of a small steel mill and a thermal electrical plant in the vicinity of the principal field in Santa Catarina.

Brazil has a huge labor pool. Rather, she has a vast reservoir of manpower. It is good human raw material and one of the major assets of the national economy. Much of it, particularly the large *caboclo* base of unskilled workers, is ill prepared for the demands of modern industry, but its ultimate potential is high. It is naturally hardy, but too often its strong body carries the germs of debilitating disease, and it needs at least enough education to enable it to count its weekly earnings, sign its name on the payroll, or read the signs and instructions on the factory walls. Also, in order to adjust itself to the strange environment of urban industry and life, it is forced to undergo a psychological revolution without undermining its own native virtues. All its traditional relationships are very personal and it finds it hard to accept the impersonal atmosphere of the modern corporation. To make the most of its new role, it has to develop a sense of ambition that is alien to its old wantlessness. And it has to be content to settle down and forget the deep urge for the road, for modern industry has no place for the drifter.

All this is strange to the new man from the back country, but the citified workers before him have long since accepted things as they are and the rhythm of the factory has become a part of their lives. Industrialization has brought with it a vast demand for mechanical skills, and for those who have them, the eventual rewards are considerable. The man of the *sertão* is ingenious in making the most of materials at hand, and the Brazilian worker in general has a natural affinity and aptitude for machines. For the ambitious and enterprising, even ancient barriers of class may yet fall down, to make way for "success stories" among the workers of Brazil.

Until the first presidency of Getulio Vargas, attempts at the organization of Brazilian labor were perfunctory. Then in 1943 Vargas, in order to strengthen his political power by the votes of the rising class of industrial workers, issued a comprehensive labor code. The provisions of the code, a translation of which has been published by the American Chamber of Commerce in Brazil, were generally too advanced for the stage of evolution of the Brazilian economy at that time. In some respects the effects of the provisions of the codes actually proved to be *contraproducente,* or contrary to their expressed purpose of serving the best interests of the laboring class. At the same time, an elaborate bureaucracy, administrative and judicial, was set up to enforce the terms of the code.

The general pattern of labor organization which was adopted tended to follow the model of Fascist Italy, with its system of state-controlled vertical federations and syndicates that were classified according to broad industrial lines. Even employers and the liberal professions were comprehended in a plan which embraced every segment of the economy. At the top of the pyramid was the federal Ministry of Labor, from which supreme authority radiated down through the successive levels of the complex hierarchy. At the same time, a political arm for the monolithic structure of labor was created by the establishment of the P.T.B. or Brazilian Labor Party. The head of the party is João Goulart, the political heir of Vargas, and popularly known as "Jango," who was vice president in the Kubitschek administration. The party largely serves as a medium for promoting the ambitions of politicians who are affiliated with it, some of whom are conservatives in search of a party, and its activities bear remarkably little relation to the class interests of organized labor. Many of the basic principles of the legislation of 1943 are contained in the federal Constitution of three years later, which is still the fundamental law of the republic.

The principal financial support of the seven federations is derived from a special tax or *imposto sindical,* which is levied on all salaried employees and wage earners at the rate of one day's pay per year. Employers are taxed according to the capital of their business. The proceeds are then distributed on a pro rata basis to the various federations and their component syndicates.

Every worker is required to carry a "labor card," which serves for identification and as a running record of his employment. One of the main features of the labor code is the provision that authorizes the fixing of a minimum wage, varying from region to region of the country. The terms of employment are regulated in great detail and include, among other items, the eight-hour working day, with payment for overtime, annual vacations with pay, the prohibition of work for children under 14 years, profit-sharing for employees, the right to strike, schedules of rest periods, safety regulations, the dispensing of medical care to workers, and special privileges for female workers, particularly for pregnant women and mothers with newborn babies.

One of the most controversial features of the code is that which concerns "security of employment." A worker who has been employed for more than a year and is later dismissed is entitled to "severance compensation" at the rate of a month's pay for each year employed. An employee who has worked for more than 10 years has permanent tenure and can only be dismissed thereafter for a "serious misdemeanor." Since the worker has the right of appeal to a labor tribunal, the odds are liable to be against the employer. The practical results of this provision are that employers are in the habit of dismissing employees before the end of the 10-year period, after which they rehire those whom they consider good employment risks, thereby eliminating the "dead wood" from their rolls.

Another provision which is open to varied interpretations is that which governs the dismissal of workers as the result of the closure of a business. In this case, barring the chance of *force majeure* as a reason for ceasing operations, an employer is obliged to compensate all "permanent" workers at double the regular dismissal rate, or two months' pay for each year of employment. The employer's dilemma, in this particular contingency, consists in his proof of *force majeure* or necessity. It is not enough to contend that the business is losing money. In the event of the transfer of ownership of an old corporation, like the St. John del Rey Gold Mining Company, which has a large body of "permanent" employees, any plans for overhauling the working force in the interest of greater efficiency are liable to entail a major cost factor in the transaction.

The domestic market for the output of industry in Brazil is dependent on buying power, knowledge of—and desire for—the particular product, and transportation facilities, which will be discussed later. The average standard of living is still low. It is impossible to express in terms of a hard currency the equivalent of a cruzeiro income. Thus to say that a sugar-cane worker in Pernambuco, who earns 40 cruzeiros a day, has a dollar pay of 22.4 cents, as he would have today, means only that he is practically outside the money economy. But there is no stability even in poverty. For, with flying inflation, there is a continuous race between pay and price, so that an employee, whether he receives 40 cruzeiros a day or 400, has no idea of what they will be worth a month hence. All he knows is that they will buy less in July than they did in June.

The low-class Brazilian spends an altogether disproportionate part of his small income on food, often to the point where he may have little left for anything else. At a higher level, rent may absorb too much of the individual's earnings. The small class at the top can buy anything, but there are not enough of them to make a market except for certain high-priced luxury goods like Cadillacs and console TV sets. A growing middle class in São Paulo and Rio has relatively high buying power and represents the hopes of the country for the expansion of her internal economy. Sometimes there is a veritable unsatisfied hunger for a product, as was demonstrated at the opening of the Sears Botafogo store in Rio, when a large stock of refrigerators was sold out on the first day. The craze for ball-point pens and small table radios and transistors is evidence of similar market potentials.

As a medium of commercial propaganda for acquainting the public with new consumer products, the effectiveness of newspaper or magazine advertising is restricted by the literacy rate, circulation figures, and geographical coverage. People who live outside the range of localized media eventually learn of a product by word-of-mouth or they may see it displayed in a store window.

The mechanics of retail trade are improving steadily, and merchandizing outlets everywhere are modernizing their appearance and methods. In the larger cities there are modern department stores, like those of Sears in Rio and São Paulo, Mesbla in Rio, and Mappin in São Paulo. The long-established chain of variety stores, known as Lojas Pernambucanas, which was founded by an American, are also an important element in retail merchandising. About 99 per cent of the merchandise sold by the Sears stores is of national origin, and the company has done much to stimulate local manufacturing to provide for its needs.

Manufactures form an insignificant share of Brazil's export trade, which is still almost as "colonial" in its content as it was two centuries ago. Beyond varying quantities of frozen and canned beef, and of pig iron, little of Brazil's industrial output is sold abroad. In 1957, 108,000 pairs of rubber galoshes, one of the oldest forms of Brazilian industry, were exported, chiefly to New York, where they have been well received.

Regardless of the chance of saturated internal markets, Brazil must, sooner or later, become a substantial exporter of finished goods. Once outside the comforting safety of her own tariff walls and labyrinthine exchange maze, and loose in a competitive field, she will have to depend on her ability to meet the international rivalries of price and quality. Foreign manufacturers who have established plants in Brazil are likely to use her as a base for supplying some of their regular markets, if conditions are favorable. In fact, "made in Brazil" sewing machines have already been exported to Chile, and Volkswagen of Brazil has made plans for shipping delivery trucks to the United States. The possibility of a Latin American "common market" might enhance the country's prospects in a new area of trade.

Many communities in Brazil are almost closed to the fruits of the nation's new industrialism by defective transportation. For example, remote interior towns, like Manaus in Amazonas, Teresina in Piauí, Montes Claros in Minas, and Cuiabá in Mato Grosso are, for all practical purposes, beyond the reach of much that is being produced in São Paulo. The alternative is long delays in delivery by primitive steamer, broken-down railroad, or rutted dirt road.

Brazil is presently engaged in renovating a collection of decrepit and piecemeal railroads, roads, and shipping lines that ill become the nation and scarcely serve its needs. Meanwhile, there is no national transportation system except in the air. Since foreigners are wont to judge a nation by its railroads, Brazilians are inclined to be sensitive about the image which their train service has left with strangers who have braved a ride on the São Luís Teresina, the Noroeste, or even the Central of Brazil. To the natives their railroads are likely to be a butt for jokes or the object of angry demonstrations, as occurred in 1959 after a particularly disastrous wreck on the suburban commuter section of the Central at São Paulo, in which 48 persons were killed and 120 injured. This wreck was the culmination of a long series of disasters in the electrified commuter service at São Paulo and Rio in which nearly 200 passengers had lost their lives in two years. As a result, the indignant public labeled the Central "the road of death."

An expression that is part of the rich folklore of Brazil is "*para inglês ver,*"—"for an Englishman to see." It means a deliberate deception, and has its origin in the era of railroad building when not all the trickery was on the side of the foreigner. According to the fable, English bankers had loaned the capital to build a railroad, but having no report of the construction work, they finally sent an agent to look over the situation at first hand. The Brazilians responsible for spending the money took their English guest into the interior, where they showed him a completed stretch of track in the jungle. Then to demonstrate to him that the line was ready for operation, they conducted him by a roundabout route to another piece of jungle several hundred miles away, where they pointed out to him another finished section of track, after which they saw the Englishman off on his way to London to reassure his principals that all was well in Brazil.

The country stopped building railroads long before the job was finished. Now it has resumed the task of filling in the gaps and extending existing lines into new territory. But when it first laid down its picks and shovels, there was not even a north-and-south railroad to bind the country together, nor is there yet a direct through land route from Rio to the Northeast, much less to the Amazon Valley. In 1959 a firm in Belém ordered a tractor from São Paulo. The tractor was not delivered by coastwise steamer, which might have entailed a wait of months. Instead, it was hauled over 4,000 miles by truck to the end of the dirt road at São Luíz in Maranhão, from where it was flown to Belém.

Most of the railroads, like the Great Western of Pernambuco, were originally built to link an ocean port with the principal towns in its hinterland. Later, as an afterthought, some of these local lines might be connected, as occasionally occurred in the northeastern states. At the best, the end results were a colossal hodgepodge of over a hundred railroads totaling about 21,000 miles. The only truly regional system was in the state of São Paulo. The efficient bottleneck of the state system was the short São Paulo Railway, which climbed the Serra da Mar from the coastal plain at Santos into São Paulo, though its terminus was further inland at Jundiaí. Well-built and operated by its British owners, who generally insisted on calling it the *San* Paulo Railway, it had the largest net income per mile of any railroad in the world. It now belongs to the federal government and is known as the Santos and Jundiaí Railway. The lines of three other companies radiated out of the city to serve the rich interior of the state, and there were also rail connections with Rio, Minas, Mato Grosso, and the three southern states. Two other state systems were the Viação Rio Grandense and the Rede Mineira, or Minas Network. The Rio Grande lines formed connections with the railroad systems of Argentina and Uruguay.

The classical, and for a long time the largest, railway system in Brazil was that of the British-owned Leopoldina. Its network of lines, whose principal terminus was at Niteroi across the bay from Rio, covered the state of Rio de Janeiro and reached into Espirito Santo and Minas.

The original nucleus of the present government system was the Central Railway of Brazil, with lines connecting Rio with São Paulo and Belo Horizonte. Its total mileage is about 2,330, and it has the largest gross income of any railroad in the country. At the opposite extreme, geographically and otherwise, is the Madeira-Mamoré Railway. Most isolated railroad on earth, it was built through the tropical forest around 257 miles of rapids on two large Amazonian rivers. The first effort to construct the line failed because of the high mortality in the working force, and it was only completed by Percival Farquhar after the experience gained in combating tropical diseases in Panama was applied to local conditions. The motive behind the building of the railroad was to provide the Bolivian Beni with an outlet for its rubber and other products, in compensation for the loss of the Acre Territory, a vacant frontier province which had been permanently infiltrated by Brazilians as Texas was by Americans. But it was built too late, for soon after it was completed the rubber boom ended. It was operated by a British company until taken over by the Brazilian government in 1930. When I rode over the line in a locomotive cab in 1923, the trip took about eight hours by the weekly mixed passenger and freight train; now it takes two days—and its days are numbered.

The federal government now owns about 78 per cent of all railroad mileage in Brazil, and actually operates 67 per cent or about two-thirds of the system. The only important railroad that is still privately owned is the Paulista, which serves the rich eastern zone of São Paulo. It is the best railroad in Brazil. Widespread dissatisfaction with the state lines led the federal government to undertake their reorganization in 1957. In the meantime, both the Joint Brazilian-American Development Commission and President Kubitschek in his five-year plan had proposed radical reforms in the national railroad system. Volta Redonda and other large industrial establishments had complained of the poor service. And according to one São Paulo newspaper, "600,000 Cariocas risked their lives daily" on the commuter trains of the Central at Rio. That same year the deficit of the federal railways was nearly 9,000,000,000 cruzeiros, a considerable sum in any currency. The schedule of rates, both for freight and passenger traffic, was too low to permit the replacement of worn-out material. Morale of the 137,000 trainmen was low, which had a further depressing effect on the efficiency of railroad service.

So, in the words of the Washington Embassy's annual *Survey of the Brazilian Economy—1959:*

> In order to free the operations of these railroads from the deficiencies caused by sluggishness of Government operation, a new corporation was created, with the greatest freedom of action, the Rede Ferroviaria Federal (RFFSA), which controls 22 different railroads and operates with a capital of 60

> billion cruzeiros. The new corporation will "administer, exploit, maintain, re-equip, extend, improve and keep in traffic all railways incorporated thereto."

One of the main features of the new railroad regime is the acquisition of more Diesel locomotives, about 400 of which have been ordered since 1957. In 1959, 56.2 per cent of locomotives on the government lines were Diesel, 25.5 per cent were electrical, and only 18.3 per cent were steam. At the end of 1957 the Export-Import Bank provided a credit of $100,000,000 for the purchase of new rolling stock. The RFFSA has also planned to abandon lines which are beyond revival, and to construct five new lines or extensions of existing lines. These would include a new line into Brasilia, in whose construction the old Goiás Railway that ends at Annapolis proved to be of little help; a line from Maringá on the outer edge of the coffee zone in Paraná to the great Guayrá falls, thus opening another link with Paraguay; and a broad-gauge trunk line to replace the present wandering meter-gauge line of the defunct Brazil Railway Company's São Paulo–Porto Alegre connection. At present, the only standard or broad-gauge lines are those of the Central, the Paulista, and the Santos-Jundiaí. Most of the rest of the mileage is meter-gauge, which circumstance is an obstacle to long-distance freight hauls in and out of the São Paulo–Rio industrial area.

Meanwhile, Brazil had taken to the road and the air with great enthusiasm. President Kubitschek's five-year plan made provision for 8,000 miles of new paved roads and 3,600 miles of asphalt paving of existing highways by 1960. Much has been accomplished toward the fulfillment of these goals. The nation is road-conscious and there is strong public backing for the massive road-building program. Previous to the new highway era, there was estimated to be 250,000 miles of "roads"—a conglomeration of old colonial trails used by mule trains, cattle drovers, and oxcarts, dirt roads, some passable only in the dry season and others well-surfaced all-weather roads, as in São Paulo and Minas, and a small mileage of superhighways, like the fine Anchieta road between São Paulo and Santos. For several years there has also been an excellent paved highway between São Paulo and Rio and another between Rio and Belo Horizonte. In addition to the new São Paulo–Curitiba–Porto Alegre highway, which I have traveled, a series of new roads converges on Brasilia. The new capital is now accessible from Rio and São Paulo, and a 1,400-mile road is now under construction between Brasilia and Belém at the entrance to the Amazon Valley, much of it through heavy jungle. This highway bears the name of Bernardo Sayao, the brilliant young engineer who was the moving spirit in its construction until his recent and untimely death. Brasilia will also be connected with the northeast coast by a long road to Fortaleza in Ceará. The lack of through east-west roads was demonstrated by the remarkable feat of two young Englishmen who crossed South America from Recife to Lima in 1958 in a Land Rover. Often cutting out a road as they went, they crossed the Tocantíns River at the long Bananal Island, which has recently been declared a national park, and eventually reached a road at Santa Cruz in Bolivia. The Brazilian government is now even considering the construction of a road from Brasilia to the remote Acre Territory, which would have to cross a series of great rivers on the way. Of much more immediate economic importance than some of these grandiose projects is the road that connects the port of Paranaguá with the junction of the Iguaçú and Paraná rivers by way of Curitiba. This road not only has opened up a rich area in western Paraná to development, but it provides a through truck route between Asunción in Paraguay and the Brazilian coast, where Paraguayan truckers are now a common sight on the streets of Paranaguá. For many years trucks and buses have traveled the long dirt road that leads from Rio by way of Theóphilo Ottoni to Feira de Sant'Anna in Bahia from where other roads reach out into the Northeast as far as Ceará and Maranhão. This is not a de luxe *caminho real,* but it is of very great importance to the economy and life of Brazil and deserves a far higher priority than it has had in the government's Brasilia-bound highway program.

One meets few passenger cars on the Brazilian roads but many trucks and buses. The truck is the most vivid symbol of the new development in Brazil, and it is not to be wondered at that the *camionheiro* or trucker is a member of a privileged class. In 1958 a total of 875,367 automobiles were registered in Brazil, including 437,207 passenger cars, 402,075 trucks, and 36,285 buses.

Airplanes have filled most of the many big gaps in Brazil's transportation system. It is doubtful if any large country has made greater progress in the field of commercial aviation. In 1922 Ralph Hinton and Pinto Martins, his Brazilian copilot, flew a plane from New York to Rio after an epic voyage of three months, during which they fell into the Caribbean and had other mishaps and delays. Later the same year, Sacadura Cabral and Gago Coutinho, two bold Portuguese airmen, crossed the Atlantic from Lisbon to Rio to receive an enthusiastic welcome from the city. Before this, Alberto Santos Dumont had inflamed the imagination of his fellow-Brazilians by flying a heavier-than-air machine in France, to become one of the great pioneers of aviation.

Commercial aviation as a business in Brazil began in 1927 with the organization at Porto Alegre of the VARIG line, which now operates a service between Brazil and New York. In the same year two European companies opened international lines to Buenos Aires by way of the Brazilian coast. One was the predecessor of Air France and the other was the German Condor, later allied with Lufthansa interests. Pan American Airways came into Brazil in 1929, and the Italian LATI company opened its service between Rome and Rio just before the opening of World War II, during which the German lines were forced to suspend their South American flights. In the meantime, Natal, on the coast of the Brazilian "bulge," had become one of the world's great "ports of the skies" and during the war served as a transfer point for the movement of American and Brazilian troops into North Africa and southern Europe. By 1944 seven national companies provided air service within the country. In addition to VARIG, they included Panair, a subsidiary of Pan American Airways, Cruzeiro do Sul, VASP, a São Paulo company, Aerovias do Brasil, later allied with Real, and two other lines. Since then, Loide Aereo has been added to the list of Brazilian companies. In the training of pilots and ground crews and in the installation of airports and facilities, much technical assistance has been given by the Civil Aeronautics Administration of the United States, a close association that persists to the present.

The best way to learn the story of Brazil's place in the sky, better than any statistics of passengers carried and miles flown, is to spend a morning in São Paulo's Congonhas Airport. There one will hear the announcements—always with a friendly *"boa viagem!"*—of planes that go to all parts of Brazil: to Aragarças and Pelotas, Itabuna and Uberlandia, Aracajú and Campo Grande, Crato and Santarém. And every half hour the shuttle planes leave for Santos Dumont Airport in downtown Rio. There may be calls for planes that are bound for far countries: Braniff and Pan American and VARIG for New York, Real for Los Angeles and Tokyo, Alitalia for Milan, Lufthansa for Frankfurt, KLM for Amsterdam, Air France for Paris, Iberia for Madrid, and other flights for London and Stockholm and Zurich.

Transportation in Brazil began with the ships that linked the isolated settlements of the long coast. For centuries, except for travels on foot or dugout canoe or horseback, the only way to move people or goods north or south from one place to another was by ship. Coastwise navigation is still almost as important to the country as it was then, but, except for the change from sail to steam, it seems to have progressed little since the age of the caravel.

The Brazilian merchant marine consists of about 1,000,000 tons of shipping, which would make it the twentieth fleet in the world. By far the largest part of it is engaged in the coastwise trade. Though it is generally considered as synonymous with the Lloyd—or Loide—Brasileiro, which has the largest share of the tonnage and the international routes, actually about two-thirds of all merchandise that moves up and down is carried in small privately owned vessels. The Costeira Company, another large shipping company formerly owned by the Lage family, whose ships had English captains, is now part of the "national patrimony."

The fleet of the Lloyd is well aged. It has ships that saw service under the Empire, which ended in 1889. Two of its ships are 73 years old and 18 have an average age of 55 years. Of over 300 ships in the coastwise service, about 40 per cent were launched before 1930. During World War I, the Lloyd replenished its fleet with some good German vessels which had taken refuge in Brazilian ports and were seized after Brazil entered the war on the side of the Allies. In the Second World War, the Lloyd lost 30 ships of over 130,000 tons to German commerce raiders. Since then it has acquired some Liberty ships from the United States and, more recently, some freighters from Poland.

In 1959 the influential daily *Estado de São Paulo* published a series about the "disastrous" state of the national merchant marine under the title, "The Great Shipwreck." It pointed out, among other things, the notorious inefficiency of its service, including the long delays that have led shippers to turn to more expensive trucking and even air freight. For example, it reports that the Lloyd's ships are tied up in port an average of 72 per cent of the time. The two government-owned lines had an operating deficit in 1958 of nearly 2,500,000,000 cruzeiros, which was covered by subsidies from an already hard-pressed Treasury. Though freight and passenger rates are unrealistically low, captains of ships have been charged with accepting "gratifications" from shippers as a condition of good handling of their cargo.

Conditions in the ports are also the object of much criticism. On the 5,500 miles of seacoast there are 33 major ports. Many of them need dredging to admit normal-sized ocean freighters.

Dock equipment is frequently obsolete or chronically out of repair, and dockworkers are probably the most difficult labor group in the country. Even in Santos, where the well-equipped harbor works are owned by a private company, the movement of freight is often delayed by the high-handed longshoremen's union. When I visited Santos in 1959, soldiers were patrolling the dock area to keep order. At that time, according to the *Estado de São Paulo,* many of the stevedores were earning more than a full professor in the universities.

Besides its coastal and international service, Brazil has an extensive network of river transport. Ocean steamers regularly ascend the Amazon to Manaus on the Rio Negro and as far as Iquitos in Peru. Rivers, like the Madeira, Purús and Negro, are always navigable for long distances by flat-bottomed steamers drawing six feet of water. The large fleet of sidewheelers that formerly belonged to the Amazon River Steam Navigation Company is now operated by the government, with the inevitable decline in efficiency. Other steamers, owned by private trading companies in Belém and Manaus, also ply on the Amazonian rivers. Other Brazilian rivers which are utilized on a commercial scale include the middle course of the São Francisco, the upper Paraguay to Corumbá and, for smaller boats, to Cuiabá, the capital of Mato Grosso, and a section of the Paraná above the Guayrá falls. There is also considerable launch travel on stretches of the larger rivers that are inaccessible because of rapids to the regular steamers. In 1958 two of my former students, Henry Ferris and John Thomson, who had entered the Orinoco in its delta, crossed Brazil from north to south in aluminum canoes, with only a short portage in the upper Tapajóz, and ultimately reached Buenos Aires by the Platine system of rivers.

The "money" for the economic development of Brazil comes from many sources, public and private, foreign and domestic. The investment capital comes from the proceeds of taxation, from government exchange operations, from foreign loans, from issues of paper currency, from direct investments by Brazilians and foreigners. Brazil can no more dispense with foreign capital than could the United States at a comparable stage in its evolution.

In 1960 direct American investments in Brazil amounted to around $1,345,000,000, most of it in manufacturing, and the balance in utilities, merchandising, mining, banks, and land. At present there is a rage of real-estate speculation in the country, prompted both by the prospect for increased values and fears of the effects of continued inflation on the value of money. There has been considerable American participation in this land boom, which has some of the features common to similar phenomena anywhere.

Whatever the long-range promise of profit, the returns on these investments have so far been modest. In 1959 the National Foreign Trade Council of New York made a protest against threats to private American investment in Brazil that were implicit in certain plans then under discussion in the Brazilian Congress, and which would have further restricted the remittance of corporate earnings or the repatriation of principal. Denying charges of "astronomical" profits sent to "Wall Street," the Council declared that in 1956 remittances represented only 2.2 per cent of total capital invested and the next year, only 3 per cent. Using 1955 as a base, the Council listed the direct contributions of the operations of American-owned firms to the Brazilian economy, including nearly $600,000,000 for wages, supplies, and taxes. At the time, 80 per cent of the total proceeds of American-owned operations remained within the country, much of it reinvested in additional equipment. According to the federal Superintendency of Currency and Credit, Brazil enjoyed the benefits of a favorable balance of nearly $900,000,000 from private foreign investments in its economy made during the previous 12 years.

British investment in Brazil began earlier than that of the United States, and in some respects has followed a different course. It was at its highest in 1930, when the total, in government bonds and private investments, amounted to £287,306,000.

By 1949, this figure had fallen by over 40 per cent, partly by the liquidation of government loans. The return on the total capital investment for the latter year was only 3.2 per cent, but on Britain's large railroad holdings no interest was paid in that year. On investments in manufacturing, mining, and utilities, amounting to about £52,000,000, the return averaged 6.8 per cent, which was twice the rate on similar investments in other Latin American countries. The British-owned railroads were later nationalized and, meanwhile, there has been comparatively little new private investment from London.

In the 1920's a series of high-interest loans were floated in the United States by investment banks for various entities of government in Brazil, including the Union itself, the Federal District, and various states.

In recent years most loans in this field have been made on a government-to-government basis. For example, the Export-Import Bank of Washington has authorized loans to Brazil to a total of about $1,300,000,000, or approximately the amount of all private American investments. By 1959 approximately $230,000,000 of the Export-Import Bank's credits had not yet been drawn. At that time, Brazil's outstanding indebtedness to the Bank was around $405,000,000. In 1953 the Export-Import Bank had opened a special credit for the payment of exchange arrears due to American companies, and two years later it established a supplementary credit to ease the country's balance of payments, of which $45,000,000 was drawn. In 1954 a group of private American banks had advanced the Brazilian Treasury a five-year credit of $200,000,000 against gold as security, and in 1958 a combination of the Export-Import Bank and private banks loaned an additional $458,000,000 to the federal government. Among specific purposes of the Export-Import Bank's loans had been the establishment of the national steel mill at Volta Redonda, the purchase of rolling stock for the state railways for a total of $100,000,000, and harbor improvements to a total cost of $51,000,000.

Besides these credits from American sources, the International or World Bank has loaned $255,000,000 to Brazil. Also, Brazil's subscription to the International Monetary Fund amounts to $150,000,000, of which she had drawn $112,000,000 by 1959 for purposes of exchange control. When she requested the use of an additional installment of her quota the same year, the Fund denied her request, except on condition that the government make specified alterations in her exchange and fiscal policies. Opinion in Brazil was aroused by the refusal, which was considered an affront to the nation, and in 1960 the balance of the Brazilian quota was made available to the Brazilian government to meet current exchange shortages in four different currencies.

It is only in recent years that the Brazilian public has begun to buy industrial securities in any quantity. A few new investment houses like the DELTEC Company have facilitated this process by providing the necessary machinery for the sale of stock issues to the individual investor. The habit of control by small groups of shareholders and the prevalence of family corporations like the vast Matarazzo industrial complex are obstacles to wider public ownership of industrials, as is also the tendency to invest in urban real estate. However, a promising beginning has been made in tapping the reserves of private savings. Unlike the United States, there is very little institutional buying of industrial stocks and bonds, and there is no trading on margins.

Commercial banks are accustomed to restrict their credit operations to short-term paper, so that in the normal course of their business they are not an important factor in furthering the nation's industrial development. In the field of private enterprise the Bank of Brazil tends to limit its lending activities to large agricultural interests.

"Brazil progresses at night while the politicians sleep"—so runs a Brazilian saying. Since government is deep in the economy, its competence is a major factor in national development and, therefore, a matter of great public concern. It not only performs the normal regulatory functions of the state, as represented by the 11 cabinet ministries, but it actively intervenes in the country's economic life to a degree that is far beyond the more or less passive role of control in the public interest. It is certainly not just another "welfare state." And much of what the Brazilian government does outside the accepted bounds of the public authority has been done on occasion by other politically orthodox nations, including the United States.

It operates important segments of the machinery of production, including mines, the petroleum industry, the biggest steel mill in the country, hydroelectric plants, an automobile factory, a chemical plant, a rubber plantation, and a key sector of the pharmaceutical industry. To the distress of shippers and travelers, it owns most of the railways and the bulk of the merchant marine. It dictates minimum-wage scales and fixes prices, regardless of state lines. It has set up some of the most complicated—and confusing—devices on earth to control the course of foreign trade and, incidentally, the value and disposal of foreign exchange. It has created a vast complex of alphabetized apparatus, designed to promote the interests of special industries that are considered vital to the public interest, like coffee and wheat, or the development of traditionally backward areas, like the Northeast and the Amazon Valley.

The massive and prolonged departure from conventional economics was not suddenly prompted by a crisis comparable to the Great Depression, which led to the New Deal with its similar intervention of government in the normal sphere of business. However, it is actually the aftermath of the Vargas "1930 Revolution," for subsequent administrations in Brazil, whatever their politics, have not made a clear break with the basic statism of the dictator. They may even have found it congenial to their own political philosophy. Moreover, they may hold that the national economy is still out of hand and that only government is capable of directing it until that day when it can move ahead under its own steam, or by "auto-propulsion," as the Brazilians say. This attitude or policy can only be justified on the assumption that the original "crisis" of the early '30's still persists in one form or another and that, in the meantime, private initiative is incapable of taking over responsibility for the economy.

This is perhaps symptomatic of a certain distrust in high places of the public-spiritedness of the nation's industrial leaders, if not of their business acumen, that may be a survival of the aristocratic tradition in government. In the upper levels of Brazilian politics there is nothing quite comparable to the successful businessman who goes into public life in the United States, like the Herbert Lehmans or Nelson Rockefellers or Will Claytons. Yet if few men of wealth go into politics in Brazil, very few of the "ruling class" leave public office the richer. Even Getulio Vargas appears to have been singularly indifferent to the material possibilities of his position.

If there has been a certain lack of economic statesmanship in the affairs of the republic and an overreliance on formalized development planning, it is because the professional has had too little place in the higher council of the state, where first-hand experience in dealing with large economic problems would be a valuable asset. There is much superior intelligence, high purpose, and dedication to the public interest at the top level of government, but its full usefulness to the nation may sometimes be compromised or invalidated, as elsewhere in the world, by the demands of practical politics, which can be a very powerful motivating force in Brazil.

At the secondary level of the hierarchy there are excellent men who are free from the compulsions of their elected colleagues. They may be high-ranking officers of the armed services who are assigned to civilian posts of power or seasoned public administrators. The military are likely to have received sound training in the economic problems of the nation at the Superior War College.

A planned economy of the magnitude and complexity of Brazil's requires the services of many economists to guide the thinking of bewildered planners. While some of them are "academicians," who may fall back on Adam Smith or Charles Gide or even Aristotle in an emergency, there has been a very definite improvement in their quality. The Brazilian Institute of Geography and Statistics has long maintained high standards as the official statistical service. The Bank of Brazil and the Getulio Vargas Foundation are both sources of much useful information on the economic questions which preoccupy the government.

One of the major economic problems of Brazil is represented by "The Bureaucracy," the army of public functionaries in the federal, state, and local branches of government. If it is oversize it is not because Brazil is outsize, but because it is a product of certain Brazilian customs or characteristics. For example, a government job, however humble, has long enjoyed a social status beyond its deserts. Strong family loyalties in Brazil have been responsible for much nepotism in public administration. And short hours in government offices have had the effect of "spreading the work," thereby creating more job opportunities. Government leaders are aware of these conditions, but have been thwarted in their urge to curtail abuses or excesses in the public service by vested interests and deep habits involved in the perpetuation of the abuses.

Doubtless a secondary factor favoring the removal of the federal capital to Brasilia was the hope for an automatic and painless curtailment of the bureaucracy, since many functionaries would probably prefer a private life in Rio to a public existence in Brasilia. When Getulio Vargas was president, he undertook to deal with the over-all question of the public service by means of a Department of Public Administrative Services (DASP), which introduced many reforms in procedures and order where there had been disorder, but has not effectively restrained the burgeoning instincts of bureaucracy. The School of Public Administration, sponsored by the United States Operating Mission (Point 4) in São Paulo and staffed by political scientists from Michigan State University, should eventually have considerable influence in improving the level of performance in government service.

The weakest link in the cycle of government in Brazil is probably the fiscal system, which one Brazilian writer has called "a monument of imbecility and unfairness." Public relations between tax collectors and taxpayers are likely to be abnormally strained. The perennial battle of wits may end in fines and recriminations, but the Brazilian tax dodger never winds up in the native equivalent of Atlanta.

The four principal sources of federal revenue are consumption or *consumo* taxes, income taxes, import duties, and stamp taxes. In 1958 about 70 per cent of all revenues came from the first two categories. Import duties, long the mainstay of the Treasury, are still an important source of government funds. Stamp taxes, an ancient tributary device, are a nuisance tax, but easy to collect through banks and other businesses. The revenue stamps have to be affixed to bank checks, receipted bills, and a multitude of other papers used in business transactions.

In 1958 the federal government spent nearly 150,000,000,000 cruzeiros, with a deficit of over 20 per cent of expenditures. New issues of paper money during the year totaled 23,300,000,000 cruzeiros, or somewhat less than the amount of the deficit. Of all outgo, about 18 per cent went to "economic and social development." The Ministry of Transport and Public Works, which operates the federal railways and merchant marine and builds the new highways, received more than a quarter of federal expenditures. The three ministries of Agriculture, Education, and Health accounted for about 16 per cent, which was only two-thirds of the combined outlay for the War and Navy Ministries. Of the entire federal payroll, which represented nearly a quarter of the total budget, the military received 3,000,000,000 cruzeiros more than all civilian personnel.

While there are bright exceptions at every level, fiscal conditions are liable to grow progressively worse as the cruzeiros and the conto descend the political scale from the federal government to the *municipio*. The raising of revenue for the support of states, cities, and lesser units of public authority is sometimes a most difficult process. The great city of Rio de Janeiro, still known administratively as the Federal District (until the capital was moved to Brasilia in 1960) is no deviation from the general rule. A principal source of income for the running expenses of government is a sales tax, but merchants are sometimes negligent in their bookkeeping. One who makes a purchase in Rio is handed a receipt for the amount. If he is a stranger, he quickly observes that the public is given to collecting sales receipts. Then, as he moves about the city, he may observe large signs that bear the words, "Your ticket is worth a million!" Putting two and two together, he finds that all this is part of a scheme by the city to recover the sales taxes owed by careless merchants. Thus, to anyone who brings in 10,000 cruzeiros' worth of sales receipts, the tax department of the prefecture gives a special lottery ticket, for which the grand prize is 1,000 contos or 1,000,000 cruzeiros, a sizable fortune for the average Carioca. On an appointed date the drawing is held in the vast Maracaná Stadium, to the accompaniment of band music and other entertainment. After the show is over, the city's tax office, which has completed the monumental task of adding up millions of sales receipts, descends on the delinquent merchants.

Political manners and morals in states and cities have bettered in recent years. Yet in a northern state atavistic impulses may occasionally break out in violence or corruption that would be frowned upon in federal circles. Once upon a time a governor went to Europe to arrange a loan for his state with French bankers. After the loan was floated and the bonds sold, it was learned that the governor had issued a duplicate set of bonds on his own, the proceeds of which he reserved as a nest-egg for his "rainy days." Another governor, suspicious of his colleagues in the state government, is said to have removed the contents of the treasury to his home each evening for safekeeping, returning them to the state house at the beginning of business the next morning. A *cause célèbre* in the history of Brazilian-American diplomatic relations was the famous affair of a land concession bounded by two rivers, which an American rubber company obtained many years ago from the government of Mato Grosso. Meanwhile, a subsequent governor of the state, who apparently found the concessionaires incompatible with his views of development, changed the name of one of the rivers, thereby reducing the size of the land grant by half. Though such refinements of statecraft are a thing of the past, the ethics of rule in certain remote quarters of the land have vestiges of free and easy undertones that would be inconceivable in the fading limelight of Rio or the sunlight of promise in Brasilia.

The old popular cynicism and easygoing indifference to the workings of politics—the "it-doesn't-matterism"—is changing. And since government has moved into his house with him, the average Brazilian is increasingly concerned with its behavior and its fitness to handle the affairs of his country. For he has begun to realize that its affairs are his business, and if it is to progress as it should, it must progress by day as well as by night.

The progress in which the Brazilian and his government are partners is now largely a matter of industrial development. Growth has been greatest in heavy industry—in the production of basic raw materials like steel and in the manufacturing industries that are dependent on them.

Of iron, the basic raw material of heavy industry and metal fabricating, there is no lack, and there will never be. Ore deposits of some 65,000,000,000 tons, calculated at about one-third of world reserves, have scarcely been scratched. Most of this weight is concentrated within the so-called "Iron Quadrilateral" of Minas, centering on Itabira do Campo, and consists of high-grade hematite, with metal content as high as 70 per cent. The peak of Cauê alone is estimated to contain 110,000,000 tons of ore or nearly enough to supply the steel mills of Brazil for 40 years at their present rate of production. I have ridden horseback over the everlasting hills of Minas, where my horse's shoes knocked sparks from the exposed surface of the endless ore beds of the iron ranges that reached to the horizon.

Father Anchieta, the famous Jesuit priest, first reported the existence of iron in large quantities to the king of Portugal. Ore deposits on the edge of the field were worked in desultory fashion from early times, and French and German mineralogists made a modest beginning with small blast furnaces in the eighteenth century, using charcoal for smelting the ores. However, the colonial market for pig iron was still small, and difficulties with financing, transportation, and labor and wood supply gradually put an end to these ventures. More were established from time to time on a similar scale, but a national steel industry was not launched in earnest until the present century was well begun. In the 1920's there was a small Swedish electrometallurgical mill at Ribeirão Preto in São Paulo that produced rods for reinforced concrete. About the same time, Belgian and Luxemburger interests built a steel plant at Sabará in Minas that has continued to operate to the present day. In the meantime, Percival Farquhar's long controversy with the government of Minas over the concession of the Itabira Iron Company held up further developments in that strategic area. By 1934 production of steel was still only a little over 60,000 tons and of pig iron a little less. Nine years later the output of steel had trebled, but it was still insignificant by any other criterion.

By this time the government recognized that the necessary expansion of national industry would be impossible without putting steel production on a stronger basis. The creation of the Companhía Siderúrgica Nacional, or National Steel Manufacturing Company, was the result. With the aid of financing by the Export-Import Bank, a full-fledged steel complex was created at Volta Redonda in the state of Rio de Janeiro, near the São Paulo–Rio line of the Central Railway. By 1958 Volta Redonda produced 548,000 tons of pig iron, 811,000 tons of steel ingots, and 622,000 tons of rails and other rolled products. Also, its coke ovens had become a major source of raw materials for the country's chemical industry.

With the prospect of growing markets and the active support of government, a strong impetus has been given to the production of steel since 1955. While Volta Redonda is still much the largest producer, about 10 other companies are either in operation or in the process of establishing steel mills. They represent large combinations of capital, Brazilian, both official and private, American, German, and Japanese. The scheduled level of output for 1963 ranges from 120,000 tons for some of the minor concerns to 550,000 tons for Belgo-Mineira, the pioneer of the industry, and 500,000 tons for USIMINAS, or Usina Siderúrgica de Minas. This company is jointly owned by Japanese, Brazilian, and American capital, with a consortium of 14 Japanese steel companies holding 40 per cent of the stock. It expects to increase its capacity to a level of 2,000,000 tons, and will specialize in the production of extra-wide steel sheets and heavy plates for shipbuilding. Other Japanese interests, now setting up a shipyard in Brazil, will offer a ready market for part of the product of USIMINAS. Its plant is in the same general neighborhood as those of ACESITA, a Bank of Brazil-controlled company that produces special alloy steels, and the Mannesmann seamless pipe plant, which is located in the ironclad hills that ring Belo Horizonte.

Several other plants are situated in the state of São Paulo. These include the Mineração Geral do Brasil, or General Mining Company of Brazil, a large producer controlled by the wealthy Lebanese-Brazilian Jafet family, with mills at Mogí das Cruzes and São Caetano do Sul; the important COSIPA or Paulista Steel Company, with a plant near Santos; and the Villares Steel Company. A factor of increasing importance in the steel industry is the Companhía do Vale do Rio Doce or Company of the Rio Doce Valley. This government-controlled entity operates the old Vitoria and Minas Railroad which provides an outlet for Itabira ores to the port of Vitoria in Espirito Santo. It also operates a steel mill at the port and is the principal link in the export of Brazilian hematite ores.

In the 20 years between 1937 and 1957, foreign shipments rose from 200,000 tons to over 3,500,000 tons, to form the nation's fourth most important export, for a value of nearly $50,000,000. A million and a half tons went to the United States, and most of the balance to Great Britain, Germany, and Canada, with smaller lots to Japan and Czechoslovakia. The Brazilians have had expectations of larger shipments to the United States, but American demand has been affected by increased dependence on the low-grade taconite ores of Mesaba and the competition of nearer ore fields in Venezuela and Labrador.

The advance of the Brazilian iron and steel industry is not only impressive in terms of its present situation as compared with that of 20 years ago. It is the largest industry in Latin America. Its production of steel is larger than that of Sweden, twice that of the new Indian industry, and about equal to that of Luxemburg or the Saar. A fuller realization of its enormous potential is dependent on the further expansion of heavy industry and on raising the living standards of the Brazilian masses. The bulk of its present output is used in the new metallurgical industries. It ends up in everything from pins and paper clips to ships, automobiles, oil derricks, bridges, large electrical equipment, towers for power transmission lines, girders for skyscrapers, rails and cars for railroads. Meanwhile, fabricating industries for consumer goods are growing. The per capita consumption of steel is still very low. The lack of coking coal is a problem for the industry, with Volta Redonda using about two parts of American coal mixed with processed bituminous from the Santa Catarina mines.

However, the steel industry is fortunate in having at its command unlimited supplies of manganese alloy metal, conveniently located near the Minas iron ore fields, where a subsidiary of the United States Steel Corporation and smaller producers have been mining manganese ores for half a century. There are also large reserves in the state of Bahia, which could be drawn on for the use of the national steel industry. Two other fields are, for the present, limited to export markets. One is the important new development of the Bethlehem Steel Company in the Territory of Amapá in the extreme northeastern corner of the country.

Exports of nearly 700,000 tons of ore a year go to the United States and now constitute, with smaller shipments from Rio, Brazil's seventh export item in value. The Urucúm field, with reserves estimated at 30,000,000 tons, is located in a mineralized butte that is situated near the Paraguay River in western Mato Grosso, but its full development awaits a solution of the transportation problem between the site of the deposits and deep-sea shipping at Montevideo or Buenos Aires.

The Brazilian automotive industry began in the 1920's with the establishment of assembly plants by the three leading American manufacturers. As time went on, the operation of these plants encountered serious difficulties as a result of exchange shortages which interfered with the importation of component parts from the United States. The national road system was still undeveloped, and most passenger cars and trucks, whether assembled within the country or imported, were used in the cities. Though roads improved, import duties remained high and exchange restrictions became more rigid, so that by 1956 only about 15,000 cars were imported into the country.

As the automobile business almost came to a halt, the Executive Group of the Automotive Industry, or GEIA, a government-sponsored organization, launched a high-power program for automobile manufacturing in the country. By offering special inducements to foreign manufacturers, it made arrangements with over 20 firms, American, German, Italian, Swedish, French, and Japanese, to set up factories in Brazil. One who drives out of São Paulo through the industrial district on the Santos highway will observe the impressive results that have already been made in establishing the new industry. By 1958 a total of 61,129 units were produced. Most of these were commercial vehicles, and half were trucks and buses, made by Mercedes-Benz, General Motors, Ford, Fabrica Nacional de Motores (FNM), a Brazilian government concern, and two smaller producers. The largest single item was the Willys Company's output of over 13,000 jeeps; 13,692 pickup trucks and station wagons were produced by Volkswagen, Ford, Willys, DKW-Vemag, and Chevrolet. Only 2,189 passenger cars in all were built, mostly by Vemag, though seven other companies were then making plans for production.

Meanwhile, though the ultimate perspective of the automobile market is extremely promising, the industry faces some trying problems for the time being. These include a shortage of skilled labor that has strengthened the bargaining power of the qualified worker, the availability of spare parts and repair services, ready access to additional working capital, and, above all, the financing of sales. Long-term consumer credit is still a novelty in Brazil, and immediate market possibilities are also limited by the effects of inflation and by the low buying power of the average citizen. Unless these bottlenecks are broken within the next few years, the market might easily become saturated, with strong pressures put on the industry to export any surplus.

Of consumer goods industries, textile manufacturing is a Brazilian pioneer, as it was in England. Its roots are deep in the cotton fields of the Northeast—and in the need for providing sacks for sugar and clothes for millions of naked Negroes. Mechanized production of better cotton goods began in Bahia and Pernambuco under the Empire but, due to the competition of Manchester cottons in the local market, made little progress. The industry had a fresh start in this century when it doubled its yardage in the first 15 years. New mills were established, not only in the north, but in São Paulo and Rio and in smaller towns like Juiz da Fora in Minas. With the development of the industry in São Paulo, cotton growing developed in the state to supply industry needs. The quality of fabrics improved and production increased by 65 per cent in the 15-year period between 1939 and 1953. By this time the national market for cottons was a monopoly of the domestic mills, and during World War II there was even a sizable flurry of exporting. However, in normal years textiles do not appear on either side of the country's foreign-trade ledger. The Brazilian weaving industry has become one of the most diversified in the world. In addition to cottons, it includes manufacturers of wool, linen, rayon, silk, and jute, all based on raw materials that are produced in the country.

Another important segment of heavy industry in Brazil is cement manufacturing. Enormous quantities of it are required for buildings and highway construction, and for dams in the new hydroelectric projects. So great is the demand that at times there is a veritable cement famine in parts of the country, as occurred during the construction of Brasilia, when cement was flown into Goiás in planes. The present industry began with a factory that was erected in 1924 by Americans at Perús in the state of São Paulo. By 1933 national output had reached a total of 339,000 tons, and by six years later imports of cement had practically ceased. Annual output of the 10 producing states is now well over 3,000,000 tons, with São Paulo in first place, followed by the states of Rio de Janeiro and Minas.

For some time Brazilians and foreigners alike have accused Brazil of living beyond her means. Her means are very great, but they are still largely undeveloped, and natural resources yet in the ground cannot pay tomorrow's bills. The country's immense reserves are human as well as material, and both need more intensive development. Brazil is too dependent on coffee and, with the present competitive situation in world markets, the coffee cycle could end as the sugar cycle ended in the 1600's when competition from the West Indies ended the profitable Brazilian sugar monopoly. Brazil must increase and vary her production, not only for export, but for internal consumption, in order to raise the low living standards of the Brazilian masses.

Inflation has continued too long and has reached the stage where social discontent might easily become a serious problem. The Brazilians are an extraordinarily patient people, but they are harried by money worries, and they cannot be expected to wait indefinitely for an easing of their problem. Some of the headlines in their newspapers are disquieting. Among those which have appeared in the past year are these: "Hunger," "Storm Signs," "Playing with Fire," "A Country Besieged by Hunger,"

"Life Is More Difficult," "Inflation and Survival," "And How Will the Poor Live?" "Between January and April Living Costs Rose 14 Per Cent."

Meanwhile, the international balance of payments continues out of balance, with the inevitable effects on the value of the cruzeiro and the buying power of the individual's budget. The devious mechanism of foreign-exchange control violates every economic law, and to those uninitiated in its mysteries, it discourages new initiative in the nation's export trade.

The answer to Brazil's dilemma is not aggressive nationalism. There is no threat of "economic imperialism" and there never has been since the republic began. The answer is certainly not Communism, which would not only wreck the nation's economy, but is antipathetic to every instinct of the most promising of the world's peoples. The country has a fund of international good will such as no other nation has. Americans and other foreigners have given bountifully of their capital and their faith to her development. Their faith in her future is so strong that, even while they complain of conditions that might be remedied, American companies do not leave Brazil but are willing to give her every chance to realize her destiny.

CHAPTER 14

The State

IN ALMOST HALF A MILLENNIUM OF EXISTENCE THE BRAZILian state has assumed several forms. For over three centuries she was a colony of Portugal, during 60 years of which she was indirectly a dependency of Spain. In 1808 the Portuguese court migrated to Rio de Janeiro to escape capture by a French army and set up its apparatus of rule in Brazil. Seven years later Brazil was declared a joint kingdom with the mother country, which she already exceeded in population. The next year the Prince Regent became King João or John VI of Brazil, Portugal, and, incidentally, of the Algarves, the half-Moorish southern province of Portugal. By that time Napoleon was living out in the Atlantic Ocean on the island of St. Helena, but the Brazilophile king delayed his return to Lisbon until 1821. When he regretfully departed from Rio, he apparently admonished his son Pedro, whom he left behind as regent, that if the Brazilians should decide to go it alone, he should accept the situation and make the most of it. In other words, if Brazil were to become independent, the young prince would be her logical ruler.

This is exactly what happened in the following year. When the Portuguese element in the government at Lisbon attempted to restore Brazil to a subordinate position in the dual monarchy, Dom Pedro threw in his lot with the local advocates of home rule. The crisis came when the prince was at Ipiranga in the outskirts of São Paulo. Raising his sword in a grandiloquent gesture, he shouted "Independence or death!" and without further ado or ceremony Brazil joined the family of nations. The act of separation took place on September 7, 1822, which has ever since been celebrated as the Brazilian equivalent of the Fourth of July and is so commemorated by the Ruà Sete de Setembro, a street in downtown Rio. The United States recognized the independence of Brazil the following year, almost contemporaneously with President Monroe's announcement of his famous Doctrine, and Portugal accepted the *fait accompli* in 1824.

With the accession of the young Braganza prince to the throne of an independent Brazil as the Emperor Pedro I there began the period of the Brazilian Empire that ended in 1889. The emperor did not live up to the hopes and expectations of his subjects. He was able and energetic but arbitrary and capricious, and he proved increasingly hostile to any liberal tendencies in the sphere of government. In April, 1831, 10 years after his father's departure from Brazil, he suddenly abdicated and returned to Portugal, where he was demoted from the rank of emperor to that of king.

On leaving Rio de Janeiro he left behind him his Brazilian-born five-year-old son who, as the Emperor Dom Pedro II, was to rule Brazil for nearly 60 years. For several years a succession of regencies governed in the boy's name. Then in 1840 the young Pedro was declared of an age to assume the throne, and the following year he was crowned as emperor. As the years of his long reign passed, he steadily grew in political wisdom, devotion of his people, and the respect of the outside world. He was a benign and conscientious monarch who accepted his role as moderator between the factions of national politics with dignity and equanimity. His personal life was blameless, and his interest in education and scholarship was sincere if somewhat dilettantish. In 1876 he visited the United States, where he was enthusiastically received, and later toured the countries of Western Europe. His international prestige was greater than that of any other ruler in the history of Latin America.

The rule of "the good gray emperor" was beset with many troubles. His government had to deal with the bitter rivalries between the provinces of the still loosely knit union and with internal disorders in various parts of the Empire. A contest with Argentina over the "Banda Oriental" of Uruguay led to open hostilities in the River Plata region, and Brazil later provided the bulk of the allied forces in the devastating War of Paraguay between 1865 and 1870. Outbreaks of indiscipline in the army were a portent of the praetorianism that was to bedevil the early period of the republic. Even the Church was a source of difficulties for the imperial government and its orthodox head. During the reign of Pedro I Freemasonry was widespread among the hierarchy. The emperor himself was an avowed Freemason and so was José Bonifacio de Andrada, his famous minister of state. Efforts of the Vatican to uproot the movement among the clergy were bitterly resisted, as was the insistence on clerical celibacy among a priesthood long accustomed to the marriage of its members. Some of the dissidents were in favor of a national Church independent of papal authority, a situation which inevitably had its repercussions in the imperial regime. To add to the preoccupations of the government, a succession of economic and financial problems threatened the solvency of the state and the stability of the economy. Finally, the growth of the abolition movement gradually undermined the very basis of the Empire and eventually led to its overthrow. The process of gradual emancipation of the slaves was well under way by the middle of the century. Abolitionists in high places, like Joaquím Nabuco de Araujo, condemned the institution of slavery on both moral and economic grounds, and the government of Brazil was under pressure from England to suppress the African slave trade. Meanwhile, the end of the traffic and preliminary decrees which cut off slavery at both ends of the life cycle doomed the institution to early extinction. However, the impatience of the abolitionists forced the issue of complete emancipation in 1888, while the emperor was absent in Europe. In May the Princess Isabel, who was acting as regent, signed the decree which freed the remaining slaves. The act was a severe blow to the already depressed agricultural region of the Northeast. Many of the large landowners, left without a labor force to work their properties, joined the growing movement against the Empire. In the meantime, sentiment for a republic was strengthened by the prospect of the unpopular Princess Isabel's early succession to the throne, burdened with a French husband who refused to speak Portuguese. The country was in turmoil when the sick emperor returned the following year, shortly to be faced with a demand for his abdication and exile.

The Empire was over and Brazil was a republic at last. It was something of a miracle that the imperial regime had survived so long. Also, in spite of all the dissensions which had wracked the state, it was a tribute to the fundamental moderation of the Brazilian temper. For Brazil had been saved from the extremes of violence that had scourged most of the Spanish-American republics since their independence. Her history had not been tarnished by a Carrera, a Melgarejo, or a Solano López. Much of the credit for the relative orderliness of her evolution belongs to the second emperor, who ruled with a firm hand that belied his gentle manner and appearance. He kept out of the arenas of open controversy, but had a genius for compromise of the passions that were aroused in national politics. He selected able ministers of state from the imperial nobility to carry the immediate burdens of public administration. In the period of confusion and disillusionment that followed the end of the Empire, there was a nostalgic resurgence of devotion to the memory of Dom

Pedro, especially in Minas Gerais. His place among the great figures of Brazilian history is now more firmly established than ever.

The republic which began in 1889 ushered in no utopia. Its creation was the almost fortuitous work of an incompatible group of civilians and military, who had no common goals or plan of action. The particular *deus ex machina* of the moment was Marshal Manoel Deodoro de Fonseca, whose principal concern was the place of the army in national affairs. He provided the necessary force for the overthrow of the Empire and became the first president of the republic. The only serious ideological contribution to the republican movement was made by Benjamin Constant de Botelho Magalhães, a zealous follower of the Positivist cult of "humanity." Other figures in the loose directorate of the new republic were the vice president Floriano Peixoto, another soldier, and Ruy Barbosa, a brilliant orator from Bahia, whose administrative talents as Minister of Finance proved to be decidedly inferior to his rating in eloquence. It would have been hard to assemble a quadrumvirate more ill suited to the task of initiating a new state and guiding it through its infancy.

The republic faced many grave problems and, after more than 70 years, still faces most of them, even if in reduced intensity. In the first place, the very basis of a democratic polity had to be established. Under the Empire there was no pretense of democracy in the government. The state was an oligarchy of large landowners, as it had actually been during the colony, and no other form of government was feasible. When the electoral laws were liberalized in 1881, only about one Brazilian in a hundred was qualified as a voter. At least quantitatively, things in that respect have improved considerably, and in the presidential election of 1960, 11,000,000 votes were cast in a population of some 65,000,000. Meanwhile, the processes of democracy are still retarded by the high rate of illiteracy, by widespread political indifferentism, and by the lack of clear-cut political issues in terms that are intelligible to the average Brazilian.

Politics in Brazil still has the character of a game. It is only lately that bold novices have broken into the arena to challenge the professional players who for so long made its eligibility rules and had a monopoly of its rewards. If the new entrants can rise above the motivation of personal ambition, the change holds considerable promise for the political future of Brazil. However, until the electorate is better educated in the issues of government and more aware of its own responsibility for the national interest, the potential advantages may be offset by the opening which it offers to practitioners in demagoguery.

The traditional realities of political organization and manipulation do not serve the national purpose of the Brazilian republic. Campaigns for the presidency and other high office are liable to involve deals between political leaders and machines on the national or state level. Expressions of policy and principle may have little to do with these arrangements, except as lures for uncommitted groups of voters. In actual practice, partnerships may be formed between groups of opposing ideologies, and a conservative candidate may welcome the support of a Communist minority in a close election. Promises of subsequent favors and division of the anticipated spoils of office are naturally stock features of this phase of practical politics. An encouraging aspect of the situation and, incidentally, a tribute to the maturity of the voting public is the growing tendency of candidates to run on a definite platform—a "program of targets" or objectives or "plan of action." However, this practice was grossly abused by Getulio Vargas in his successful appeals for the support of the Brazilian masses.

A comparable phenomenon to nineteenth-century American political bossism is the prevalence of bossism or *caudilhismo* in Brazil. Sometimes these political machines are deeply entrenched in a state, where their power depends on the allegiance of local politicians who command large blocs of voters. A current example is the dominant faction which represents the political tradition of Getulio Vargas in his native state of Rio Grande do Sul. These state machines sometimes play a large part in national contests for the presidency, candidates for which are usually former governors of states.

Brazil is a federal republic of 21 states and four territories. The territories—Amapá, Rio Branco, Acre, and Rondonia—lie along the northern or northwestern rim of the country and are ruled by governors appointed by the president of the republic. The states vary greatly in size, population, economic and social development, and political power in the union. Some of the northeastern states, by reason of their dependence on subsidies and other favors from the national treasury, are, in a sense, wards of the federal government, and their political status is diminished accordingly. At the opposite extreme are the key states of Minas Gerais and São Paulo, which have long exerted an influence in national affairs out of proportion to their numerical position in the federation. They hold nearly a quarter of the population of the nation and possess most of its agricultural and industrial wealth. As a recognition of their superior status, they have generally rotated the presidency between them, with an occasional concession for appearance's sake to one of the other states, as in the case of Epitacio Pessoa of Paraiba. Of 10 civilian presidents, five have been Paulistas and four have been Mineiros.

The state of São Paulo has held a very special place in the political life of Brazil. At times it has almost been an *imperium in imperio,* a nation within a nation. Its flag was displayed on school buildings above that of the republic. It made arrangements regarding immigration and other matters with European governments that virtually had the force of treaties. Its primacy in the union was recognized by the diplomatic emissaries of foreign nations, who had the habit of visiting São Paulo shortly after they had presented their official credentials at the Itamaratí in Rio. In São Paulo they were received by the president of the proud state and escorted through the streets of its capital with much pomp and display of power. The state had a formidable army of its own, and on two occasions—in 1924 and 1932—it revolted in open war against the central government. In one of these struggles the largest armies ever to take the field in Latin America were engaged. Since it bears a disproportionate share of the financial burden of the national government, São Paulo has expected preferential treatment for its own economic problems, particularly those related to the coffee industry.

Minas Gerais, its co-partner in power, owes its high precedence in the nation to a combination of factors, among which are a large population, a strong and remarkably well-balanced economy, and a solid and politically minded citizenry who are instinctively cautious, clannish, and conservative. Other states whose voices are liable to be listened to with respect or attention are Rio Grande do Sul, rebellious and vigorous frontier community; Bahia, which its people refer to as "the Virginia of Brazil," patriarch of the states, revered for its history, and reputed for the lush fluency of its orators and writers; and Pernambuco, brash and unpredictable, with undercurrents of radicalism and an urge for violence, and with a certain priority of prestige over its more backward and slower-moving sister states of the Northeast.

Another problem which Brazil has shared with the other countries of Latin America is that of militarism. The military did not find their proper place in the state during the Empire and the republic inherited the problem, which was only aggravated by the events of the transition period. Only three presidents have been military men. Two of them, Deodoro da Fonseca and his vice president, Floriano Peixoto, ruled the republic during the first five years that followed its inception in 1889. The third was Marshal Hermes da Fonseca, nephew of the first president, who held office between 1910 and 1914. Not one of the three was suited to the demands of the presidency. Their patriotism was unquestioned, but by temperament and the traditions of their class they were unfitted for the tasks of governing a republic whose bases were essentially civilian in character. They were high-handed and impatient in dealing with the inevitable elements of opposition in their government. In their counsels they favored their military colleagues and spurned the advice and co-operation of civilian leaders who were more competent in the critical fields of economic policy and public administration. The armed forces got out of hand, and the early history of the republic is replete with a chronicle of military disorders that took the form of barrack revolts, mutinies, and local civil wars. Interservice rivalries led to a major rebellion of the Navy against the Peixoto government in 1893, and several years later units of the fleet mutinied on two occasions in Rio harbor.

In time the curse of praetorianism and its attendant turmoils abated as discipline was established in the armed forces and the military accepted civilian responsibility for the governance of the nation. Gradually the armed forces assumed the role of defenders of constitutional government against those who would violate its principles. It was in this capacity that military leaders twice forced the resignation of the dictator Vargas. The military gained much in professional standards from the training of an American naval mission and a similar mission of French army officers, headed by General Gamelin. Moreover, the officer corps of all three branches of the service now have the benefit of excellent high institutions of training. The Brazilian armed forces also earned new pride in their position in the state as a result of their very creditable combat record in World War II.

The progress of democratic government in Brazil has been retarded by the lack of meaningful political parties. The early parties of the republic, like Ruy Barbosa's Civilista Party, have disappeared, and bewildered voters in national elections are now confronted with a confusing array of a dozen parties, none of which has deep roots. Most of the parties date from the first Vargas regime and represent the views of opposing factions of that era. They are generally founded on vote-getting opportunism rather than on any broad and clear-cut lines of fundamental doctrine that would appeal to the convictions of the voter and resolve his doubts instead of intensifying them. The result is that choice is liable to be made on the basis of personalities rather than on the vague or even spurious platforms.

The four leading parties are generally identified by their initials, and include the UDN, the PTB, the PSD, and the PSP. The UDN or National Democratic Union was founded in 1946 by a coalition of anti-Vargas groups. Its political philosophy is right-of-center, with definite reformist leanings. Its most active support comes from professional men and the middle class in general. Among the party's principal figures are Juracý Magalhães (Magellan), governor of Bahia, and Carlos Lacerda, first governor of the new state of Guanabara, a newspaperman who gained fame as a bold enemy of Vargas. The PSD or Social Democratic Party was founded the same year, largely by consolidation of pro-Vargas machines in the states. Whatever real tenets it has are basically conservative. It still has a strong following and a large bloc of seats in the national Congress. Another product of the political turmoil of the same year that followed the unseating of Vargas was the Social Progressive Party or PSP. It was the personal instrument of Adhemar de Barros, ex-governor of São Paulo and later mayor of its capital city, and exponent of *Varguismo,* who ran third in the presidential elections of 1960. Principal carrier of the Vargas banner is the PTB or Brazilian Labor Party, organized by the dictator himself toward the end of his 15-year "term," to perpetuate his hold on the working classes. Its permanent head is João Goulart or "Jango," an intimate associate of Vargas for most of his political career and self-designated bearer of "the word." He was vice president during the Kubitschek administration and was re-elected to that office in 1960, as a by-product of the Brazilian custom of candidates for the two highest places in the government running independently of each other. Beyond its vague appeal to organized labor as guardian of the Vargas tradition in national politics, the Brazilian Labor Party offers no clearly defined program and affords a convenient refuge for extremists of various political denominations. For harried voters who cannot find an acceptable answer to their political yearnings in these four major parties, there are further alternative choices among about eight other groups, including a Christian Democratic Party and a Brazilian Socialist Party, all of which hold a sizable total of seats in the national Congress.

Among the veritable chaos of parties which came into being during the protracted Vargas era were the Integralists and the Communists. The Integralista Party was the creation of one Plinio Salgado. Appearing during the Second World War, before Brazil had declared itself on the side of the Allies, it was frankly Nazi-Fascist in its ideology and methods. Its followers wore green shirts and jackboots and constantly paraded about Rio in Hitler-like demonstrations. Their antics might have been laughed off in true Brazilian fashion if the movement had not grown to dangerous proportions. Meanwhile, the Axis powers were greatly pleased by these fantastic goings-on in Brazil, but when they interfered with the plans of Vargas he ordered the suppression of the party. The Integralists thereupon made a desperate attempt to take over power one night by attacking the Guanabara Palace. Only the president and his family, with a few intimates, were in the palace at the time, but they managed to hold off the assailants with firearms until soldiers of the local garrison arrived on the scene.

The Communists proved to be a much more serious menace. During the first years of the Vargas regime they were organized as the PCB or Brazilian Communist Party. Under the skilled leadership of Carlos Luís Prestes, this group eventually became the best-disciplined and most tightly organized political organization in Brazil. Prestes was a former army captain who took advantage of the Paulista revolt of 1924 to gather a company of hard-bitten rebels and social malcontents for a spectacular display of opposition to the existing status quo in Brazil. He led his flying column on a two-year trek through the back country, not unlike the early march of Chinese Communists through the interior of China. Their numbers decimated in constant guerrilla fighting, they were at last defeated by federal troops, and the remnants of the column were broken up. The leaders scattered into the neighboring countries, only to appear several years later as heads of a more formidable group, schooled in Communist techniques and ready to participate in the free-for-all struggle for power that seemed to be ushered in by the rise of Vargas. After a prolonged stay in Moscow, Prestes organized the National Alliance of Liberation in 1934 and announced himself as champion of the Brazilian masses against their only too manifest wrongs. However, Vargas, who had his own ideas about social reform in Brazil, resented the intrusion of the Communists into his chosen field of policy. Prestes was arrested and removed from circulation until 1945, at which time Vargas himself was removed from power. In the elections of that year the Communist vote was 10 per cent of the total. As a mark of his political rehabilitation, Prestes was elected to the Senate and 15 of his partisans won seats in the lower house of Congress. In the elections two years later the Communists raised their quota by an alarming margin. The Dutra government was by now gravely concerned by the growth of Communism, particularly after Prestes announced that, in case of war with the USSR, he would take arms on the side of Russia. In 1947 the Supreme Court declared the Communist Party or PCB illegal. Prestes and all other Communists were removed from public office, but with the inevitable result that the party moved underground, where it continued its agitation. The party profited from the removal of the Vargas censorship of the press and other publications, and openly carried on its propaganda throughout the country. With a tolerance peculiar to the Brazilian temper, Prestes, who was respected even by his political enemies, was sentenced to house imprisonment in a pretense of "hiding," only to reappear again in 1958, 34 years after his original recognition as the leader of Brazilian Communism.

In the meantime, operating under the slogan of "business as usual," the Communists carried on their work without let or hindrance. Presumably in order to identify themselves more closely with the interests of Brazil, they are ultra-nationalistic. They follow a bitterly anti-American line and lose no opportunity to oppose a closer entente between Brazil and the United States. They agitate for the establishment of diplomatic relations with Russia and for the promotion of increased trade with the Communist bloc of nations.

For 24 years, from 1930 to 1954, a third of the history of the republic, Getulio Vargas dominated the political life of Brazil, whether as president or, *in absentia,* as a more or less private citizen on his ranch in Rio Grande do Sul. His bustling ghost still sits at the council table, and each year, on the anniversary of his birth, the little people whom he championed do honor to his memory. They smother his statues with wreaths and, kneeling, all but pray to him as to an uncanonized saint. But each year fewer of his simple devotees appear before the banks of flowers and the lighted candles at the commemorative rites.

His dictatorship was a new phenomenon in Brazilian political life. Previous presidents may have acted arbitrarily on occasion, as the Fonsecas did, but they generally observed the rules and amenities of power. Most of them were conscientious chieftains and two or three were leaders of real distinction. Even if inert or blundering at times, or harboring corrupt and self-seeking followers in their camp, at least they did not threaten the fundamental structure of the state.

But Vargas was something else. His will was the government of Brazil. He combined in his own personality the functions of president, congress, and governors of the states. He made the laws by decree, dictated a constitution for the republic, and as sole source of executive authority, enforced the laws of his creation. Yet he was no baleful ogre, like so many of the conventional dictators of Latin America, no paranoiac monster like Hitler or strutting little Caesar like Mussolini. His personal image was that of the grown-up farm boy from out of the south, homey and smiling and friendly, a sort of gaucho Huckleberry Finn of the pampas, but who ultimately went bad in the big city. He usually had his way, but he did not enforce his rule with firing squads or by incarceration in loathesome dungeons or exile to the jungle. He did not even exile his enemies to Paris, as some of his Spanish-speaking colleagues were in the habit of doing with their opponents. Nobody ever tried to assassinate him, though he liked to wander alone through the streets of Rio like some tropical Harun-al-Rashid. He did not indulge in prolonged ratiocination, but, a shrewd judge of human nature, he acted on the spur of calculated impulse and capitalized on his instinctive premonitions of the inevitable. He left the drafting of the philosophical charter of his "New State" to more contemplative aides, like Francisco Campos. He was bored by the reading of long state papers, and sometimes dozed off during the tiresome process, only to be nudged by the reader when it was time to fix his signature to the document. He was a supreme opportunist and probably had few deep political convictions. But he had an overweening obsession for power and preferred not to live when it finally slipped from his skillful hands. He proved to be a master manipulator of men and situations.

He underwent his apprenticeship in practical politics in his native state and later served for a while as Minister of Finance in Rio. His great opportunity came in 1930. It was customary for the outgoing president to name his successor, and in that year Washington Luiz violated the unwritten code by selecting Carlos Prestes, a fellow Paulista, as the next president, thereby arousing the ire of the Mineiros, whose turn it was at the Cattete Palace. The powerful machine in Belo Horizonte thereupon threw their weight in favor of Vargas, whose partisans promptly proceeded to Rio and seated him in the presidency. Secure in the support of Minas and Rio Grande, the newcomer went about the task of transforming Brazil. The Depression was on, and the mass of the population rallied to him as their savior from the economic ills and other troubles which the people ascribed to the current clique of politicians. Two years later, São Paulo, humiliated by the blow to its prestige as the once-dominant state of the union, revolted against the new regime, only to be defeated by the federal army.

As the details of Vargas' program unfolded, the full implications of the change became evident to the nation. To break the power of the state political machines, Vargas virtually dismantled the federal mechanism of the republic. He invoked the instrument of "intervention" to remove state governors whom he supplanted with his own appointees. He dismissed the national Congress and ruled by decree, to the infinite confusion of lawyers and administrative officials. Only the judges of the Supreme Court held out against the arbitrary exercise of his will by refusing to recognize the constitutionality of much of his peremptory and often conflicting legislation. He suppressed criticism of his rule by high-handed censorship of opposition views. When the end of his term neared, he showed no intention of holding elections. Instead, he called a constitutional convention, which drafted a new constitution, replacing that of 1891, and then, under cover of a "national emergency," proclaimed him president for another five years. When the war began in Europe, although public opinion was on the side of the Allies, Vargas, whose attitude toward the Axis powers was suspect, showed no inclination to abandon his policy of neutrality. It was only after the earnest urging of advisers like Oswaldo Aranha and representations by the American ambassador that Vargas consented to a declaration of war. Thereafter the Vargas government prosecuted its place in the war with vigor. The United States was permitted to utilize a series of strategic bases and air transfer points like Belém, Natal and Recife, which were vital to the conduct of the war in North Africa and southern Europe. The Brazilian Navy and Air Force performed a useful service in patrolling the long coast against German submarines and surface commerce raiders, and a Brazilian expeditionary force of six divisions fought side by side with the American Army in the campaign in southern Italy.

By now Vargas had put into effect his comprehensive program of social reform, whose accomplishments were represented by an advanced labor code and social security legislation. Though these measures strengthened his hold on the long-forgotten Brazilian masses, his growing defiance of all restraints on his dictatorship, particularly after the end of the war, brought the opposition to his rule to a head. When he again avoided the holding of national elections in 1945, elements in the general staff of the Army combined with civilian leaders in a sudden coup that forced his resignation. He calmly accepted the ultimatum presented to him one night in the palace by General Goes Monteiro, head of the Army, and his colleagues and retired to his home in Rio Grande do Sul to await the turn of events that would restore him to power. His opportunity came as the dull and matter-of-fact Dutra administration drew to its close in 1950. Chosen by his own Labor Party as its candidate, Vargas made his appeal for support to the working classes whom he had befriended and was re-elected to the presidency.

But the old magic was gone, and the period of the Getulian restoration proved to be a prolonged Götterdämmerung. The President was surrounded by an inferior group of advisers and there was much corruption in the public service. Vargas tried to recover his former position by adopting policies of extreme nationalism, as in the petroleum industry, and he reiterated his concern for the welfare of the masses. A series of scandals and blunders ultimately sealed the doom of his government. The Rio police, which were headed by his disreputable brother, murdered an officer of the Air Force and wounded Carlos Lacerda, a newspaperman who had openly criticized his rule. When a delegation of the military again asked for his demission, Vargas realized that the game was up, and on the night of August 24, 1954, he committed suicide. The government was taken over by João Café Filho, the vice president, who proceeded to eradicate all the remnants of the Vargas regime from the administration of the republic.

The Brazilian Constitution dates from 1946, the year after the overthrow of the first Vargas regime. It is the sixth of its kind since independency in 1822. The first constitution was drafted the following year, but was thrown out by the temperamental young emperor, Pedro I, who substituted for it a document more to his liking. That was in 1824, and, with extensive amendments 10 years later, it did service throughout the imperial period. Then in 1891 the initial constitution of the republic was drawn up and put into effect. The constitutional convention which drafted it was largely dominated by the great jurist, Ruy Barbosa. It drew heavily on the constitution of the United States, an influence which pervades much of the present Brazilian Constitution. It survived until 1934, when Getulio Vargas replaced it with one which embodied much of his political and social philosophy.

Translated in Fitzgibbon's *Constitutions of the Americas,* the national charter of 1946 occupies more than three times the space of the constitution of the United States. Like most similar documents in Latin America, it contains much material ordinarily left to legislative enactment. For example, it grants pregnant women employed outside the home time off with pay before and after delivery. In fact, the basic provisions of the Vargas labor code are preserved in considerable detail. Some of its features also recognize certain political processes that are common to constitutional law and administrative practice in the rest of Latin America, such as the right of the central government to intervene in the affairs of a state or province and to declare a "state of siege" in time of political disorders. As a safeguard against *"continuismo"* and dictatorship, presidents and state governors can only be re-elected after the interval of a term. One of the first sections of the Constitution expressly forbids a war of conquest, or war under any circumstances, unless all the possibilities of arbitration or peaceful negotiation have been exhausted, "regulated by any international organ of security in which it [the Union] may participate." The relative areas of jurisdiction between the federal and state governments are defined in much detail, including the sources of taxation reserved for each. In this connection, the Union is empowered to levy taxes on "income and profits of whatever nature," and on the "transfer of funds abroad." At least 60 per cent of direct taxes levied on the consumer, including gasoline taxes, are to be turned over to the states and municipalities. Property taxes, except on urban real estate, and inheritance taxes, are a monopoly of the states. The states are also permitted to tax exports at a rate not to exceed 5 per cent *ad valorem*. All units of government may tax increases in property values resulting from improvements by public works. The basic division of powers within the government is expressed in the following terms: "The branches of the Union are the legislative, the executive and the judicial, independent and harmonious among themselves."

A national Congress is composed of a Chamber of Deputies and a Senate. The provisions which govern the two houses of Congress and their respective fields of action follows in general the corresponding sections of the American constitution. Deputies, whose minimum age is 21, serve for four years, and senators, who must be 35 years old, have an eight-year term. There are three senators from each state of the Union. As in the United States, either branch of Congress may establish special commissions of inquiry or investigation. The Senate is required to annul any federal legislation which has been declared unconstitutional by the Supreme Court. The president shares with members of the Congress the power to initiate laws. Authority over the national budget is shared by Congress and the president with a federal Tribunal of Accounts, whose functions are somewhat similar to those of the Bureau of the Budget in Washington.

The term of the president is five years. Only one president, Rodrígues Alves, has been legally re-elected after the required lapse of one term. Most of the president's powers are similar to those of his American counterpart. One of his most important prerogatives is "to maintain relations with foreign states." In the exercise of this function he has at his command one of the ablest foreign offices and diplomatic corps in the world, whose high traditions of efficiency were established by the famous Baron of Rio Branco, long head of the Itamaratí, Brazil's Ministry of Foreign Affairs. The president also has the power of veto over legislation, is commander-in-chief of the armed forces, and at an annual joint session of Congress delivers an address on the state of the Union. However, he cannot leave the country without the express permission of Congress.

The Brazilian judicial system is headed by a Supreme Tribunal, whose members are required to be men "of notable juridical knowledge and spotless reputation." It has managed to remain above the sometimes turbid currents of national politics and to maintain high standards of probity and wisdom in its deliberations and decisions. There is also a federal court of appeals, as in the United States, and there are military, electoral, and labor courts on the national level. Over the entire judicial system is the Attorney General of the republic.

The Constitution contains a lengthy series of provisions regarding the rights and civic status of the individual citizen, including specific definitions of nationality and citizenship. For example, anyone born in Brazil has Brazilian citizenship unless the parents are in the employ of the government of their country. Literate Brazilians, both men and women, more than 18 years of age, and able to speak Portuguese, are qualified voters, and voting is "obligatory" for all who meet these requirements.

Among the rights expressly guaranteed by the Constitution are equality before the law, the free expression of thought, the secrecy of correspondence, freedom of religion, freedom of assembly and association, the inviolability of the home, freedom from arbitrary arrest and imprisonment, with the safeguards of *habeas corpus,* immunity from the death penalty or imprisonment for debt, trial by jury for certain crimes, and freedom from arbitrary taxation. Exceptions to these guarantees are generally on reasonable grounds of public interest, though during a "state of siege" there are restrictions on freedom of assembly and in other areas, like propaganda, which affect the security of the state.

The Constitution assures "the right of property," but permits expropriation "for public necessity or utility, or for social interest," though "with prior and just indemnification in money." It also declares that "the economic order shall be organized in conformity with principles of social justice, conciliating the liberty of initiative with the value of human labor." It further states that "everyone is assured work that enables a dignified existence" and that "work is a social obligation." The provisions "Concerning the Economic and Social Order" reflect the persistent influence of Vargas. For example:

> The Union may . . . intervene in the economic spheres or monopolize specified industries or activities. . . . The use of property shall be conditioned upon social welfare. . . . The law may . . . promote the just distribution of property, with equal opportunities for everyone. . . . The law shall restrain all forms of abuse of economic power, including unions or groups of concerns, either individual or social, regardless of their nature, which have as a purpose the domination of national markets, elimination of competition, and arbitrary increase of profits.

Other sections of the Constitution cover a variety of unrelated matters: The family is declared indissoluble. Financial aid is to be given to large families. Everyone has a right to education. "Support of culture is a duty of the state." "All Brazilians are obligated for military service," but, unlike Cuba, women are exempted. Government employees may retire on full pay after 30 years. And the royalties of authors and the salaries of journalists and professors are exempt from taxation!

A perennial Brazilian problem, finally resolved by the construction of Brasilia, has been the location of the national capital. The colony was originally ruled from Bahia or Salvador, but in the eighteenth century the seat of government was moved to Rio de Janeiro, where it remained through the period of the Empire and until April 21, 1960, at which time Brasilia was formally inaugurated as the capital of Brazil. The idea of moving the capital from the coast into the interior of the country was an old one and was even enunciated in the 1820's by José Bonifacio, the leading statesman of the early Empire. The first constitution of the republic, promulgated in 1891, provided for a large federal district in the state of Goiás, to which the capital was to be transferred. However, none of the subsequent administrations got beyond a vague endorsement of the project, if they took notice of it at all, until President Juscelino Kubitschek, elected in 1956, espoused the idea with enthusiasm.

The motives for moving the capital inland from Rio were several. In the first place, the site on Guanabara Bay was a reminder of the time when the population of Brazil was largely confined to a narrow coastal strip. Its situation was a deterrent to the development of the interior, whose accelerated growth was one of the most urgent needs of the nation. Moreover, Brazilians had become increasingly aware of the fact that Rio was unsuited to be the capital. They called it another Capua, a hedonistic pleasure ground, where the serious conduct of public business was no longer possible. Besides ascetic considerations, the support of an overgrown and underworked bureaucracy was a heavy drain on the hard-pressed federal Treasury. Over a century ago, Professor and Mrs. Agassiz commented thus on the Brazilian predilection for government jobs:

> The exaggerated appreciation of political employment prevailing everywhere is a misfortune. It throws into the shade all other occupations. . . . Every man who has received an education seeks a political career, as at once the most aristocratic and the easiest way of gaining a livelihood.

President Kubitschek presumably calculated on the likelihood that a large proportion of government functionaries would prefer to remain in Rio rather than submit to the austerities of life in the back country.

After a survey of the relative advantages of five different areas in the interior, the present site of Brasilia was selected as most suitable for the purpose. It is located near the sixteenth parallel on the central plateau of the state of Goiás. In a straight line it is about 650 miles from Rio and about twice as far by the road which leads through Belo Horizonte. Since the city is situated at about 3,500 feet above sea level, the climate is moderate. As in much of Brazil, there are distinct wet and dry seasons, with much reddish dust during the rainless months. Most of the rolling country of the new Federal District is covered with a light growth of scrub forest alternated with coarse grass. When the project was initiated the only practicable connection with the coast was by air.

In justifying the massive and costly venture, the example and experience of previous fiat capitals were stressed. Brazil itself had created two such capitals, Belo Horizonte in Minas Gerais and Goiania in the state in which Brasilia is situated. Other examples which were quoted included Washington, Canberra in Australia, New Delhi in India, St. Petersburg in czarist Russia, and Ankara in Mustafa Kemal's Turkey.

Once the fateful decision was made and approved by Congress, an open competition was held for the planning of the city. The plan accepted was that presented by Lucio Costa, a well-known Brazilian city planner. In its final form the basic design followed the general pattern of an airplane—or dragonfly. The design of the buildings was the work of the distinguished—and ultramodernistic—Brazilian architect, Oscar Niemeyer.

The plans involved many revolutionary features. For example, all streets have overpasses at crossings. A series of small local streams were dammed to make a large crescent-shaped lake which when filled will almost surround the city. Residential and shopping areas are laid out to provide localized facilities for the needs of an eventual population of 500,000 people. A Plaza of the Three Powers contains the executive offices, the chambers of the federal courts, and separate halls for each house of Congress, with tall office buildings for their members. Opposite this "heart of Brazil" is a long mall or esplanade, with a double row of steel-framed buildings for the various ministries or federal departments of government. The Palace of the Dawn, which is the executive mansion, is located at some distance from this center of the nation's political life. A long avenue was reserved for foreign embassies, with a signboard marking each lot with the name of a country with which Brazil maintains diplomatic relations. The location and design of business establishments, such as banks and office buildings, are strictly regulated to conform with the over-all plan of the city.

The actual construction of Brasilia presented serious problems. General supervision of the work was in the hands of a special entity known by its initials as NOVACAP, an abbreviation of "New Capital," and headed by Dr. Israel Pinheiro, now the first prefect or mayor of the city. The president's determination to complete the project before his retirement from office in early 1961 raised the question of deadlines for completion of buildings and public works. In default of a through railway connection with Rio and São Paulo, large quantities of materials were trucked to the construction site over an unimproved road from the terminus of the line at Annapolis. Cement, steel girders, and bricks were flown in by planes. With a labor force of over 30,000 men, work went on in three shifts, for 24 hours a day seven days a week. The majority of the workers were hardy *caboclos* from the northeastern states. Natural pioneers, they drifted in overland, their belongings in a suitcase or in a sack on their back, sleeping at night by the side of the road and already hardened to the primitive living conditions of the early months at Brasilia. Some continued on, to work on the long highways that were a-building or to settle on a patch of ground along the new roads.

If the little men entered into the spirit of the president's great scheme, there were many in Brazil who criticized it as a waste of money or a "Pharaonic dream." They prophesied that, if it were not finished when the president left office, his successor would abandon the new capital and Federal District to the Indians and the jaguars, and some day archaeologists would uncover its moldering ruins as another Angkor or Copán.

While Brasilia was still unfinished, the *Cidade Libre* or Free City near by was a going concern. It became a center of community life for thousands of construction workers, a "hangout" for truck drivers between trips, and an unpublicized tourist attraction for those who flew in from the coast to view the rising glory of Brasilia. It was a Wild West town of one-story clapboard buildings, with unpaved streets that were either dusty or muddy and that at night were dimly lighted. As unconventional as Brasilia was stylized, the Free City offended the sensibilities of the planners, who vowed to raze it from the earth as soon as their model city was ready for occupancy.

Brasilia was not quite ready when it was inaugurated in an impressive ceremony on the date set for its opening in April, 1960. Some of the furniture and fixtures in the government buildings were still missing and there were many loose ends to take care of. But it had progressed so far that now there was no turning back. Cost what it might, this would henceforth be the capital of Brazil, and Brazilians would eventually be as proud of it as had been the men who built it from nothingness to a greatness befitting their land.

SUPPLEMENTARY READING LIST

FOR THOSE WHO WISH TO READ FURTHER IN THE GENERAL field of this book or on particular phases of the country and its civilization, the following materials are suggested:

GENERAL

Bastide, Roger. *Brésil, Terre des Contrastes.* Paris: Librairie Hachette, 1957.

Freyre, Gilberto. *Brazil: An Interpretation.* New York: Alfred A. Knopf, Inc., 1945.

———. *New World in the Tropics.* New York: Alfred A. Knopf, Inc., 1959. Commentaries by the leading Brazilian sociologist.

Hill, Lawrence F., ed. *Brazil.* Berkeley and Los Angeles: University of California Press, 1947.

Nash, Roy. *The Conquest of Brazil.* New York: Harcourt, Brace and Company, 1926. An appreciative and sensitive study by an American who spent several years in Brazil as forester and U.S. government official.

Smith, T. Lynn, and Marchant, Alexander, eds. *Brazil: Portrait of Half a Continent.* New York: The Dryden Press, Inc., 1951. A symposium by a group of American and Brazilian scholars on various phases of Brazilian civilization.

HISTORY

There is no satisfactory history of Brazil in English. A sound but dull chronicle of events is available in *History of Brazil,* written by José Pandia Calogeras, a Brazilian finance minister. The translation by Percy Alvin Martin was published by Duke University Press, Durham, N.C. For certain eras of Brazilian history, see:

Boxer, Charles. *The Dutch in Brazil, 1624–1654.* Oxford: Clarendon Press, 1954.

Freyre, Gilberto. *The Masters and the Slaves.* New York: Alfred A. Knopf, Inc., 1946. An interesting study of the slave society of colonial Brazil.

Haring, C. H. *Empire in Brazil: A New World Experiment with Monarchy.* Cambridge, Mass.: Harvard University Press, 1958.

There is much useful information in the Brazilian chapters of the textbook histories of Latin America, including those by Hubert Herring, Mary Wilhelmine Williams, J. Fred Rippy, A. Curtis Wilgus, Alfred B. Thomas, Charles E. Chapman, John A. Crow, Helen M. Bailey and A. P. Nasatir, and Donald E. Worcester and Wendell G. Schaeffer.

ECONOMIC GEOGRAPHY

James, Preston E. *Latin America,* chapters 11–18. New York: The Odyssey Press, Inc., 1959.

———. *Brazil.* New York: The Odyssey Press, Inc., 1946. The Brazilian section of an earlier edition of the above book, with some additional material.

AMAZONIA

Bates, Henry Walter. *The Naturalist on the Amazon.* New York: E. P. Dutton and Company, Inc., 1910. This book, first published in London nearly a century ago, and reprinted in the Everyman Library, is the classic work on the natural features of the Amazonia.

Lecointe, Paul. *L'Amazonie Brésilienne.* 2 vols. Paris: Augustin Challamel, 1922. This encyclopedic work by a French scientist, who resided in the Amazon Valley for many years, is still the best source of information for the region.

Wagley, Charles. *Amazon Town: A Study of Man in the Tropics.* New York: The Macmillan Company, 1953.

RURAL DEVELOPMENT

Smith, T. Lynn. *Brazil, People and Institutions.* Baton Rouge: University of Louisiana Press, 1954.

EDUCATION

Faust, Augustus F. *Brazil: Education in an Expanding Economy.* (U.S. Department of Health, Education and Welfare, Bulletin No. 13.) Washington, D.C.: Government Printing Office, 1959.

LITERARY AND INTELLECTUAL HISTORY

Putnam, Samuel. *Marvelous Journey: A Survey of Four Centuries of Brazilian Writing.* New York: Alfred A. Knopf, Inc., 1948.

Verissimo, Erico. *Brazilian Literature: An Outline.* New York: The Macmillan Company, 1945.

LITERATURE

Cunha, Euclides da. *Rebellion in the Backlands.* Chicago: University of Chicago Press, 1957. Brazil's most famous historical novel, translated by Samuel Putnam and published as a paperback by the University of Chicago Press.

PEOPLE AND CULTURE

Azevedo, Fernando de. *Brazilian Culture.* (Translated by W. Rex Crawford.) New York: The Macmillan Company, 1950. A comprehensive and scholarly discussion of the national character and culture, and of their regional variations.

Tavares de Sá, Hernane. *The Brazilians: People of Tomorrow.* New York: The John Day Company, 1947. Frank and interesting comments on the Brazilian character and society by a Brazilian who has spent much time in the United States.

For the story of the Negro in Brazil, see:

Pierson, Donald. *Negroes in Brazil.* Chicago: University of Chicago Press, 1942.

Ramos, Arthur. *The Negro in Brazil.* (Translated by Richard Pattee.) New York: Associated Publishers, 1939.

ECONOMICS

The most useful material on the economic development of Brazil is in periodicals and pamphlets. Leading sources are: The U.S. Department of Commerce, various agencies of the Brazilian government, the United Nations, the Office of Foreign Agricultural Relations of the U.S. Department of Agriculture. For valuable background information, see:

Kuznets, Simon Smith, and others, eds. *Economic Growth: Brazil, India, Japan.* Durham, N.C.: Duke University Press, 1955.

Wythe, George. *Brazil: An Expanding Economy.* New York: 20th Century Fund, 1949.

GOVERNMENT AND POLITICS

Fitzgibbon, Russell H., ed. *The Constitutions of the Americas.* Chicago: University of Chicago Press, 1948.

MacDonald, Austin F. *Latin American Government and Politics.* New York: Thomas Y. Crowell Company, 1954.

Szulc, Tad. *Twilight of the Tyrants.* New York: Holt, Rinehart, Winston, 1959.

A NOTE ON PRONUNCIATION AND SPELLING

THIS BOOK CONTAINS MANY PORTUGUESE WORDS, CHIEFLY place names. The author believes that the reader unfamiliar with the sound of this language, particularly as used in Brazil, will derive some reward and satisfaction from the feeling that he is mentally pronouncing these words with a reasonable degree of correctness. For this purpose there follows a brief, tabulated guide to the approximate pronunciation of the Portuguese language.

Letter

a	*aba:* like *a* in "f*a*ther"
e	p*é:* like *e* in "l*e*t"
i	R*i*o: like *i* in "mach*i*ne"
o	t*o*da: like *o* in "n*o*te"
u	*u*ma: like *oo* in "b*oo*t"

Portuguese vowels have a nasal sound either when marked with a til (~) as in S*ã*o, or when followed by an *n* or *m,* as in co*n*to or ca*m*po.

c	*c*ima: like *s* in "*s*ing" before *e* or *i*
c	*c*afé: like *c* and *k* in "*c*a*k*e" before *a, o, u*
c	Igua*c*ú: like *s* in "*s*ing"
ch	*ch*á: like *sh* in "*sh*e"
g	*g*elo: like *z* in "a*z*ure" before *e* or *i*
g	*g*ato: like *g* in "*g*ate" before *a, o, u*

gu	*gu*ía: like *g* in "*g*ate" before *e* or *i*
h	*h*ora: not pronounced as in "*h*our"
j	*J*aneiro: like *z* in "azure"
lh	i*lh*a: like *lli* in "mi*lli*on"
nh	Cu*nh*a: like *ny* in "ca*ny*on"
qu	*qu*ero: like *k* in "*k*ite" before *e* or *i*
	*qu*anto: like *qu* in "*qu*ite" before *a* or *o*
s	ca*s*a: like *s* in "ro*s*e" between vowels; in other cases like *s* in "*s*ister"
x	*X*ingú: like *sh* in "*sh*e"
z	zelo: like *z* in "lazy"

Letters not listed in the above table are pronounced similarly in Portuguese and English.

In 1943 there was an orthographic and diacritical revolution that left its marks on the printed word in Brazil. However, since this is not a linguistic treatise, any detailed consideration of the changes made would only confuse the reader. The aftereffects of the reform are chiefly apparent to those foreigners who were introduced to Brazilian geography before 1943 and now find "Goyaz" spelled "Goiás" and "Nichteroy" spelled "Niteroi."

INDEX